Health, happiness, sexual v... coming of loneliness depe... take positive steps to achieve them. Our lives must be led in a way that does not abuse both our bodies and minds. Most important of all we must take control of our own destiny and not abdicate responsibility for our actions and well-being to others. In *A Way of Living*, Michael Wheatley examines nutrition, diseases, happiness, diets and the sexual life to show how each facet of our life relates to others and how all are dependent upon good health and a good diet. He gives a comprehensive guide to health foods and a healthy diet and hints on where to obtain them.

To Dennis + Mollie
With love + best wishes
and all the best wishes
for the future.

Michael Wheatley

25th June 1985

A Way of Living

A Way of Living

How to achieve natural health

MICHAEL WHEATLEY

London
UNWIN PAPERBACKS
Boston   Sydney

First published in Great Britain by Transworld Publishers Ltd. 1977
First published by Unwin Paperbacks 1982
This book is copyright under the Berne Convention. No reproduction without permission. All rights reserved.

UNWIN® PAPERBACKS
40 Museum Street, London WC1A 1LU, UK

Unwin Paperbacks,
Park Lane, Hemel Hempstead, Herts HP2 4TE, UK

George Allen & Unwin Australia Pty Ltd.,
8 Napier Street, North Sydney, NSW 2060, Australia

© Michael Wheatley 1977, 1982

ISBN 0 04 613048 9

Set in 10 on 10½ point Plantin
and printed in Great Britain
by Hazell Watson & Viney Ltd, Aylesbury, Bucks

HEALTH FOOD STORES

Health Food Stores are to be found in most towns. The majority of products mentioned in this book can be purchased there. In the UK the National Association of Health Stores, Bank Passage, Exchange Walk, Nottingham will give the address of a local store. In Australia general information will be given by The Natural Health Society of Australia, 1st Floor, 131 York Street, Sydney, NSW 2000.

The following manufacturers and distributors in the UK, although not engaged in the retail trade, will be able to supply details of their products and the address of their local stockists: Mapletons Ltd, Garston, Liverpool; Granose Foods Ltd, Stanborough Park, Watford, Herts; Brewhurst Health Food Supplies Ltd, Byfleet, Surrey; Modern Health Products Ltd, Davis Road, Chessington, Surrey; Health Stores Wholesale Ltd, 100 High Street, Croydon, Surrey.

Suppliers of a comprehensive range of health foods and supplements in Australia include Hygenic Food Supplies Ltd, 97–99 Ryedale Street, West Ryde, NSW 2114; Vitamin Supplies Pty Ltd, 51–55 Warrah Street, East Chatswood, NSW 2067; Caloric Control Foods Pty Ltd, 172 Halden Street, Lakemba, NSW 2195. Vitamins, cell salts, food supplements and organic cosmetics are supplied by Blackmore Laboratories Pty Ltd, 26 Roseberry Street, Balgowlah, NSW 2093.

Wholewheat flour and other cereal foods produced by the following are available in most parts of the country or can be obtained direct from the mills: Allinson Ltd, Queens Mills, Castleford, Yorks; Dean's Water Mill, Lindfield, Sussex; W. H. Marriage & Sons, Chelmer Mills, Chelmsford, Essex; W. Prewett Ltd, Stone Flour Mills, Horsham, Sussex.

Contents

Introduction	*page* 13
Nutrition	23
Diseases	55
Happiness	111
Living Alone and Planning a Diet	149
Health Foods	201
Stepping Stones to Health	253
Sex	303
More Food For Thought	365
Index	369

1. Introduction

'Since we learn from our critics, I too am willing to be criticised.'

Michael Wheatley.
Orange Cottage,
Epping Green,
Essex,
England.

FOOD FOR THOUGHT

IN the modern world health, happiness, loneliness and sex have been fashioned into weapons and their exploitation is a thriving industry. That at least is the case in the West. In the East the strong family system and a philosophy of goodwill solve many of these problems and a strict code of ethics governs sex, or so it was up to recent times. For the West, therefore, it seems opportune at this moment to write a book directed at these subjects because they are important ones and so much rubbish is talked about them by their exploiters. It is also opportune now because people are losing faith in religion and so have nowhere to turn for guidance about their happiness or health. I hope therefore this book will redress the balance in favour of those who find themselves bewildered by a world which is moving so fast that it seems to have lost sight of the reason for existence.

Your immediate reaction to what I have just said may well be that it is perfectly permissible for each of us to be responsible for his own health, happiness, security and sex and to a great extent I would agree with you. But unfortunately we are not complete masters of any of these things because from the day we are born, we are fed food and ideas over which we have very little control. In this manner our bodies and minds are formed and we receive a basis for a way of life. Next we are thrown upon the world which we imagine has our best interests at heart, and it is not until we have received our first setback that we discover how untrue this is. Society is principally interested in what it can get out of us, in the form of labour, cash, talent or the like. We are left to seek our own health in a world which profits more from our ill-health, to find happiness which is confused with pleasure, to try to dispel our own loneliness and to resolve our own problems of sex. It is an unequal struggle, but today we know a great deal more about keeping the body and mind healthy than we ever did before; and now that sex has come out into the open we are able to see it for what it is instead of what once it was alleged to be. So we must learn how to deal with these problems, and all we need to know are a few fundamental facts.

In the West everyone is alone to fight for himself. I have fought such a battle and won, but it was a long and exacting process which required considerable determination as well as courage. In writing this book I have no axe to grind: I do not seek to make money from your health, happiness, loneliness or sexual desires. If you want to survive as an individual, to be free in your own right to live your own life and to resolve your own problems, then this is the book to help you. But please remember that I can do no more than give you the facts; you have to put them into practice.

Today both physical and mental health have been handed over to the State in many countries and as a result people have sacrificed their responsibility, by surrendering to drug-peddling, knife-wielding doctors. We have enslaved ourselves to the State and whittled away our self-respect as well as our ability to stand on our own two feet. I too wanted the people of my country and the world to be healthy, and I too thought this was the way to do it. But I realize now that I was wrong, that we were all wrong, because the millions spent each year by National Health Services are only frittered away in palliating the symptoms of disease instead of tackling the problem at its cause: the nation's devitalized health. That is what this book is really about, to show you how you can achieve health and to direct your attention to this positive accomplishment instead of merely pandering to the symptoms of disease.

In saying this I am not absolving the State from its general responsibility for the nation's health, nor for such specific fields as cleanliness and drains, pollution and food processing or anything else which affects our health externally. In any case, medical care must be available to everyone who cannot afford it. But otherwise it is our own affair, the test of what we are. The strong and healthy will survive and the weak will not. Those who have the wits will find out what it takes to survive and doubtless the others will serve them. That is how a virile world works.

If you are wise you will learn now because it takes time to acquire the habits and for the effects to be felt, because health and happiness do not come from a bottle nor are they effected by a surgeon's knife, they are part of our way of life, a way of living. For that reason we have a lot of re-thinking to do before starting on the positive course of seeking health, instead of the negative one of staving off disease. It is an entirely new approach, a mental attitude which takes arms against a sea of troubles and by opposing ends them, instead of accepting an inevitable state of ill-health which is suppressed from time to time when it becomes unbearable.

The majority of people are born healthy and it is only their abuse of their bodies and minds which causes a breakdown. Our bodies are made to be self-repairing, to fight disease and to remain healthy; 85% of all disease is self-determining so the odds are very much on our side. But survival is a state of mind and to survive we must be independent, it is no use handing over the responsibility for our health or our happiness to the State. If you rely upon others for your life you only survive as long as you are needed and that applies to people or countries, animals or objects. Hence the survival of the fittest, those who are independent and can survive alone; it is the weaklings who need protection and help.

The quest for happiness is somewhat different from that of health but the same principles are involved because happiness also is not something which can be given to anyone, in part it involves one's own self-respect in finding it. When I came to the East last year I hoped I would be able to discover the origin of that solid core of peace which seems to run right through the Orientals, and now I am nearer to knowing the answer. It is not one thing but many, but principally it is each individual's control over his own mind and an appreciation of what is important and what is not. Some of it comes from the family system and the rules and regulations which govern it so that everyone knows exactly where he stands, the rest is based on human relationships. All of this they are taught and learn by heart. The West has no equivalent so each person must find his own happiness – and it is necessary to know how.

Fortunately it is never too late to learn and the body can be rejuvenated from the most appalling state of degeneration, as can the mind be re-educated to understand the basic needs of mental health. But you yourself have to make this possible by understanding what it is necessary to do and then doing it. No-one else can do it for you. It has been said before that it takes a lifetime to learn to live and that is not far from true, so we must make use of the wisdom of those who have gone before us and draw upon modern discoveries for our physical health. For those without the time to undertake the enormous amount of study involved, I offer you this book which is presented as concisely as possible so you can extract the vital facts and see clearly what is required of you to be healthy and happy.

I was told by my doctor that there was nothing more he could do for me, but at the same time I knew I had not recovered from my third attack of jaundice. Realizing I might never again feel well enough to enjoy life as I had in the past, I set about the task of curing myself through correct eating. As a first step I discovered that I did not even know what the protein foods were nor what were carbohydrates, I had not the least idea where vitamins were to be found and minerals had hardly entered my calculations. Things such as anti-stress factors and enzymes I had never heard of. Later I learned that the mind rules the body and is blindly obeyed and that the will to live and enjoy life, and the spirit with which to do it, are things for which no food can serve as substitute. There is no doubt that we can die as quickly from a lack of the will to live as from lack of food, yet our state of mind can keep us going beyond the limits of physical endurance.

Now life is mostly habit and habits are things we do not notice because they become automatic. That is why it is so dangerous to acquire the wrong habits and why it is difficult to break any of them. But if we are going to be either healthy or happy we must inspect our way of life and discover what are wrong habits and what are right ones. In this context we would do well to inspect Peter Fleming's list of things which civilized people have and primitive ones do not. It includes: money, firearms, soap, medicine and tin-openers. With these items we are destroying ourselves.

You may wonder whether it is worth acquiring a high degree of health and developing one's mind to achieve perfect peace. I would urge a little extra effort now to evaluate our habits and establish the right ones as an insurance against a miserable old age and as a means of achieving a certain pleasure in daily life.

I realize that breaking habits is difficult and it is hard for us to see them in perspective or appreciate them for what they are. That goes for the good ones as well as the bad, for our virtues as well as our vices, our eating or our thoughts, even our daily life. We must therefore inspect them very closely and find out what they are based on, and whether there is not something better which we should substitute in their place. Most of the prophets of the past took away from life everything they had until they were left with nothing, then they were able to see clearly not only what was right and what was wrong, but also what was needed and what was not. I am not suggesting that you go to these lengths because you might find it difficult and harmful to live on one grain of seed each day as Buddha did, but I am suggesting you learn the rudimentary principles of proper eating and mental health. It is true to say that the more you take away from life the more you add to it. The more you simplify your life and reduce it to the bare essentials the more you are likely to enjoy living.

Telling people not to do things is tantamount to encouraging them to do them, because human nature is perverse and always wants to taste forbidden fruit. What I want to try and do in this book, is to help people understand why they should adopt certain habits of eating and thinking, and show them how to incorporate those into their daily life.

To accomplish this I have broken down A WAY OF LIVING into seven sections to make it more easily assimilable, the first of which is basic nutrition. In this I propose to outline what is known about food so you can refer back to it throughout the rest of the book, because you must understand what food is composed of before you can learn how to use it to achieve better health.

The next is about diseases, for when you have failed to put into practice what you learned earlier, and have created some sort of imbalance within your body. When our defences are down, changes take place inside us and we develop what are called diseases, which are named after the symptoms in whichever part of the body they appear. Curing disease is not generally a difficult matter if you can discover the cause of it instead of treating the symptoms, and usually the cause is eating the wrong foods. So we are back to nutrition again.

However, no amount of correct eating can cure an unhappy

mind. What is wrong with the mind must be put right, after which you must follow a simple plan of right thinking and proper values. When our defences are down changes take place inside us which make us vulnerable to viruses and bacteria as well as causing vitamin and mineral deficiencies. Now the body is built to do battle with the former providing the right raw materials are at hand, but it cannot cope with the latter unless vitamins and minerals are supplied from outside. Hence curing disease really comes down to giving the body the weapons it needs and sufficient rest.

In the fourth section I want to tell you how to plan your diet, and I shall devote this section to people who live alone because they are the ones who always seem to be in need of a square meal. It will also be necessary to include some philosophy and some positive thinking because a correct diet is not the only requisite for alleviating loneliness. This section tells you how to put into practice the knowledge I have given you in the first section, because it is not enough to know how a car is made or what it is capable of doing, one also has to learn how to drive it before one can go anywhere.

Next comes an explanation of the contents of a health food shop. Very often people become diseased because the food they eat has been processed and certain vital elements have been removed. In order to regain health it may be necessary to discover those missing elements and take them for a period of time. To maintain health it is necessary to eat every element of food in order to keep the delicate balance of nature, even cooking it can sometimes destroy what you need. To help people find what they want in a health food shop I shall explain in detail the goods on sale, and why they are necessary.

Despite my explanations, I still find that some people are unable to correlate all the information and then actually settle down to live by it. I will therefore give you the stepping stones which are necessary to carry out my programme and they include ones for individuals, families, towns, cities, counties, nations and the world.

I have added a section on sex because so much misery is caused by its abuse, and people can ruin their lives by not knowing enough about it. This most normal of all desires can easily become perverted and turned into a vice. The urge for sex, like that for alcohol, increases little by little, and over-indulgence of either can harm the body and mind.

These facts of life you need to know, all of them, for your daily living. Of course there are heaps of learned tomes on philosophy and nutrition, but people will not translate them into a way of living, so there is a need for this.

I do not want this to be a lengthy book: what I shall try to do is give you the broadest possible view, because to confine oneself to one school of thought is not enough. Originally Europe was the leader of the world in nutrition, due to the great Vienna school of medicine, and our philosophy came from ancient Greece. Now the Americans are ahead of the world in nutritional research, even if most of them do not put it into practice. Their problems appear to be caused by those who are determined that people shall not help themselves because their own livelihood depends on them being helped.

Of course human nature works against us all because the comfortable security of our habits becomes a rut and once the wheel of our daily life is caught there it is an effort to dislodge. Eggs and toast and tea are an Englishman's breakfast, soya bean milk and an oilstick are for the Chinese, coffee and croissants for the French, coffee and chuffa for the Spaniards, and none of them would think of changing. Their fathers had the same food before them, and probably their grandfathers and great-great-grandfathers. Eating is a habit even if one can afford a choice, so it may be really necessary to see one's grave before being frightened out of the rut. That is what happened to me. I had never given the matter much thought before, or even suspected that food could be the cause of the various ailments I regularly suffered from. I cannot begin to describe to you the difference this new way of life has made to me, physically, mentally and from the point of view of my own personality. May you also be able to find the same benefit, because it makes life worth living no matter what your circumstances are.

2. About Nutrition

ABOUT NUTRITION

About Nutrition	25
Protein	26
Carbohydrate	27
Fats	29
Vitamins	30
Vitamin A	32
Vitamin B	33
Vitamin C	34
Vitamin D	36
Vitamin E	37
Vitamin K	39
Minerals	39
Calcium, Phosphorous and Magnesium	42
Sodium, Chlorine and Potassium	44
Iron, Copper and Cobalt	46
Zinc and Sulphur, Iodine and Manganese	48
Water	49
Enzymes	50
Anti-Stress Factors	51

NUTRITION

Nutrition is food for living,
For energy, health and repair,
It creates and maintains the body,
If selected and balanced with care.

But that's only part of the story,
At least in this present day,
Because food which is dead is divided,
Its life-giving agents destroyed.

Half-foods are the cause of most illness,
They do not supply what we need
To digest and make use of their contents,
The result is what's called disease.

Pain and distress are the symptoms
Which attract our attention right there,
A cry to supply what is missing,
Whole food is the certain cure.

ABOUT NUTRITION

NUTRITION means nourishment, in other words food, and its purpose is to maintain life. Without a daily supply we must live off our reserves, therefore we must eat ourselves, and there is a limit as to how long we can continue to do that. What we eat largely dictates our state of health, but regrettably in the modern world food and its preparation often becomes merely a status symbol. Primitive people however are not led astray by such vanity and therefore eat simply to benefit their health, providing they can afford to be properly nourished.

What is the nutritional difference between the rich man's diet and that of primitive people which so much affects the health? Basically one eats mostly processed food, and the other consumes it as nature produced it: brown rice and whole grain flour, sugar from the cane instead of refined, fresh vegetables and fruit instead of canned, practically no meat and lots of exercise in the fresh air.

That is the case in some parts of the world where industry has not taken away people's identity and turned them into masses, bringing such enormous problems of organization and care that nature has broken down and modern science is still unable to cope. On how we answer that problem will depend the future of the human race, its happiness as well as its health. Some people may have to be taken from the factory floor and the land subdivided to produce a solution, because there is no doubt that given the land and the water we can feed ourselves. But more important even than the supply of food is the knowledge of what to eat to keep healthy, because everything has to be learnt. When you think of the trouble we take to learn so many unimportant facts, why is it that what actually keeps us alive is omitted from the syllabus? Let me therefore correct this error now by telling you what food consists of and what elements in it are needed for optimum health.

The fundamental facts about nutrition are agreed by all, that vital living food is the basis on which we live and keep our health. Recent discoveries only serve to show in more detail the specific action of various vitamins and minerals, enzymes and intrinsic factors. From that premise it should only be a question of studying in what quantity and combination we should take our food. However by analysing food we have discovered a number of its principal elements and in particular those which vitally affect our health.

Basically food consists of protein, carbohydrate, fat, vitamins, minerals and water. It also contains enzymes, anti-stress and intrinsic factors which we are gradually learning more about each year, but for most practical purposes this is all we need to know to remain healthy. Each food in its natural state contains some or all of these elements and if it is particularly high in any one of them is referred to as that type of food, such as a protein or carbohydrate food. Let me therefore start by explaining what these elements are and what they do for you.

PROTEIN

Protein is what we are principally made of. It forms the building blocks which nature uses to create our muscles, organs and glands. It is also a component of bones and teeth, skin, nails and hair, of blood cells and serum. It is therefore vital to the continual repair, maintenance and working of the body, and without it life would not go on.

Protein differs from other food elements in that it contains nitrogen which the others do not. It is made up of amino acids, and the amount and combination of these determines its value. Some protein is complete which means it will support life and growth on its own, while some is incomplete and therefore will not. The difference is that complete protein contains the eight essential amino acids (ten for children) which the body cannot synthesise, while incomplete protein does not. However if eaten at the same meal different incomplete protein foods can all combine to produce an even better result, hence the ability of the vegetarian to be so healthy.

Broadly speaking, animal food contains complete protein and vegetable food does not, although combining several of the later will make them complete. Thus a small amount of animal food with lots of vegetables is an ideal combination, although a large variety of vegetables without the animal food can be even more so. The only fatal mistake is to have one or two vegetable foods alone, unless you know exactly what you are doing.

Milk, meat, eggs, poultry and fish are the principal complete animal foods, not forgetting liver, kidneys, blood and other organs. In the vegetable kingdom soya beans, brewers' yeast, almonds, sesame seeds, combinations of seeds and nuts or combinations of vegetables will all suffice. If too much protein is taken the excess nitrogen must be eliminated from the body, so it is wise to keep to about one gram of protein per kilogram of body weight (roughly half a gram per pound). Special cases such as stress, pregnancy, surgery, illness, poor digestion or growing children need more.

Incomplete protein consists of beans, peas, lentils, gelatine, some nuts and all grain (rice, wheat, barley, rye etc), most vegetables and fruit. It is therefore necessary either to combine many of these foods together or take some complete protein with them.

Protein deficiency symptoms include: anaemia, flabby muscles, slow healing, fatigue, edema, bad nails or skin or hair, lack of antibodies to fight disease, inadequate protection by the liver from poisons, an imbalance of acid or alkaline or of water in the tissues.

Protein, therefore, is the first consideration in our diet, and we must know where it is coming from, and in what quantity, to be certain we are healthy. Since eggs and milk are the only two foods which are complete in every food element except vitamin C we would be wise to include these, although for those who know enough about nutrition and have the means to eat properly, they would probably be best eaten sparingly from middle age onwards.

CARBOHYDRATE

The energy of the sun is used to synthesize carbon dioxide from the air and water into carbohydrate in plants. Thus in turn we also obtain our energy from the vegetable world or from animals who have eaten it. The trouble comes when we interfere with that carbohydrate by removing some of the elements nature put there for its digestion and use. We then create an imbalance within our bodies and disease is caused, not immediately, but over a period of time. By continuous use disastrous effects will result. The golden rule with carbohydrate is therefore always to eat it as it appears naturally in food, in fruit and vegetables, in whole wheat, brown rice and other unprocessed cereals, in whole raw milk and honey. Any other sort will do harm and eventually cause disease.

The majority of the world obtain their carbohydrate from cereal grains such as rice, wheat, barley, millet and others and thus satisfy their calorie need for energy. If this enormous quantity of grain was eaten whole in its natural state, instead of having most of the goodness processed out of it, the whole picture of world health would be completely changed, as most diseases are either degenerative in origin or come from food element deficiencies. So heed this warning and avoid white sugar, white flour and white rice, but by all means eat them as whole foods.

Carbohydrate consists of three groups: simple sugars such as glucose which comes from sweet fruit and certain vegetables and roots, and fructose from honey and other ripe fruit. Double sugars such as sucrose, maltose and lactose come from refined sugar beet and cane, also milk, some fruit and vegetables. Complex sugars are those such as starch (the form in which plants such as grain, legumes, rice and potatoes store carbohydrate), glycogen, which is how animals store it, and cellulose which can only be utilized by ruminants. The simpler the sugar the easier it is to digest, because all sugars have to be broken down into glucose before they can enter the blood stream and so be used.

We store carbohydrate in the form of glycogen in our livers and muscles which can be rapidly transformed into glucose for energy. To create energy the glucose is oxidized, leaving the byproducts of carbon dioxide and water to be eliminated by our lungs and in our urine. Enough glycogen is stored in our body to last about half a day after which we start to break down body fat and protein to make energy. Thus the no-breakfast eaters are able to survive till lunchtime but they would be very weak in the afternoon if they did not have an adequate lunch.

Refined white sugar not only causes tooth decay but is considered to be one of the major causes of heart disease and some gastrointestinal complaints. Unfortunately processed carbohydrates satisfy the appetite and therefore people think they are being properly nourished – this is the cause of most malnourishment in wealthy countries. That is also the reason why desserts, puddings and sweet foods are usually served at the end of a meal. But sweets of any sort, from dried fruit to candy, cakes and puddings can become an addiction and an excess of them can do harm and produce a lack of energy, although this is less likely if they are unprocessed. But even concentrated natural carbohydrate such as honey, molasses and dried fruit is not good in large quantities.

Unused carbohydrate is stored in our bodies in the form of fat but if we are healthy and lead a normally active life this does not build up in excess, because the amount of carbohydrate which we actually absorb is strictly regulated. That is why healthy people can eat as much as they like and not put on weight, and why the Georgians in Russia consider fat people to be ill. Excessive carbohydrate or fat cause water retention, if they are absorbed, and this in itself is unhealthy. We must therefore either become healthy or carefully inspect our carbohydrate intake to ensure that we eat it only as nature presents it to us.

FATS

These are the most potentially dangerous food in our diet, and the cause of many premature deaths. Yet we need fat in the right form for proper health, calm nerves and beautiful skin, quite apart from other body functions. Fats are one of the three building materials for maintaining and creating life, as well as producing energy, the others being protein and carbohydrate.

There are two types of fat, unsaturated fatty acids which appear in the vegetable world and do us nothing but good, taken in reasonable amounts, and saturated fatty acids which come mostly from animal sources including milk and its products as well as eggs and meat, and which can be harmful.

Like carbohydrate, a small amount of fat is necessary to create energy and maintain all the body functions, but an excess is harmful. The danger of animal fat is in its processing and heating, because by removing some of its coefficients it cannot be properly utilized by the body, and thus causes untold damage. Diseases of the heart caused by hardening of the blood vessels, liver and kidney troubles, disorders of the digestion and respiration can all come from eating excessive animal fat or from fat when it has been processed or continually reheated.

We should therefore concentrate on eating enough unsaturated fatty acid in our diet, because it is this which will prevent prostate disorders in old age, maintain all the functions of the brain, liver, kidneys and other glands as well as helping to prevent skin eczema and other blemishes of the skin. Since this type of fat is essential to health it is sometimes called Vitamin F, so always take a tablespoon of vegetable oil daily or eat some nuts or seeds. Soya beans are also a good source as are wheat germ, rice germ or the germ of any other grain, and therefore the whole grain itself. Unsaturated fatty acids can help to reduce cholesterol build up and can sometimes contribute towards its removal from the blood vessels. Fat is necessary for the complete combustion of carbohydrate, otherwise acid is formed which must be eliminated from the body.

Fat is also necessary for the absorption of the fat-soluble vitamins A, D, E and K from the intestines, but the taking of mineral oil will strip these vitamins from the intestines. Rancid oils and fats have much the same effect. Be sure therefore to take about $2\frac{1}{2}$ ounces (70 grams) of fat a day and try to have it in the form of cold-pressed vegetable oil or from beans, nuts or seeds. The fat from milk and its products is suitable for children but not so good for grown-ups. Keep to the liquid fats rather than the solid ones.

VITAMINS

The word vitamin was invented to mean that vital element in food, a deficiency of which makes the difference between health and a state of disease. Their function is mostly to do with the utilization of food which underlines the importance of food in health.

Now vitamins have their enemies, perhaps amongst those

who make their living from other methods of tackling disease, or even those who envisage the world being able to master its own health and therefore also disease. From time to time one reads in the press veiled attacks on vitamins which can undermine the confidence of the public in taking them.

There is no doubt that taking vitamins can vastly improve one's health and it is almost true to say the more the merrier. This certainly applies to the water-based ones, C and B (providing all the components are taken in the right proportions). Of the fat-soluble ones, D is best taken in the form of sunshine, you must find the exactly right dose of E for your complaint, and A is best taken in food form. Too much fish liver oil (A and D) or synthetic Vitamin D must be guarded against, both for children and adults; otherwise be guided by the following pages.

Since vitamins are all interdependent you need to take all of them. Just taking one for a few days will do little good. When you have been taking them all for several months, in food and capsule form, you will begin to notice a tremendous difference in your health. If you continue to take them for a matter of years every part of your body will start to function as it should. Start the vitamin habit before you are thirty, because in your forties degenerative diseases can begin and these are frequently caused by vitamin deficiencies.

Vitamins are present in all raw food but they are easily affected by sunshine and heat and can be washed and processed away. Therefore take your fruit and vegetables raw to ensure an adequate supply of vitamins as well as sufficient enzymes which are what turn food into flesh. Remember that the water-soluble vitamins B and C cannot be stored by the body and must therefore be taken daily. A, D and E can be stored but since we use them all the time they need replacing.

When you learn the many different roles vitamins play in maintaining health, you will understand why a generous supply of them can only improve your health and well-being. In order to prevent vitamin wastage, fruit and vegetables are best stored in the fridge. Ideally both are best eaten immediately they are picked.

During disease vitamin requirements are vastly increased and it is then necessary to take them in drug doses (very strong).

This will help fight disease and speed recovery. It is also worth remembering that vegetarians who do not eat eggs or dairy produce usually suffer from a Vitamin B_{12} deficiency after a few years, and that their health can be greatly improved and even saved by taking it.

VITAMIN A

Since it is fat-soluble this vitamin is stored in the body and therefore in theory it is possible to take too much, however this mostly applies to infants with over-generous mothers. 50,000 units appear to be about the maximum dose for adults over a long period, 20,000 for children and 10,000 for infants. However if toxicity does occur from excess, Vitamin C will quickly detoxify.

Vitamin A is principally found in yellow or orange coloured fruit and vegetables and green leaves. Liver, dairy products, egg yolks, apricots, carrots, sweet potatoes are particularly good sources, so are spinach, chard, turnip tops and beet greens.

This vitamin is famous for its effect on night blindness and sensitivity to bright lights, but all vision is improved by it (plus Vitamin B_2 with the whole B complex). It is also the skin vitamin for dryness, pimples, whiteheads and other blemishes. A deficiency can quickly be spotted by roughness or pimples on the outer part of the upper arm, legs, thighs, back and shoulders. Other signs of this deficiency are dull hair and dandruff, and finger nails peeling and breaking.

Vitamin A also helps to fight disease by assisting in the production of antibodies and white blood cells, and in its effect on all the mucous linings such as those of eyes, mouth, intestines, lungs, kidneys and urinary tract. Children need it for proper growth, and for skeletal and tooth formation mostly through calcium absorption. The thyroid and other glands need it for proper functioning as do the reproductive organs. It is a must for pregnant mothers and it helps to prevent the formation of kidney stones and those in the gallbladder and pulp. Squinting can be caused by lack of this vitamin.

Vitamin A is sometimes referred to as the youth vitamin because an abundant supply can add at least ten years to the prime of life and also because of its effect on the skin and internal organs. Clench your hand and see whether there is a yellow tinge below the skin before the blood rushes back. If there is, you have enough Vitamin A.

VITAMIN B COMPLEX

This vitamin was discovered by a Dutch physician in the East Indies who found that chickens which were fed only on white rice died, but that when given the polishings as well they remained healthy. In spite of this discovery the majority of people in the East still live mostly on white rice. It is the same story with white flour which is the staple food in the West.

Vitamin B is a group of compounds referred to as a complex. It is unwise to take individual members of the complex separately because they can create a deficiency of the ones not taken. This however is not the case with B_{12} and pantothenic acid which can both be taken on their own. Otherwise it is better to take preparations of the complex or to take it in the form of food, or to stimulate its production in the intestines with yogurt.

B vitamins are water-soluble and cannot therefore be stored in any appreciable quantities in the body, so should be taken daily. Antibiotics, sulphur drugs and sleeping pills destroy the bacteria which make these vitamins in the intestines, and in America you can sue your doctor if he does not tell you to take B complex supplements after prescribing these things. Yogurt, sour milk and abundant raw vegetables will help to restart the process.

The greatest cause of Vitamin B deficiency and the consequent diseases and lack of energy is white flour, and white sugar. By removing nearly all this vitamin in their processing, the body automatically creates a deficiency by robbing all its reserves to try and digest these incomplete foods. By eating what is processed out of them, the wheat germ and the molasses, we can replace the deficiency, but how time-consuming and how expensive. Other concentrated sources are liver and brewer's yeast, but egg yolks, peanuts, milk, organ meats and all fresh fruit and vegetables supply adequate amounts. Brewers' yeast creates gas when first taken but this disappears after a few weeks.

Of the many deficiency symptoms, here are a few: Irritability and nervous disorders, and resultant sleeping problems. Depression (to the degree of suicide) and lack of calm. Constipation and fatigue, and poor liver function, particularly for alcoholics. Cracked lips, sore mouth and abnormalities of the tongue. Bad digestion, poor memory and anaemia. Some heart diseases and blood vessel degeneration. Impure blood and skin eruptions. Lack of energy is nearly always the first sign of this deficiency.

People sometimes complain that B complex supplements are not doing them any good. This could be because they are not taking a large enough quantity or an adequate preparation, or because they are not including plenty of concentrated food sources as well. Both food and supplements are necessary, not only to obtain a large spread of the complex but also because a long-standing deficiency takes enormous amounts of the B vitamins to fill it. During illness larger than usual amounts are needed daily. Do not take individual B vitamins separately, except in the isolated cases I will describe later in the section on diseases.

VITAMIN C

This vitamin was discovered while investigating scurvy amongst sailors, which it was found to cure. It is one of the cheapest vitamins to manufacture and in some countries it is sold for half the price that is asked for it in other parts of the world. It is the best-known vitamin (also being called ascorbic acid) because it occurs so abundantly in citrus fruit, practically all other fruit, sprouting seeds and some vegetables. Most animals synthesize it themselves except guinea pigs, monkeys and humans.

Since it is water-soluble it is only stored in the body in small quantities, particularly in the adrenal glands, the pancreas, liver, pituitary, kidneys, spleen and thymus glands, so it must be taken daily. The amount needed varies according to whatever stress is being undergone, and the amout of toxins inhaled, eaten and produced within the body. For example smokers need extra large amounts, as do people under surgery and those who are ill, therefore it is impossible to state even an approximate daily requirement. Vitamin C is destroyed while performing its tasks in the body, therefore the tissues need to be saturated during disease before it is prudent to reduce the dose. Since any excess is eliminated in the urine this can be safely done. In illness 1 gram every hour or 3 grams every 3 hours may suffice. I personally take at least 1 gram daily after each meal.

Vitamin C is also a complex since it consists of the bio-flavonoids as well (sometimes called Vitamin P) which predominate in brightly coloured fruit, grapes, rose hips and buckwheat, but absorbic acid alone will always suffice. The first signs of Vitamin C deficiency are bruises, bleeding gums, loose teeth and an inability to overcome infection. In such cases the tissues must be saturated with half-hourly 1 gram doses or even more until the symptoms disappear. This advice should always be followed whenever this vitamin is called upon for assistance.

Vitamin C maintains the integrity of the capillaries and tiny blood vessels, thus preventing harmful substances entering them. It assists in overcoming infections by rendering bacterial toxins harmless, by inhibiting bacterial growth and by destroying viruses and bacteria. Snake bites and those from other poisonous animals can be neutralized by this vitamin but if life is at stake (and it often is) it is necessary to have intravenous injections (calcium will then assist its effect). But obviously do not rely upon Vitamin C, go immediately to a doctor.

Otherwise the chewable sort of Vitamin C is easily assimilated. Its protective action against disease is to stimulate the production of anti-bodies and white blood cells, as well as assisting the adrenal glands. Fevers can often be swiftly reduced with Vitamin C as can serious illness be assisted, such as encephalitis, meningitis, poliomyelitis, virus pneumonia, tetanus, mumps, prostate infections, and hepatitis.

Vitamin C is a must for healing wounds (cuts or surgery), for all liver troubles, certain types of arthritis, all stress diseases (plus B complex), to help reduce cholesterol levels, as an anticoagulant, to fight allergies, reduce damage from X-ray treatment, stimulate the thyroid gland and to help in schizophrenia and diabetes. It aids in the assimilation of iron and acts as a diuretic. This is an impressive list and it is by no means complete because Vitamin C is also needed for making the dentine of teeth, for bones, cartilage and connective tissue. It helps varicose veins, haemorrhoids, nose bleeds, haemorrhages and bruises. Convalescents should always take it, as should those with anaemia.

Fresh fruit and some vegetables are the principal source, or it can be bought as ascorbic acid or in health food shops as rose hips or acerola berries. The white pith of citrus fruit contains more than the pulp. Dairy products, meat, eggs, fish and poultry contain only minute quantities but human milk has a little more. Since heat and light accelerate the oxidization of this vitamin, fruit and vegetables are best stored in the fridge. Peeled or chopped fruit or vegetables oxidize especially quickly and Vitamin C can easily be washed away with cooking water or by soaking. It is always wise to take some Vitamin C additional to food sources.

Children particularly need it for growth and for its action with oxygen which gives endurance (as for all of us). On sea voyages sprout some seeds such as mung or soya beans, even wheat or barley to ensure a natural supply as well as taking absorbic acid. Anyone wanting to acquire immunity to disease should take this vitamin, therefore it should be a must for us all. Since Vitamin C is recycled by the kidneys, it tends to be in short supply in those with damaged kidneys.

There is practically no diseased state which this vitamin will not help, so we should have it constantly at hand and have our tissues always saturated with it. Antibiotics and other drugs are commonly used to do what Vitamin C can do cheaper, better, without danger and to the lasting improvement of health. Vitamin C is the best first aid for almost any disease.

VITAMIN D

This vitamin is formed by the action of sunlight on the oils in our skins. There is no other really reliable source, although it is found in fish liver oils and minute amounts in butter and milk, eggs, tuna fish, herrings and liver. It can now be manufactured synthetically but this is the one vitamin which it is dangerous to take in excess, so follow the directions. However it can be stored by the body since it is fat-soluble, so a summer's supply will help you through the winter.

Children have the most urgent need for this vitamin because normal growth will not take place without it and bowed legs, knock-knees, pigeon chest, receding chin, large forehead and crowded or buck teeth result. Rickets is the classic Vitamin D deficiency disease because of its effect on calcium and phosphorus utilization, therefore many calcium or phosphorus deficiencies can be traced to Vitamin D deficiency.

Our energy supply is affected by lack of this vitamin because sugar is not burnt up efficiently, and nerves and brain function is also affected by inadequate calcium and phosphorus. Dental caries and the general health of our teeth are thus affected by Vitamin D deficiency, and so are our bones, especially the jaw. Broken bones and poor sight need Vitamin D, as do bone diseases such as arthritis.

Do not overlook your Vitamin D requirements and take some sunshine regularly. If this is not possible, rely on fish liver oils or even synthetic preparations, because your body needs this vitamin, particularly in winter.

VITAMIN E

This is usually referred to as the sex vitamin, but it could be as truly called the heart vitamin. It was discovered while searching for the cause of infertility in rats. It was found that a deficiency causes irreparable damage to the male reproductive organs and temporary damage to those of the female. The world authority on Vitamin E is the Shute Foundation in London, Ontario, Canada which has done interesting work with tens of thousands of people with heart disease, liver troubles, diabetes and problems of infertility.

For the heart, it can act as an anticoagulant in blood clotting, reduce hardening of arteries and helps phlebitis, varicose veins and haemorrhoids. Since it improves muscle tone it can, in some cases, actually help the heart itself, quite apart from its oxygen qualities.

Before and after surgery Vitamin E should be given to prevent dangerous blood clotting, to prevent scarring, phlebitis or haemorrhoids. It will help prevent the scarring from burns if applied externally and internally. All scar tissue can be softened and sometimes completely removed both inside and outside the body. This particularly applies to kidney disease, stomach ulcers and cystitis scars. This vitamin also helps prevent wrinkles of the skin.

By its oxygenating qualities Vitamin E assists the liver to detoxify poisons and therefore helps all liver complaints. Female frigidity has been cured by its use as well as infertility, premature births, miscarriages, and menstrual disorders. Malfunction of the thyroid gland or pituitary and all cases of shock and therefore stress (through adrenal glands) are assisted by it. The unpleasant effects of change of life can be modified, and endurance can be greatly increased.

All forms of arthritis benefit from taking Vitamin E as do cataracts, kidney and gall stones, even anaemia (through blood regenerating action). Calcification of the soft tissues can be prevented and sex interest can be retained longer, and sometimes regained. This vitamin improves all glandular health and increases the production of hormones.

Vitamin E is generally sold by International Units if it is natural and by milligrams if it is synthetic. It is labelled d alpha-tocopherol if natural and di alpha-tocopherol if synthetic. It is important to find exactly the right dose for your complaint, so start with 100 i.u's daily and gradually build up because taking too little will have no effect. When you are cured, 100 i.u's daily is probably enough as a prophylactic dose, although this varies according to the amount of unsaturated fatty acid eaten. On the other hand it may be necessary to take high doses all your life. Vitamin E is destroyed by rancid oils and fats, by lead and iron salts and by mineral oil taken as a laxative. Sunlight oxidises it in food.

The germ of cereal grains is the best food source, therefore the oils of wheat and rice germ, also sunflower and sesame seeds, soya bean and cotton seed (all best cold-pressed) are valuable. Green vegetables contain a little Vitamin E as do avocado pears. Therefore eat only whole grains, nuts, seeds, soya beans and have green leafy vegetables daily.

Heart disease is as common today amongst the young as the old, and degenerative diseases are the lot of everyone, but they could all be prevented with Vitamin E, and all can be corrected at least in part by it. But small doses may not be sufficient, it may be necessary to take four, five or six hundred units daily.

VITAMIN K

This is the blood-clotting vitamin and therefore important in treatment of haermorrhaging. It is fat-soluble and small amounts are stored in the liver. Deficiencies are uncommon because it is synthesized in the intestines and contained in green leaves and liver.

Infants are born without it but since more than 10 milligrams are toxic to them, medical advice should be taken before giving it to them. Adults can take 10 milligrams safely. Sulfa drugs and antibiotics interfere with synthesis of this vitamin (as with Vitamin B) but this can be restarted with yogurt and sour milk.

Can anyone in their right senses, having read these facts about vitamins, possibly disregard them? The filling of a vitamin deficiency is not such a difficult matter, whether you take whole food or supplement your diet with capsules. Is it not worth studying these facts to find out how you can cure your own vitamin deficiency diseases, and then following the advice in the rest of the book to build health? You would not only save yourself a lot of trouble but also a lot of pain, worry and discomfort too. Vitamins are needed, they are essential to health and they are all there in the food which nature has to offer us. We disregard them at the risk of our health and in the certainty of ultimately becoming ill.

MINERALS

Minerals are as vital as vitamins and as essential for health, but they are frequently overlooked because of the better-known vitamins. Also they are less easy to administer since they have to be in the right proportions, and therefore nutritionists and nature-cure practitioners tend to rely upon food sources. However in the middle of the nineteenth century Dr Scheussler discovered that by taking minute homeopathic doses of the twelve principal mineral combinations which exist in the body, the daily imbalances could be corrected and health restored. He also stated that almost every disease causes or is caused by an imbalance of minerals, which can be put right by his method of application. He then proceeded to enumerate in minute detail the exact mineral deficiency symptoms. If you buy a copy of 'Dr Scheussler's Biochemistry' by J. B. Chapman from your health food shop you will discover the genius of his work.

Long-standing and acute mineral deficiences can also be dealt with by the Scheussler method. Occasionally supplements of mineral combinations can help if taken for only a short time, but it is essential to know their proportions and relationships with other minerals, even with other vitamins. My advice therefore is to check your diet for adequate quantities of minerals and to keep a box of the 12 mineral cell salts developed by Dr Scheussler always at hand for daily imbalances. This is what I do myself and rarely a day passes when I do not call on his wisdom. For taking additional supplements, advice is given further on in this book.

During a recent tour of England when I called on many health establishments and consulted numerous people who should have known better, I was greeted with blank faces when I asked them how they administered minerals. The reason was that they never did administer them nor prescribe them. Perhaps they were under the impression that the seven principal minerals are normally adequately supplied in food and that the trace minerals are hard to come by. But this is by no means the case as they would have discovered had they studied Dr Scheussler's work, or indeed probed more deeply to find the cause of their patients' complaints. Let me explain further.

About 4% of our total body weight consists of mineral elements which is not much, when you consider that up to 70% is water and the rest solid matter. Of this 4% most of the weight comes from our body skeletal structure, including jaw, head, ribs, back bone and long bones, all of which contain calcium and phosphorus which leaves only 25% of the 4% for the rest.

Five other minerals account of most of the balance: potassium, sulphur, sodium, chlorine and magnesium. The remainder are known as trace elements because they are only required in minute quantities, but they are as essential to health as the others. The better-known are: iron, manganese, copper, iodine, cobalt, fluorine and zinc, but the list also includes chromium, molybdenum, selenium, aluminium, arsenic, barium, boron, bromine, cadmium, lead, nickel, silicon, stronium and vanadium.

Minerals are found in organic compounds, in inorganic ones and as free ions. The skeletal structure contains most of the body's calcium, phosphorus and magnesium, and the soft tissues most of the potassium, sodium, chlorine and sulphur. Minerals generally tend to regulate the body's activities such as muscle contraction and relaxation, nerve response, water balance, acid-alkaline equilibrium and the metabolism of food, to name but a few. Calcium, phosphorus and magnesium work together to build and maintain the bony structure, whereas iron, copper and cobalt all function together in the blood and do so inadequately without one another.

Thus, generally speaking, minerals tend to group themselves together for their particular functions and that is the way I intend to deal with them now:

1. Calcium, phosphorus and magnesium are all involved in bones, teeth, nerves, circulation, heart-beat, blood and digestion.
2. Sodium, chlorine and potassium regulate the water balance, osmotic pressure, digestion, acid-alkaline balance and to some extent nerve and muscle irritability.
3. Iron, copper and cobalt play a vital part in the blood as haemoglobin, necessary for oxygen transportation, energy production and prevention of anaemia.
4. Sulphur and zinc are essential for digestion, also for hair, nails and cartilage.
5. Iodine and manganese are both needed for proper working of the thyroid gland and its important role in physical and mental health.

There is a constant exchange of minerals in the body, even in the bones. The soft tissue cells maintain a high degree of activity and the glands continually use minerals for hormone production. Those that are not needed are eliminated in the urine and faeces by the bowels and kidneys, as well as through the skin. Very often we do not have enough of these essential elements and health can greatly be improved by rebalancing the body's supply. This is reasonable when you realize that minerals work with enzymes to turn food into flesh, bones, teeth, glands, nerves and to make energy. In fact proper nutrition is impossible without them because food would not be correctly digested or utilized.

An adequate daily supply of minerals should be easy enough to obtain through a normal diet, but some minerals are difficult to absorb and utilize and others are not over-generously supplied in nature unless a very varied diet is eaten. However the water we drink can be a great help in providing many of them, if we live in a mineral-rich district. A daily amount of seaweed, either dried in the form of kelp from health food shops, or in its natural state as sold in some countries, provides essential iodine and other minerals. Fresh vegetables, nuts and seeds, whole cereals and liver come next on the list, and are anyway musts for proper nutrition.

Milk and eggs are the only two complete foods which contain all our daily needs, and of course they contain plenty of minerals, particularly calcium and phosphorus in milk, and iron in eggs. Brewers' yeast, which is such a valuable food for health, also contains many minerals, and fruit is useful for its alkaline effect. To this list should be added salt for sodium and chlorine, but it must only be taken as sea salt or specially prepared biochemic salt. Also it should only be taken between meals with a little water, never with food and not more than 4 grams daily. Dr Scheussler's biochemic mineral salts can correct the hourly imbalances in any particular organ or other part of the body.

CALCIUM, PHOSPHORUS AND MAGNESIUM

These are all primarily found in the bones, therefore an acute imbalance can be rectified by taking bone meal. However too much calcium for children or adults can cause an imbalance of magnesium, which, amongst other things, is nature's tranquillizer. Calcium is used for the contraction of muscles, for a steady heart-beat, blood-clotting, circulation and memory, normal relaxed nerve responses, cell permeability, the activation of some enzymes and to prevent anaemia. Calcium is necessary for growth, and for proper nutrition, and is essential for convalescents since it helps with food utilization. It can also de-sensitize pain and induce sound sleep. If too much is taken in the form of calcium phosphate for too long it can cause calcium deposits, and that is dangerous for blood vessels and spurs on the joints can result.

Its partner, phosphorus, is needed also for energy production, glandular secretions and all body fluids. It also plays a part in maintaining the acid-base balance, regulating the transportation and metabolism of fats and carbohydrates and the utilization of calcium for bone and teeth formation. Both minerals need hydrochloric acid in the stomach to dissolve them, and Vitamin D and unsaturated fatty acids for absorption. A malfunctioning thyroid gland will also upset their usage. If enough protein is eaten, phosphorus will certainly be adequately supplied, but possibly not enough calcium, which can be obtained from bone meal, eggshells dissolved in lemon juice or milk. The relationship between the two should be $1\frac{1}{2}$ parts phosphorus to 1 part calcium.

70% of our magnesium is found in our bones, the rest plays a part in the contraction of muscles and in regulating the heart, nervous and skeletal tissues. It is also needed for energy production. Anyone consuming excessive concentrated carbohydrate such as alcohol, white sugar, even white flour and white rice or dried fruits can cause a magnesium deficiency. This is characterized by a craving for sweets or alcohol, by irritability or nervousness, even convulsions, abnormal heartbeat and possibly insanity. Magnesium has been known to correct angina and coronary problems, to reduce cholesterol levels, melt kidney and gall stones, and protect people from the effects of stress.

Milk and dairy products supply enough calcium and phosphorus for growing children, but later in life they are less frequently taken, and the calcium in pasteurized dairy products is less easily available. Other sources are almonds, soya beans, sesame seeds, whitebait, mustard greens, broccoli, leafy green vegetables and kale. Most fresh vegetables contain some, as well as most fruit, particularly dried figs. Bone meal and dissolved eggshells are a concentrated supply. Do not take it for granted that you obtain enough calcium in your diet because you may well not. Boil down some bones for stock or include some skim milk in your diet.

Magnesium is to the plant what iron is to the blood. It is found in leafy green vegetables, in nuts and seeds, eggs, legumes and citrus fruit. Whole cereal grains also provide some but there is little in white flour. In the case of serious deficiency, Epsom salts are a concentrated source.

SODIUM, CHLORINE AND POTASSIUM

Sodium and chlorine combine to make common salt, but since table salt can be unhealthy it should only ever be eaten as sea salt, or specially prepared biochemic salt, which have enough other elements to make them non-toxic to plasma. Sodium and potassium play vital roles inside and outside the cells of the body, and it is the constant tension between these two which portrays vibrant health. If too little potassium is eaten sodium will replace it in the cells and many troubles ensue.

Sodium is one of the vital nutrients of the body because without it normal cell division cannot take place, and therefore malnutrition and anaemia follow. Too much is dangerous. Salt is one of the least understood food elements. So many people pour it on to their food and into their cooking, with disastrous results. Unfortunately some symptoms of excessive salt intake are the same as for a deficiency. In both cases you become excessively thirsty, either because of too little water in the body, or because of too much salt, which the water can help to eliminate through the kidneys.

Without any salt the body would not retain water, because this is what distributes it. The blood would dry out, internal secretions would not take place and there would be no hydrochloric acid in the stomach which is necessary for digestion. There would be too much or too little water in many parts of the body, and a watery and bloated appearance which would be accompanied by drowsiness, langour and watery exudations or excessive dryness. This is because salt transports water round the body and ensures an equal distribution.

Any dry surface in the body is usually a salt deficiency symptom, so is drowsiness and unrefreshing sleep as well as low spirits. The eyes discharge watery mucus and water easily, you lose your sense of taste and smell and your nose runs. There is excessive saliva in the mouth, the lips crack, blisters appear round the mouth, so do cold sores, the tongue and mouth become dry. Water comes up into the throat from the stomach, you become violently thirsty or ravenously hungry but have an aversion for bread.

The acid deficiency in the stomach causes indigestion and you crave salt. There is constipation from dry bowels. The skin has watery blisters and thin whitish scales, it is greasy on the forehead and where there are sweat glands. It is sore in the bends of the knees and elbows. The hair is dry and falls out. Insect bites are troublesome: they can be treated externally with salt. You develop nettlerash and violent itching after exertion, eczema appears on the eyebrows, behind the ears and at the hairy margin of the scalp, hang-nails grow. The blood becomes thin and watery, causing anaemia (which also needs iron, copper, calcium, Vitamin B_{12} and correct food).

Salt can be used externally with excellent results, not only for insect bites but for healing (witness sea water for this). It can be used as a gargle or spray for catarrhal infections. The stress of cold weather or swimming in very cold water can cause an imbalance which is particularly noticeable in the morning.

Damaged kidneys cause a permanent deficiency, and the first stage of stress is always the elimination of salt (surgery, accidents or shock). Prolonged stress such as worry, or internal disease, causes retention of salt and therefore water.

Salt is always best taken between meals with a little water. 4 grams a day (about one scant level teaspoon) is normally enough but excessive sweating, diarrhoea, vomiting or urination cause abnormal losses. It is best not taken with food.

The first stage of a cold can be greatly helped by a little salt, as can most infections where there is inflammation and a bloated appearance. Bags under the eyes are usually caused by salt imbalance, so are abdominal or leg cramps. The cells of the body can neither be nourished properly nor eliminate their wastes (both by osmosis) without salt. Excessive gas in the stomach or intestines can also be caused by salt deficiency, as can lung infections and ulcers of the eyes. Sunstroke and heat cramps cause a salt deficiency, as do severe burns. There is a feeling of hopelessness and muscle weakness without enough salt and it can even be the cause of death.

A gross excess of salt is used as a method of suicide in the East, even an accumulative excess causes high blood pressure, thus cortisone therapy is dangerous. Since vegetarians only obtain minute quantities from their food they sometimes need additional amounts. In theory perhaps this is not necessary but in practice I have found it to be so. Otherwise muscle meat, milk, cheese, bread and eggs contain a little and all food which is preserved with salt.

Potassium is the great antagonist of sodium and their constant interplay is vital to health. Too little potassium and too much sodium cause waterlogging in the cells, because sodium replaces potassium inside the cell. This is dangerous. Potassium is essential to maintain the sodium balance, and if necessary to drive out excess. It also works with sodium in osmosis (the feeding of the cells), in preventing constipation, maintaining body alkalinity, growth, digestion, normal sleep, prevention of fatigue, and muscle contraction. A deficiency leads to slow and irregular heart-beat and even damage of its muscles, the kidneys enlarge and bones become brittle.

Whole grains are rich sources of potassium, so are molasses, potatoes, almonds and other nuts, figs, brewers' yeast, most fruit and leafy green vegetables. The refining of food causes loss, and cooking in water sends most of it down the drain. Choose potassium-rich foods to ensure that the sodium/potassium balance is maintained in proper proportions. Remember that excessive urination can cause a deficiency of potassium, and so can diarrhoea, but not excessive sweating. Medical advice should always be sought before taking extra potassium as the right balance must be maintained.

IRON, COPPER AND COBALT

Every cell of the body depends on iron for its oxygen, but copper is necessary before it can be utilized so the two must always go together. Cobalt is a component of Vitamin B_{12} which is essential for normal blood formation, therefore it is also a must with iron and copper.

Iron removes some of the carbon dioxide from the cells and plays a part with enzymes. A deficiency causes anaemia but this can often be corrected by copper alone since the iron may be present but not being utilized. However anaemia may also persist without cobalt in the form of Vitamin B_{12}. Rich red blood therefore depends on these three minerals as well as food and our blood supply is what feeds our cells, gives us energy, repairs and builds our body and maintains our mental activity.

Iron also gives strength to the walls of the blood vessels, and it is vital for taking oxygen to diseased parts of the body, particularly inflammations. An abnormally flushed face needs iron, so do fevers, quick full pulse, hot dry skin, pain and redness. A rush of blood to the head often calls for iron, so does inflammation of the eyes, conjunctivitis, red eyes (accompanied by a burning sensation like grains of sand in the eyes), nosebleeds, sore throats of singers and orators, loss of voice and hoarseness. Bronchitis and respiratory infections need iron, also haemorrhoids, heart palpitation, rheumatic pains, stiffness from cold, strains and sprains, back pains, congested blood flow.

Although iron is recycled from the breakdown of the cells and some is stored in the muscles and liver, we must still have a daily supply to satisfy our needs. Infants in particular would use up the supply they were born with if only fed on cows' milk (mothers' milk contains $2\frac{1}{2}$ times more) after six months. Vegetarians should watch their diet carefully for iron and be certain to take Vitamin B_{12} to prevent anaemia. Non-vegetarians find it in muscle meat, liver, kidneys, egg yolks, bone marrow, oysters and clams. It is also plentiful in the vegetable kingdom if you look for it: molasses, peanuts, almonds, pineapples, loganberries, apricots, figs, prunes, dates, wheat germ (therefore whole grains), soya beans, brewers' yeast, sweet potatoes, green leafy vegetables and parsley.

Iron needs hydrochloric acid for absorption (therefore salt) and is helped by Vitamins C and E. Iron compounds such as ferrous sulphate and gluconate are toxic and even fatal in doses exceeding 900 milligrams, also they destroy Vitamin E in the intestines, therefore it is best to rely upon food sources. Liver extract or dessicated liver are also convenient sources.

ZINC AND SULPHUR

Sulphur is important as a blood cleanser and conditioner, also for digestion through the bile and liver. It helps maintain healthy skin, nails, hair and cartilage. All protein contains some, also cabbage and sprouts as well as garlic, onions and leeks.

Zinc helps growth and food absorption. It is found in the liver, pancreas and thyroid glands but more particularly is needed for the male sex glands and the prostate. Some pumpkin seeds will supply your daily needs, otherwise sea foods, oysters, wheat germ, brewers' yeast and liver supply a little. Zinc can help to normalize the prostate even late in life so it is a valuable mineral.

IODINE AND MANGANESE

Iodine is principally associated with the thyroid gland and a deficiency causes goitre. Minute amounts are needed but without them the thyroid malfunctions and we lose our zest for work and play, have no mental or physical energy and put on weight easily because of poor metabolism. Skin, hair and nails are also affected by the thyroid and it helps maintain health, a trim figure and an alert personality. Other symptoms include abnormal reactions to heat and cold, hands and feet which are never warm enough, mental and physical sluggishness, decreased sexual urge, faulty memory, a constant desire to sleep and early ageing.

Lack of iodine can also produce an overactive thyroid gland which makes people highly-strung, excessively nervous, intolerant of heat, have clammy hands and protruding eyes and causes irritability and difficulty in sleeping. To normalize the thyroid gland see under diseases. The best food supply of iodine is sea weed (dried kelp) or oysters, sardines, shrimps and other sea food, also eggs, spinach, oatmeal, baked potatoes, milk, cabbage, radishes, tomatoes, watercress, apple seeds and oranges. Sea salt also has some iodine.

Manganese is needed also for the proper working of the thyroid gland and a deficiency can cause lack of maternal instinct. Manganese is concentrated in the liver, pancreas and adrenal glands. Green leaves, peas, beets, egg yolks and nuts supply adequate amounts as do whole grains and most meats.

That about covers the principal minerals, but it is worth adding that the body needs to remain alkaline and this is achieved mostly by calcium, magnesium, sodium and potassium as opposed to phosphorus, sulphur and chlorine which are acid in reaction. We need a ratio of four parts alkaline to one part acid for healthy cell activity. This is why one should not eat too much acid-forming foods like meat, cereal grains, eggs, fish, sugar and food preserved with it, cheese, walnuts, and peanuts. Eat lots of fresh fruit and vegetables which are nearly all alkaline as are milk, brewers' yeast, most nuts and seeds, most dried fruit and honey. All protein is acid and the excess nitrogen needs to be eliminated.

Therefore our health depends on our mineral balance, because an acid body brings many troubles. This balance is not difficult to achieve if we eat lots of fresh fruit and vegetables, most of them in their raw state so as not to lose any of the vital vitamins and minerals. If you are in any doubt about eating enough alkaline foods you should add to your diet nuts and seeds, brewers' yeast and occasionally honey and dried fruit, possibly milk in small amounts (but only unpasteurized).

However, proper nutrition does not depend on one food element such as minerals, but on all of them in their right proportions. Protein, carbohydrate, fat, vitamins, water and air all work together with minerals to produce health as I will describe later. Before ending this section let me add a word about some other essentials.

WATER

It is easy to overlook such a common substance but a good supply or a bad one can greatly influence health. The best source is the food we eat, principally fruit and vegetables and in fact if you are properly nourished and healthy you will never need to drink any water. I have been living in the tropics for the past eighteen months and no liquid has passed my lips except the minute amount I have with my salt twice a day. The body is so designed as to retain water in the intestines and other tissues for when we need it, such as to keep us cool.

However most people are not that healthy and by drinking a little water between meals can help to eliminate poisons or excesses of any kind, which is mostly the reason we feel thirsty. But be careful because too much water can also eliminate vitamins, minerals, protein and other valuable food substances in the urine.

86% of my diet is water (mostly fruit, vegetables, nuts, seeds, yeast and soya beans) but more than 55% of everyone's diet is water, and we also make it as a by-product of metabolism. Sodium chloride, sodium phosphate and sodium sulphate control the distribution, metabolism and elimination of water in the body and can be effectively taken as mineral cell salts (Dr Scheussler), so if you have these there is no need to worry.

Never drink water with your meals as it dilutes the gastric juices essential for digestion. Only ever drink when you are thirsty. If you have any problems eliminating water from your body immediately take advice. Untreated spring water is the best or that which is sold as mineral water, because it contains therapeutic qualities. City water is usually over-chlorinated which adversely affects digestion, but it is better than drinking foul water. If necessary boil it to be on the safe side. Artificially softened water should be avoided.

Cold running water also has remarkable powers of cleansing wounds, reducing fevers and bringing blood to sprains, boils, inflammations, insect bites and burns which I will deal with at greater length under diseases.

ENZYMES

Enzymes are what turn food into flesh, hair, nails, bones, nerves and blood and produce all the other chemical reactions necessary to a healthy body. They are therefore essential for every function of our body. Each enzyme has a particular job but most are concerned with turning food into whatever it is required for, such as energy, maintenance or repair. Enzyme activity depends to a large degree on whether its desired environment of acid or alkaline is present, upon the heat it needs and upon whether the protein, minerals and vitamins are at hand to make the chemical reaction possible. Other enzymes control the life cycle, growth, ripening processes and decomposition of plants. An enzyme oxidizes Vitamin C in fruit and vegetables and thus destroys it, which is why such food should be put in the fridge quickly because heat is necessary for this oxidizing action.

Enzymes are mostly destroyed above blood temperature which is the best argument for eating all your fruit and vegetables raw. I do, so do a great many other people and they taste much better this way. The enzyme in milk which is used for assimilating calcium and phosphorus is destroyed when it is pasteurized (heated). Other enzymes are produced within our bodies but the older we get the weaker does this supply become, until our final hour when they spring into action to decompose our body. They can be preserved indefinitely in food which is dried below blood temperature or deep-frozen. Dormant enzymes in dry rice and other grains have been found to contain active enzymes even after three thousand years in the Pyramids.

Raw liver is rich in enzymes, so are sun-ripened fresh fruit and vegetables. Boiling water is a certain killer for enzymes, so use the minimum heat and the juice of the vegetable itself to cook it in, if you must. The more enzymes you obtain from your food (exogenous ones) the less you have to produce inside your body, therefore save your body the extra work because the older you grow, the less easy does that process become.

There is also an enzyme known as the intrinsic factor which is essential for the utilization of Vitamin B_{12}. In pernicious anaemia the stomach has become so unhealthy that it cannot secrete this enzyme or hydrochloric acid so B_{12} must be injected. Eating liver, wheat germ and yeast will all help these secretions.

ANTI-STRESS FACTORS

These vitamin-like substances are found in liver, wheat germ, brewers' yeast, kidneys, soya beans and green leafy vegetables (even cooked ones but not juices), and are essential to repair the ravages of stress which causes so many of the modern diseases. Ill people particularly should work as many as possible into their diet. Everyone can improve their health and resistance with them.

3. About Diseases

ABOUT DISEASES

About Diseases	59
Your Medicines	63
Rest and Relaxation	65
Fresh Air	65
Breathing	65
Sunshine	66
Exercise	66
Water	67
Whole Food	68
Vitamin Therapy	68
Vitamins A and D	69
Vitamin B Complex	69
Vitamin C	70
Vitamin E	70
Vitamin F	71
Vitamin P	71
Mineral Therapy	71
Calcium, Phosphorus and Magnesium	72
Sodium, Chlorine and Potassium	73
Iron, Copper and Cobalt	73
Sulphur and Zinc	74
Iodine and Manganese	74
Trace Elements	74
Minerals Generally	74
Fasting	74
Homeopathy	76
The Mind	76
Special Foods	77

  Wheat Germ Oil, 77   Liver, 78   Green Vegetables, 78
  Yeast, 78   Soya Beans, 79   Garlic, 79   Juices, 79
  Nuts and Seeds, 80   Charcoal, 80   Lecithin, 80
  Ginsen 80

SPECIFIC DISEASES

Abscesses, 83
Acne, 83
Alcoholism, 84
Allergies, 84
Anaemia, 85
Arthritis, 86
Beauty, 87
Blood Sugar, 87
Bones, 88
Bronchitis, 88
Bruises, 89
Burns, 88
Cancer, 89
Cataracts, 90
Change-of-life, 90
Chilblains, 90
Colds, 90
Cold Sores, 91
Constipation, 91
Convalescence, 91
Cramp, 92
Dandruff, 92
Depression, 92
Diabetes, 92
Diarrhoea, 93
Emotions, 93
Energy, 93
Eyes, 94
Flu, 94
Fevers, 94
Glands, 94
Gout, 95
Gums, 95
Hang-Nails, 95
Headaches, 95
Heart, 96

Indigestion, 96
Insomnia, 97
Jaundice, 97
Joints, 98
Kidneys, 98
Lips, 99
Mental Health, 99
Memory, 99
Metabolism, 99
Mumps, 100
Muscles, 100
Nails, 100
Nerves, 100
Neuritis, 101
Pain, 101
Piles, 101
Poisoning, 102
Prostate Gland, 102
Respiration, 102
Rheumatism, 102
Scars, 103
Sex, 103
Shyness, 103
Sinus Problems, 104
Skin, 104
Stress, 104
Sunstroke, 105
Teeth, 105
Thirst, 105
Thyroid Gland, 106
Tongue, 106
Twitching, 107
Ulcers, 107
Varicose Veins, 107
Water Retention, 108
Warts, 108

DISEASE

In healthy flesh
No virus, germ
Can ever take a hold,
'Tis only when devitalized
The root begins to grow.

To cure disease
And rotting flesh
Requires the same fair hand,
For nature only can undo
What ignorance began.

So take your food
Straight from the ground,
Devour it while it's live,
This way it can and always will
Ensure your body thrives.

ABOUT DISEASES

WHAT are called National Health Services in most countries should in fact be called National Disease Services because that is what they are concerned with and the function they perform. Curing disease and achieving health are two completely different things because curing disease does not necessarily mean becoming healthy, although becoming healthy does mean curing disease. Would it not be more sensible therefore to concentrate our attention on the national health which might then practically eliminate the nation's diseases? One is positive and lasting while the other is a continual drain on the exchequer and can never accomplish what people are seeking, namely health. However doctors are trained for at least seven years to learn the names of diseases and how to deal with their symptoms, yet they only learn about nutrition for a few weeks of that time and this is where the real cause of disease mostly lies.

Why do we not read about health in the Press nor hear about it on the radio and television? Does that not seem rather strange? We read about some new wonder drug the moment it has been invented, but not about the positive steps for building health. Are we expected to know how to be healthy without being taught? Is this knowledge considered to be dangerous for us and if so why? Although animals seem to know by instinct how to deal with their ills and keep themselves healthy, our senses have become so perverted by civilization that they no longer transmit the truth. The chances of remaining healthy with so many semi-foods on sale are not very great and be quite sure of one fact, that disease comes from not being healthy even though this may be only a very temporary state.

Now health is not only nutrition as I said earlier, it is a whole way of life and thinking, but proper nourishment and rest are the best way of tackling disease unless a fast is called for. In days gone by much of disease was caused by people not having enough to eat and thus developing deficiency and degenerative diseases. Even today this is still the case, not because people do not have enough to eat, but because they eat semi-foods which cause deficiency symptoms and degenerative changes. Of course living conditions have improved and the two great allies of disease, damp and cold are less prevalent and the dirt diseases have mostly been eliminated. We are left with the problems of the missing elements of food and an unhealthy way of life.

To bear this out let me tell you about a doctor friend of mine who has his clinic in his own house in a little village. Every time I call there, I find people lying on their backs having blood transfusions. He explains that many of his patients have some form of anaemia, and that this is the best cure for them. It does not take much imagination to see what he is in fact doing for them, namely giving them a decent meal with all the necessary food elements because that is where all digested food ends up, in the bloodstream. He had overlooked copper without which the iron, so necessary in anaemia, cannot be utilized, or Vitamin B_{12} without which blood cannot be formed, or salt without which cell division cannot take place, or calcium without which proper nutrition is impossible, quite apart from fresh air and exercise, because he was never taught about them in medical school.

Had he been educated in a positive attitude to health he would not have wasted so much of other people's precious blood, or their money. The body is built to fight infection and to be self-repairing, and all it needs is the raw materials to do the job. These raw materials are principally food with the addition of fresh air, sunshine, exercise and a healthy mind, and those are the medicines I have to offer you here. The body is one entity and when one part of it goes wrong it is because we have maltreated or abused it as a whole, and therefore we must try to put it right by tackling the whole and not the individual part. For that reason the cause must always be found and the body as a whole restored to health.

You may wonder why, with all this talk about disease, I have not so far mentioned that ominous word germ. The answer is because germs themselves are not the cause of disease, but the unhealthy body onto which they fall. Germs are there most of the time and it is only when our defences are down that we are unable to cope with them. These defences consist of the whole body, including the mind, which must not only be healthy but positively want health. For that reason I have no patent medicines to offer you, only what nature provides us with to maintain health and a deficiency of which has been proved to cause disease. This is not a journey into the complicated world of chemistry, but into the comparatively easy one of eating and living, because those daily tasks were not meant to be arduous. There is ample material to draw on, because man has studied his eating and living habits in minute details over many thousands of years with a remarkable degree of success.

It is true that we have learnt to prolong life, and that we now know a great deal more about the workings of the body, but we are too preoccupied with theories which we do not necessarily know as facts. In the past man did not try to prove why, because he did not anyway have the scientific instruments, and the only proof was that it worked and continued to do so. Now we attack the symptoms of disease and when those have disappeared we say the person is cured, whereas we may have only driven it deeper into the body. What we are doing is to interfere with nature which we only partly understand. We would do better to stick to nature and those known facts than to flirt with new theories every month.

I have before me thirty volumes of a Chinese work compiled more than three hundred years ago, stating exactly what food and herbs cure what symptoms. I also have innumerable American books stating which elements in food have been used to regain health from a multitude of diseases. I have the famous Swiss and German books which are derived from the great Vienna school of medicine and which form the basis of the European natural healing. I have books on the findings of Dr Scheussler which state specifically and in detail exactly which symptom can be corrected by which of his 12 mineral cell salts. I have books on the homeopathic principles of curing like with like, many of which I have used and proved myself. None of these books is able to qualify by scientific proof why what they say works, and if they were I should doubt them, and lose confidence in their content. What we all want to know is what works, and that it has been proved to be effective over the years. That at least is all I am concerned with and what you will find in this book.

No one in their right senses pretends that drugs cure disease, although they do sometimes relieve symptoms which enables the body to heal itself. At least 85% of all diseases are self-determining, which means that they cure themselves given a reasonable chance in the right circumstances. More than 90% of our diseases are self-inflicted or degenerative in origin, and can be put right in the same way as they were caused. The other 10% could be prevented by proper health, because there is such a thing as immunity to disease and it is within our grasp. One way of achieving it is through raw food eating plus a sensible way of life

Most animals must eat what they can find when they find it, and when they are ill must rely upon their senses to put themselves right. This usually entails curling up in a corner and not eating. What a different picture from us mad humans who rush around with bottles of patent drugs or drown our painful symptoms in stiff doses of alcohol, when a day in bed without food but lots of water would probably do the trick.

However such a simple cure does not always work, and in days gone by those with the means were sometimes sent to Switzerland for what was referred to as the air. But that was only part of what Switzerland had to offer, because it also had food grown by the best principles of organic husbandry, a stimulating climate, the most beautiful scenery and a peace which has to be felt to be understood. That is nature cure, a mental, physical and moral tonic supplied by daily life as a way of living.

So the prevention and cure of disease really lies in the health of the body, and the way to approach the body is through the head. It is there we take our food and drink, breathe in air, make our decisions to exercise or rest, relax and enjoy ourselves and it is there that sleep takes place which affects the whole body. From our heads also come negative responses such as hate, fear and resentment, as well as the positive ones of compassion, patience, honour, self-restraint and truth.

There are two main groups of professionals dealing with disease: physicians, surgeons and psychologists on the one hand, and nutritionists, biochemic practitioners, naturopaths, herbalists and homeopaths on the other. The first group, the doctors of medicine, are taught about disease when it has appeared in the body and practically nothing about nutrition, health or the allied sciences. The nutritionists and their group make a study of health because they know that in a perfectly healthy body disease cannot take root.

Since I am not a doctor of medicine I will not touch upon that, and anyway I believe it to be too negative. After all a surgeon can only cut what is offending and/or replace it, and a physician can only alleviate the symptoms and make the patient more comfortable by drugs and bed rest. Neither of those rebuild health, whereas the whole approach of the nutritionists and their group is to do just that. When they have done their job, disease should not only be cured but further disease should be prevented, and the patient at last be independent of doctors and without a further thought for his health or ill-health.

In general, nutritionists study food in relation to health, biochemic practitioners study minerals, naturopaths fasting and diet, herbalists herbs, and homeopaths the art of curing like with like. They all overlap, and it is true to say that they really all follow the same path but that each specializes in his own subject. However there are cranks and others who are bigoted, but that you will find in any field of study. That is why I want to give as wide a picture here as possible. Homeopathy and herbalism are more specialist fields and require reference books but I hope that what I say will be endorsed by them as well.

What I have to tell you is mostly simple, common-sense general knowledge that everyone should know, things that every child should be taught at school and practise in his daily life. With this small amount of knowledge you should be able to overcome your daily variations in health and never become really ill, providing you also do as I have suggested nutritionally and as a way of living. These facts are not disputed by any reputable authority and have been put to the test by nutritionists and their group throughout the world.

YOUR MEDICINES

First come rest and relaxation, because they create the right circumstances within which healing can take place. Next comes fresh air, because oxygen is needed in every process of the body, particularly for detoxifying. After that breathing, to increase the vital oxygen supply and eliminate the wastes. Then sunshine, because it is the very source of life and nothing would exist on this planet without it. Exercise because it keeps the body processes going. Water to eliminate the poisons and keep everything moving. Whole raw food because it is the blood supply which nourishes every cell of the body. Vitamins because without them health is not possible. Minerals to convert that food into body tissues with the assistance of enzymes. Fasting to rest the internal organs, thereby giving the body a chance to heal itself. Homeopathy because like does in fact cure like. A healthy mind because it controls the body. Special foods because they have been proved to do the job, and are needed when the body is under stress. Herbs because nature put them there for the purpose of healing.

This is neither an expensive nor a difficult list of requirements. Eight out of the fourteen are free, two are normal parts of your diet which leaves only four as additional expenses, and they need not cost much. Offset that against hospital expenses and the loss of earning time, the misery of ill health and the inconvenience to everyone, and you have a bargain. No longer is it necessary to lie in a heap on your bed feeling sorry for yourself because we now know how to put ourselves right.

The birds of the air and the beasts of the jungle are not forever consulting doctors and going to hospital. Diseased animals die quickly, usually without much pain, but many humans linger on for years at an enormous cost in suffering and cash to themselves and the community. What is wrong with us or our way of life? The answer lies in my list of medicines.

I remember very clearly when a girl friend of mine gave me some cuttings from her geraniums. The first time I received a lovely, bright red, healthy looking specimen but the next time, when she no longer loved me, I was given the opposite. Not to be outdone by the pique of a woman's love I transplanted it in fresh soil to which I added some horse dung, and before the week was out my sickly plant was nearly as beautiful as the other. That is what we too need to do for ourselves. It is as simple as that.

REST AND RELAXATION

The first thing nature forces us to do when we feel ill is to rest, which relaxes us and thus leaves all our energy free to fight disease. Unfortunately however there are many degrees of feeling ill and for most people it has to be severe before they will put their feet up. But always it should be a prerequisite for curing disease: to conserve one's energy and eliminate stress of any kind. Usually it is best to go to bed and even sleep but whatever happens do not rush around, and eliminate any form of stress, particularly that of cold. If you do not do this you are not giving your body a fair chance of throwing off whatever is troubling it, so it may become worse and even develop into something serious. Rest therefore should be your first consideration when feeling ill.

FRESH AIR

We rely upon it for our oxygen of which we must have a constant supply, because without it we die within a few minutes. Oxygen is the fire of life which not only gives us physical and nervous energy, but renders poisons harmless, keeps us warm and makes the life of every cell of the body possible. Fresh country air is full of it and sea air is even better because ozone has an added molecule. Stale air of any sort has less oxygen, plus harmful impurities, so fresh air must always be sought. By night and by day a constant supply is necessary because lack of it predisposes colds, although draughts can cause them. If you live in a town take a regular supply of country air each week, the change of scenery will also help.

BREATHING

The Yogis believe that deep, regular breathing influences the health of the body and mind. That I am sure is correct, but if we cannot make the effort to master this art we should at least remember that by completely emptying the lungs (which we seldom do) we can cure many catarrhal, sinus, bronchial and even toxic troubles. To do this you go on breathing out quite slowly till there is no more breath to come. I often do it as I walk in the country, forcing the air out with each step I take, trying to squeeze my lungs empty. I feel that there is almost no diseased state which this will not help, because every process of the body depends upon oxygen, from the utilization of food to the elimination of wastes.

SUNSHINE

All animal life depends upon it because the vegetable kingdom would not exist without it, and all animals obtain vegetables either directly or indirectly from animals which have eaten them. For human beings sunshine is not only a mental tonic, but a physical necessity because it makes Vitamin D in the oils of the skin. It also relaxes the mind and body and gives simple pleasure. Light of any sort has an enlivening effect and lack of it a depressing one. In nutrition the sunshine foods (fruit and vegetables) are considered to be the foundation of health as well as the best medicine, and the basis on which most of the famous cures have been done. If you are lucky enough to live where there is some sunshine try to get out in it every day or at least as often as possible. In the winter exercise daily in the daylight or even buy a sun lamp, otherwise you must find a regular source of Vitamin D from the health food shop.

EXERCISE

The heart and circulation need it, so do the liver, kidneys and other internal organs, digestion and elimination are helped by it, the lungs and therefore the oxygen supply are assisted by it and it is necessary for the muscles. In fact it is not possible to be healthy without exercise, and one of the quickest ways to the grave is to dispense with it. Those people who continue to take exercise right up to their dying day live the longest. For mental workers it is relaxation, and for standers and sitters a necessity for their circulation and hearts.

Make it a part of your daily routine, whether you are young or old. Without it the heart muscle will fail and the other muscles will weaken, the circulation will gradually block up, the glands will receive insufficient blood flow and the oxygen intake will be inadequate. Exercise need not be excessive but it must be regular. This particularly applies to those with poor constitutions, frequent cold-getters, the sickly, heart patients and for anyone who wants rugged health.

WATER

The body comprises up to 75% water and without it we should die in about 80 hours. The best water comes from fruit and vegetables which contain up to 95% Next comes spring water or what is sold as mineral water (medicinal) in most countries. Normal city water is usually too highly chlorinated or fluorinated. The worst kind is artificially softened water which will almost certainly give you heart disease quite quickly. Insufficient water in the body causes constipation, dehydration, dry skin and slow digestion, but these symptoms are usually due to a deficiency of salt without which water could not be distributed or held in the body. The elimination of poisonous wastes could not take place without water. If you drink at meals it dilutes the digestive juices, and too much liquid can cause loss of the water-soluble vitamins, minerals, protein and other nutrients in the urine. A good water supply provides valuable minerals, particularly calcium and trace minerals, but it is best only to drink when you feel thirsty. If you are excessively thirsty it may mean you are either taking too much or too little salt or that you have too much sugar in your bloodstream (diabetes), all of which the water helps to eliminate. People who eat only raw fruit and vegetables, nuts, seeds, yeast and the like retain enough water in their intestines and do not need to drink any. Excessive carbohydrate eaters, particularly of the refined sort, are always thirsty and retain too much water, as do compulsive fat eaters. At spas and health hydros you are often given a litre of hot mineral water an hour before each meal with only the most beneficial results.

Cold running water or sea water can be used externally most

effectively for health. Animals lick their wounds to keep them clean and to help the healing process but water is equally good and has the added advantage of attracting blood to that spot (which is needed for healing). Cold running water is the best first aid for burns, sprains, sunburn, insect bites, inflammations and cuts. Swimming in the sea or any other cold water is helpful for arthritis and poor circulation and will reduce the temperature in fevers, providing the patient is strong enough to swim. Swimming also helps to build up a resistance to colds and to establish a robust constitution. Sea water is always a great healer. Wherever water is applied it attracts the blood and that is an essential part of healing, quite apart from its cleansing qualities. Nature cure practitioners use hot and cold packs with marvellous effect.

WHOLE FOOD

Now we come to the corner-stone on which health is built, because food creates our blood supply which nourishes every cell of which we are made. Nothing is more important in health or disease, but it must be WHOLE food as supplied direct from the animal or ground, because any form of treatment from the time it is picked or killed till it reaches our mouths detracts from its value. Nutritional elements in food are extremely susceptible to heat, sunlight, water and the knife or hammer, in fact we would be healthier if we ate in the fields! The value and usefulness of food lies in its wholeness, any other sort is dangerous and a potential killer. It follows that raw food holds the secret to proper eating and nutrition.

VITAMIN THERAPY

In a diseased person the need for vitamins drastically increases, therefore they must be administered in drug (i.e. very strong) doses. This is partly due to the incidence of stress, the activity of germs and the presence of toxins, but also because the body's fight for survival requires these extra amounts. The need for a particular vitamin predominates in certain diseases, as you will see in the following pages, although usually more than one is called for. However since all vitamins are interdependent and there are only four principal ones plus Vitamin D, you would be wise to find a reliable source of each and never be without them.

People often wonder why it is necessary to take additional vitamins if they are properly fed. The answer is that in disease they definitely speed recovery and the need for them is much greater, and in normal health they give you super-health. These facts have been proved by all nutritionists and since any excess of B and C is easily eliminated, there is no danger. Synthetic Vitamin D can be taken in excess, so can fish liver oil (A and D) and it is important to find the right dosage of Vitamin E. Care should be taken in selecting the right brands, and the manner in which they are administered, because too little of some will do no good at all.

VITAMINS A AND D

These are best bought together in the form of fish liver oils, the halibut being stronger than the cod, but carotene is also a good source (of A only). Vitamin D is now satisfactorily manufactured synthetically. 100,000 units of Vitamin A have been taken daily for six months without toxic effects, but 50,000 is more than enough for long-term massive doses. Any toxic effects can be rendered harmless by large doses of Vitamin C. Food sources should form one's principal supply in health or disease, so concentrate on orange and yellow fruit and vegetables, green leaves and liver.

VITAMIN B COMPLEX

These are normally synthesized in our intestines but the process can be disrupted by sulfa drugs, antibiotics and certain other chemicals. Since the stress of disease calls for large quantities of these vitamins, an additional supply is essential. Look carefully at the label of the product you buy to check that there is a large spread of the individual B vitamins. Never take individual B vitamins separately as they are inclined to create a deficiency of the ones not taken. Pantothenic acid seems to be the exception, which is fortunate since it is the anti-stress vitamin. Strong doses of B complex are not recommended over long periods, but during illness it is vital. Liver, yeast, wheat germ (or the oil) or yogurt are the best concentrated sources when ill.

VITAMIN C

This is best taken in the form of rose hips or acerola berries but additional ascorbic acid is usually necessary, particularly during illness since all the tissues must be saturated before bacteria, viruses and their toxins can be completely neutralized. When the tissues are saturated, which means that the other jobs have been done and the symptoms have gone, you can reduce the dose. Hourly or even half-hourly doses of 1, 2 or even 3 grams may be needed initially until the symptoms subside. The chewable sort of ascorbic acid is better than the effervescent. It is also advisable to eat oranges, lemons, blackcurrants and other food sources during illness. Vitamin C is destroyed while performing its task so take massive doses from food, concentrated natural sources and as ascorbic acid.

VITAMIN E

This is best bought as D-Alpha-tocopherol, distilled from natural vegetable oil sources and is sold by International Units. The synthetic sort is usually sold in milligrams and labelled DL-Alpha-tocopherol. Too little of this vitamin will do no good at all, so it is necessary to find exactly the right dose by starting with 100 iu's daily and gradually building up till the effective dose is found. For diabetes and heart disease it will probably be necessary to take large doses for the rest of your life, but in other cases it can be reduced to a topping-up dose. Wheat Germ Oil or even Rice Germ Oil should also be taken and in health this alone may be a large enough supply of Vitamin E, but remember that an excess of vegetable oil increases the need for this vitamin. Although it is usually specific in its action, its oxygen-sparing role makes it invaluable for healing of all sorts (internally and externally). Also remember that rancid fats, mineral oils and iron compounds destroy it in the intestines, and the refining of most foods removes it (particularly wheat, which is where the majority of the world should obtain their daily supply). It is always advisable to take a food source as well as capsules.

VITAMIN F

This is not strictly a vitamin, and is usually referred to as the unsaturated fatty acids, but since it is essential to health and cannot be synthesized in the body, it is sometimes rated as a vitamin. It is necessary for cell multiplication, thus repair and growth of all tissues and as you will see in the following pages, many diseases can be cured or prevented by it. The best and most easily available supply is the oleaginous nuts, seeds and beans or their cold-pressed oils, also olives and avocados. Two dessertspoons from all sources is enough or about the same amount as you need of protein (1 gram per kilogram of body weight). In cold weather more fat is needed but too much will increase your need for Vitamin E and may put on weight.

VITAMIN P

This is known as the bioflavonoids which occur in all brightly-coloured fruit and vegetables as well as grapes, buckwheat and sweet potatoes. Natural concentrates are available in health food shops and are an invaluable aid whenever Vitamin C is taken. It has been stated that there is no diseased state in which Vitamin P will not help and it is specific for some. The Swiss have analysed it and manufacture a highly concentrated form called Venoruton P_4 which is useful in disease, particularly varicose veins and haemorrhoids. Being water-based, the quantity does not matter except that it must be adequate.

MINERAL THERAPY

Minerals have been fully explained in the Nutrition Section but their application needs careful study. Perhaps it is best to go back to Dr Scheussler who discovered that there were 12 mineral combinations which could deal with most of man's daily maladies. As his research progressed he found that the smallest, most finely triturated doses, had the best effect. Ultimately he developed a system for triturating (grinding and spreading) the minerals and administering them in what we now call homeopathic doses. Nearly every symptom which is known as disease will respond to one or other of his mineral cell salts.

From my own experience, and that of millions of others, I cannot overestimate the importance of these completely harmless common elements of our own bodies, which Dr Scheussler has taught us to use in re-balancing our daily deficiencies. They need time to study and some experience in using, but the longer you use them the more miraculous do they become. This method of taking minute doses of minerals should deal with the important function they play in enzyme cooperation and in cellular deficiencies, but for larger deficiencies you must go elsewhere as I will now explain.

CALCIUM, PHOSPHORUS AND MAGNESIUM

Carefully prepared powdered bones of animals will supply calcium and phosphorus in the right proportions, or they can be rendered down in the form of soup. Other than that, pulverized egg shells soaked in lemon juice or the stalks of all vegetables are a good source. However, if the following conditions are not met, no amount of calcium can be utilized by the body, as is often the case in arthritis and other bone problems: a healthy thyroid gland, sufficient stomach acid (salt and B complex), Vitamin D, the enzyme phosphatase (from unpasteurized milk, pasteurized contains none, or the bran of grains), adequate unsaturated fatty acids (vegetable oils).

Too much saturated (animal) fat causes insoluble calcium soaps in the intestines and thus appalling deficiencies. Magnesium is also found in bones and green vegetables, nuts, seeds, eggs, legumes, citrus fruit and the germ of grains. These various combinations of calcium, phosphorus and magnesium are best used as a daily supply or to replace deficiencies. Too much milk is not wise after childhood because of the fat, nor is too much calcium for that matter.

SODIUM, CHLORINE AND POTASSIUM

Never use chemically manufactured common table salt as it is not good for you. Only use sea salt or what has been biochemically balanced and prepared. Never take it with food as it speeds up the digestion as well as adversely affecting it. Take half a level teaspoon in a little water twice a day between meals, thereby ensuring it will do you no harm and that it is available for all the various body functions which it performs. Four grams a day is generally considered enough under normal conditions. For more information about sodium chloride see the Nutrition Section.

Potassium is the mineral we principally throw down the drain when cooking vegetables in too much water for too long. See the Nutrition Section for best food sources, otherwise Potassium Chloride can be bought at the chemist and mixed with an equal amount of sodium chloride (salt) to regain the correct balance. If however sodium has replaced potassium in the cells (ie you are water-logged), then potassium alone must be taken. Always ensure adequate potassium as the sodium is easy to obtain.

IRON, COPPER AND COBALT

All artificially manufactured iron salts are toxic and should only ever be taken for very short periods to fill an iron deficiency but the best method is to rely upon liver, egg yolks, dates, bone marrow or the other foods mentioned in the Nutrition Section.

Since iron cannot be utilized without copper, this is essential in minute quantities. Some soils are deficient in it, otherwise it is found in all iron-rich foods.

Cobalt should be taken in the form of Vitamin B_{12} which is found in liver, egg yolk, milk and meat, or for vegetarians can be adequately supplied synthetically. In pernicious anaemia it must be injected as the stomach cannot absorb it.

Vitamins C and E help absorption of all these minerals as does stomach acid.

SULPHUR AND ZINC

Usually sulphur is best taken from vegetable-rich sources as it is toxic in other than minute amounts. See the Nutrition Section.

Zinc is also best taken from food sources, but this supply must be assured as it is easily overlooked and refined food contains practically none.

IODINE AND MANGANESE

Seaweed is the most reliable source either as kelp (dried) or as the real stuff. Some salt is now iodized and of course all sea salt naturally contains it.

Manganese is best taken in food.

TRACE ELEMENTS

Minute amounts of these other minerals are adequately supplied providing whole food is eaten in good quantities, but if there is any doubt, specially prepared capsules can be bought.

MINERALS GENERALLY

Those who live on whole food will usually not be deficient in minerals but it is necessary to keep an eye on your calcium supply, to ensure that you are taking enough salt but not too much, and that your iron intake is adequate. It is also worth checking on the mineral content of the local soil, because if that is deficient in one or more minerals so will you be. Since a mineral imbalance, however small, is nearly always one of the causes of disease you would be wise to have mineral cell salts at hand. Do not forget that without minerals food would be without value.

FASTING

This is what nature tells us to do in certain cases of illness and we disregard these instructions at our peril. Since this is such a big subject you would be well advised to buy a book about it, either *Fasting Can Save Your Life* by Herbert Shelton or *Everybody's Guide to Nature Cure* by Harry Benjamin. For a short fast it is quite easy to drink the juice of an orange in a glass of water every two hours or just the water, but nothing else whatever. This you can do for two or three days, or a week or even two with perfect safety. Reduce your activity and take a lot of rest. The American school do not believe in taking enemas during fasting and I agree with this. If your bowels need to make elimination they will do so, otherwise they are best left to follow their natural course. You may have heart palpitations and a headache from the build-up of toxins in the body, but that does not matter. On the other hand any more serious symptoms should cause you to break your fast or consult an expert in fasting.

Breaking a two-week fast is best done on half a glass of juice every two hours for the first day, then a whole glass the next. Eat three pieces of fruit at each meal on the third day, work in some salads and other vegetables as well as the fruit on the fourth and take small normal meals on the fifth, gradually enlarging them till you are eating proper meals by the end of the first week. Guard against overeating after that, because this is a normal inclination, but equally see you are properly nourished otherwise your recovery will be slow and inadequately accomplished.

One-day fasts can be done on water or juice and water every two hours or one type of fruit at each of the three or four meals (the quantity is not important) or even fruit and milk. I do a fruit fast once each week and feel much better for it – or rather I notice the adverse affects if I do not do it. The purifying effect on the blood is the most beneficial regular spring-cleaning, as well as its cleansing effect on the intestine from the throat to the anus. By using the Vitamin C saturation technique you can greatly help to purify the system during a fast. Any kind of fruit or vegetable juice is suitable for fasting, but you must only have one sort throughout the whole fast.

One of the objects of a fast is to rest your internal organs so that the body is free to concentrate on healing itself, but it also rests the mind and all the other parts of the body.

HOMEOPATHY

This is the principle of healing which uses the law that like cures like. A lot of snake venom will kill but a minute amount can cure, as also a lot of something which makes you sick can be neutralized by a small amount of the same stuff. This art has been developed to a very fine degree and over a very wide range of diseases, but it requires the use of reference books and the advice of a homeopathic chemist. In England this is possible, as homeopathy has now been accepted as part of the National Health Service.

THE MIND

This I will deal with at greater length in the section on Happiness later on. Here I principally want to stress that the mind does in fact control the whole body and therefore all the secretions of our glands, the absorption of our food and the reactions of our nerves. Yoga is the development of the power of the mind over the body, so is Buddhism and both of these disciplines can be responsible for a contented and happy mind and body. Of course food is necessary for the maintenance of the nerves, glands, brain and all parts of the body, and nothing the mind can do will replace this need. But equally no amount of nourishing food will keep you healthy if your mind is distressed. It is also worth remembering that people who cannot afford to become ill or who urgently do not want to, usually remain healthy. Of course the reverse is also true, those with empty minds and lacking in purpose frequently find themselves in a doctor's care.

Our emotions originate in the mind and are controlled there and can play havoc with the body, causing untold misery and disease. The mind needs self-discipline and a sound philosophy as well as the right physical and mental nourishment from a healthy blood stream and positive thinking. Since blood sugar supplies its energy this should be kept at a constant optimum as in good health (see later on).

From the mind comes relaxation and enjoyment, sleep and

contentment, fear and hate, love and laughter, so we must learn how to deal with our minds. Simple rules like never letting emotions fester and discussing one's troubles, or even writing them down, can all help. Learn the method of coping with problems and think ahead progressively. Pay particular attention to the section on Happiness.

SPECIAL FOODS

There are certain foods which have exceptional value in disease because of their properties. By eating them you can not only help to shorten the period of illness, but also save your body from many of the ravages of disease. The most important group of these contain what is called the anti-stress factor. Disease of course is stress, so is anything which harms the body or damages, breaks down or destroys the cells, such as anxiety, overwork, lack of sleep or exercise, fear, excesses of all kinds, temperamental or environmental difficulties, extreme cold or heat, surgery, accident or shock, loud noise, blinking lights, rarefied air, electric shock, X-ray, infections from viruses or bacteria, reactions to drugs or chemicals, burns, fasting, the frustrations of enforced immobility, exhaustion, toxins or mineral oils, deficient or excessive diets.

One's body always reacts to stress in the same manner, and particularly needs pantothenic acid and the other B vitamins, protein, Vitamins C and E as well as the anti-stress factors. Under the heading Stress later in this section I will discuss this further. I confine myself here to the special foods which contain the anti-stress factor and exceptional nutritional qualities.

WHEAT GERM OIL

If there was only one nutritional supplement I was allowed to give a sick person this is the one I would select. Fresh wheat germ itself is also good. It contains the highest natural concentration of Vitamin E, has lots of lecithin, Vitamin B Complex, and unsaturated fat as well as the anti-stress factor. Yet this is the vital part of wheat which is removed and fed to animals. It is the same story with rice, once the outer covering has been removed. The vital point about wheat germ oil and other germ oils is that they be cold-pressed and completely pure, which you can usually tell by the smell. Much of what is on the market is not genuine although it may contain a few drops so it can bear the name.

LIVER

This is the next wonder food because of its B Complex (including B_{12}), Vitamin A and anti-stress factor content. It also has iron, copper and many other minerals. This is the ideal anti-anaemia food, the blood-building and regenerating food. Eat it fresh, do not keep it and cook it as little as possible at the lowest temperature (even eat it raw if you can). Dessicated liver tablets or liver extract are next best to the fresh product. Kidneys are also good food.

LEAFY GREEN VEGETABLES

These are a must for everyone daily for their anti-stress factor, iron and copper, abundant vitamins, potassium, calcium and other minerals, enzymes, stored sunshine and their proved beneficial effect on health, energy and resistance to disease. Eat them raw, if you can, mixed with a little cold-pressed vegetable oil. Never let a day pass without having some.

BREWERS' YEAST

Two dessertspoons of this invaluable food taken last thing at night or first thing in the morning will build resistance to stress and disease as well as nourish you. The B vitamins and iron are its particular assets, plus minerals and the anti-stress factor. Torula yeast is the most pleasant to eat, but any form of dried brewers' yeast is suitable. If it creates gas this will only last a couple of weeks and then disappear. Mix the yeast into a paste with water or milk (never anything else) or let it mingle with your saliva when taken dry. If eaten when there is any form of sugar in the stomach it will ferment this.

SOYA BEANS

Whole soya beans are amazingly valuable in disease or health. For vegetarians they supply first class protein with the right kind of fat, they are also a storehouse of Vitamins A, B, E and F, plus lots of minerals and the anti-stress factor. They are best eaten whole (cooked) or as full-fat flour, but other preparations are also good.

OTHER SPECIAL FOODS

Outside the anti-stress foods there are others which should always be kept available and even eaten daily. Garlic, nuts and seeds, fruit and vegetable juices, charcoal, lecithin and ginsen are all medicinal foods.

GARLIC

This is nature's antibiotic and the great intestinal antiseptic. It has been used to lower blood pressure, relieve toxins in the heart area, improve digestion and assimilation, treat cancer, loosen catarrh, help lung troubles, heal wounds as an ointment, ward off the plague in the Middle Ages and prevent pneumonia, typhus, T.B. and diptheria as well as many other diseases. Providing your digestion is good your breath will not smell after it. If it does, parsley neutralizes the odour. Alternatively eat it last thing at night mixed with some other food or as capsules. There is no greater prophylactic food than garlic and it should be taken daily for this reason.

FRUIT AND VEGETABLE JUICES

Some incredible cures have been performed with just carrot, cabbage or other vegetable juices. The secret is to live on them for a few days (only one kind) and have nothing else. After that you can take them as additions to the diet. Juices are also useful because people enjoy drinking them, whereas they may balk at the whole vegetable. Fruit juice is a bonus to health and should always be available, in sickness or in health. Fruit juice is best drunk immediately after preparation. If you wish to keep it, store it in the fridge.

NUTS AND SEEDS

These contain the element of new life apart from valuable vitamins, minerals and essential unsaturated fatty acids. For skin troubles, glandular functions, vitality and youth these should be taken daily. Without them it is difficult to have a complete diet unless whole grains are eaten.

CHARCOAL

This can be bought from the chemist, or simply burn a piece of toast and eat that. Diarrhoea and digestion, impure blood such as boils and other eruptions respond to charcoal. For that reason it is an essential medicine.

LECITHIN

This is essential for proper absorption and therefore nutrition, for the utilization of fats and cholesterol and for liver health. Since it is removed from most processed food it is necessary to take it additionally. In middle age it helps the heart, liver, blood vessels and beautifies the skin. Since it promotes phosphorous utilization it also helps that of calcium and therefore is useful for arthritics. For the young it is not so necessary but later on it is vital.

GINSEN

This has been used as a general tonic and medicine in the East for centuries because of its wide range of properties. It is known in the West principally for its sex-rejuvenating qualities, but it is also used as a general rejuvenator, for respiration and kidney troubles, for diabetes and fatigue, for increasing body heat in winter, for nervous disorders such as insomnia, neurosis and fatigue and for many other things which I will discuss in the Health Food section later. Be sure to buy the genuine product without added stimulants. If you want to retain your youth and reproductive powers, take some ginsen annually.

HERBS

Although herbs do not constitute food they do have enormous value in treating disease. Their study is a life's work but there are many excellent books on the subject, and herbal societies exist in most countries whose aim is to propagate their use. Never overlook this natural medicine.

BOOKS

As supplementary books to this section, buy *Let's Get Well* by Adelle Davis or any of her books about nutrition and child care.

Fasting Can Save Your Life by Herbert Shelton (published in U.S.A.) is invaluable as are his books on nutrition.

The Earth Heals Everything by Justine Glass (published in England) is the story of biochemistry and explains minerals as well as nutrition.

Dr Scheussler's Biochemistry by J. B. Chapman is the best book of several on mineral cell salts (published in England).

Food is Your Best Medicine by Henry Bieler (published in U.S.A.) explains the value of your glands.

Better Sight Without Glasses by Gaylord Hauser tells you how to regain your eyesight naturally (published in England and U.S.A.).

Good Health and Happiness by J. Ellis Barker shows how diseases are caused and can be prevented (published in England).

Books on *Yoga* and *Buddhism* teach you how to treat the mind.

There are also classics on nutrition but they are long, learned and complicated and not for the everyday reader.

SPECIFIC DISEASES

With these medicines, the elements that keep us alive, we should have no difficulty in curing most of our ills. Our bodies are composed of cells, each of which has intelligence and to a degree is a world of its own. Each cell selects from the blood stream exactly what type of nourishment it requires (and they all want something different) and provided it is there, the cells remain healthy.

These medicines, which are also the normal nutrients of the body, are not a matter of opinion like the scientific methods of treating disease which change rapidly. These medicines have formed the basis of our nourishment, and therefore our lives, since time immemorial. It is only since we started to interfere with them for the greed of gain that trouble began. Before that dirt and insufficient food caused most disease, as well as cold and damp, lack of rest, faulty habits and insufficient air and sunshine. Since therefore these are the cause of disease, we can attack the cause and eliminate disease which must be our object. The symptoms which are treated by modern medicine are of no importance except to draw our attention to the cause.

With these medicines people have recovered from their death beds to live long, happy and fruitful lives but they have always changed their habits of eating and living after their recovery. So when you have followed the suggested therapy in the following pages do not think the matter is ended there, because it has only just begun. What caused your disease was faulty eating and living and the only thing which can prevent it occurring again is to correct your eating and living habits. So follow the instructions carefully and do not omit any part of them, because the body is a whole and all of it is interdependent, so is food.

Learn how to use vitamin and mineral therapy, work the anti-stress foods into your diet, clean out your mind, cultivate the art of relaxation and breathing, take some exercise regularly, enjoy some sunshine and swimming, fast once in a while, study homeopathy, herbs and the Scheussler biochemic system, and above all discover how to eat for health with the assistance of the nutrition sections in this book. You will then no longer have to spend money on being ill, you will not be a drain on your country's national resources and you and your whole family will be much happier because of your good health.

Do not think I have overstated the requirements in this book, do not think that just a little Vitamin C will do the trick because it will not, the tissues must be saturated when you are ill. Do not blame Vitamin E because a minute dose does not work but go on trying till you find the dose that does. Do not do everything I say and forget the mind because you can never be well until it is tranquil. Also do not expect to be well in a day or two, because what may have taken you ten or twenty years to bring about will take more than a few days to put right.

Remember that raw goats' milk, fresh fruit and untreated honey saved the life of a girl dying from chronic indigestion in Zurich in 1895, when the same foods cooked were not digested (this was because of the enzymes in raw food). Also remember that one way of building immunity to disease is by eating abundant raw food. Health is a whole way of living and only by treating it as such can we acquire positive health.

Abscesses

Boils and carbuncles need the same treatment. The cause is constitutional, an unhealthy body and bloodstream.

Biochemic mineral salts will cause suppuration, then start the healing process and also cleanse the blood, but otherwise they must be lanced to drain the pus.

Vitamin B Complex is also a blood cleanser, particularly brewers' yeast. Vitamin C helps eliminate poisons. Vitamin A is always essential for skin health and for making antibodies to fight disease. Improve your diet to regenerate the blood.

Hot wet dressings cause suppuration, whereas hot dry ones prevent suppuration and draw poisons. Dress frequently and keep clean under cold running water. A moist antiseptic dressing allows complete suppuration and prevents scabs from forming.

Abscesses and the like need the fundamental treatment of rest and proper nourishment because the body is run down.

Acne

This is a skin disease consisting of pimples and other blemishes on the face. Adolescents have one sort but there are others also.

Vitamin A is for skins and Vitamin B Complex for cleansing the blood. Unsaturated fats (vegetable oils) are particularly needed and can often cure alone.

See also under Skin in later pages.

Alcoholism

Whatever its original cause, this ultimately becomes a nutritional problem because of its effect on the liver and other internal organs, and because of the nutritional deficiencies it causes.

Vitamin B Complex is the first vital need because of the deficiency caused by taking so much unbalanced carbohydrate. Vitamin C in enormous doses is needed to eliminate the poison of alcohol and to help with the blood sugar. Vitamin E will also help detoxify and prevent permanent damage to internal organs. An accumulative magnesium deficiency may be partly the cause of compulsive drinking and no alcoholic can be cured until his diet and his health is improved. In extreme cases it may be necessary to take magnesium oxide, otherwise mineral cell salts will help, or alternatively bone meal or other magnesium-rich supplements.

Without the stimulus of alcohol and its carbohydrate, the blood sugar must be maintained at a constant level which can only be achieved by correct eating and the elimination of refined carbohydrate such as white sugar, white flour and alcohol. Raw fruit, whole grains, honey, sweet potatoes and other whole food sources of energy should replace the unnatural supply.

Drinkers are difficult to live with, even for themselves. Their brains and bodies gradually degenerate and they usually lose their wives and families and end up alone and ill.

Allergies

These are mostly stress diseases from overwork, fear, excesses of all kinds, temperamental and environmental difficulties or any other stress. Healthy individuals, protected by anti-stress foods, are unaffected by them. They can be caused by injections of drugs, vaccines, serums, etc, by skin cosmetics, insect venoms, poison ivy, etc, or through the mucous membranes from food, bacteria, moulds or histamine.

The following are some of the symptoms: skin rash, eczema, hives, hay fever, asthma, sinus trouble, headache, runny nose, digestive disturbances, as well as all the symptoms of adrenal gland exhaustion.

Rest and avoid stress as immediate precautions and follow the Vitamin C saturation technique. Vitamin B Complex with extra pantothenic acid is needed, also Vitamins A and E. If you can discover the offending allergy eliminate it.

See also under Stress in later pages.

Anaemia

This has many causes but always the blood is poor and must therefore be regenerated. The only way this can be done is through food or food elements, either by mouth or injection in serious cases. Vegetarians are particularly susceptible to it because Vitamin B_{12} only appears in food of animal origin, however they can be cured by taking it (in synthetic form) either by mouth or in acute conditions by injections. After about four years vegetarians exhaust their reserves of B_{12} and can ruin their health for lack of it, and even reach a state beyond repair. It is very questionable whether the body can synthesize B_{12} however adequate a diet, unless of course it contains milk products and/or eggs.

Iron, which causes the red colour of blood through haemoglobin, is the missing element in anaemia, although often there is enough of this but it cannot be utilized for lack of copper. For both of these liver is the best source, as it is for B_{12}. Also see mineral section under Iron because inorganic iron is all toxic and destroys Vitamin E in the body.

Salt deficiency anaemia also exists because cell division cannot take place without it. Follow the instructions for salt in the mineral section extremely carefully because salt is toxic but enough must be taken each day (4 grams in and out of food and cooking).

Calcium and the biochemic mineral cell salt silica are needed for anaemia resulting from poorly nourished states. Fresh air, exercise and sunshine will also help those who are malnourished or with poor constitutions.

Anaemia from overwork, mental strain and many other causes can be helped by biochemic mineral cell salts but essentially one must start with food. Liver is the most certain cure.

Vitamins C, E and B Complex will greatly assist blood

regeneration and are natural companions of iron. Green leafy vegetables, pineapples, apricots, dates, raisins and prunes have special blood-building properties, plus all the other iron-rich foods.

Young girls, people who are cooped up without enough sunshine, air or exercise, vegetarians, most women (because of menstruation), people living on copper-deficient soils and those suffering from poor assimilation are all susceptible to anaemia. Everyone would be wise to eat anti-anaemia foods because good red blood is the life stream which feeds the cells.

Arthritis

There are many kinds of arthritis. Arthritis is basically a degenerative disease, so its cause is deep-seated and long-standing, but in one or two cases it is emotional in origin and therefore release from this suppressed emotion will bring relief. Dr Bircher-Benner at his clinic in Zurich has had some successes in treating completely bed-ridden osteoarthritics by diet, so has Herbert Shelton in America. I believe that a raw food diet is the surest method, but usually there is faulty metabolism of calcium which must be corrected, and possibly ulcerated teeth which can sometimes be cured with minute amounts of plaster of Paris (calcium sulphate). Constipation is another predisposing factor which can best be overcome with lots of fresh fruit and vegetables which are the basis of the raw food diet, or with brewers' yeast plus Vitamin B Complex. Any other failure in the elimination of the body's wastes or poisons must also be corrected.

Biochemic mineral cell salts can sometimes be invaluable for treating the swelling and discomfort of the joints. Vitamin C can help in the neutralizing of poisons and lubricating the joints. Vitamin E can assist in preventing calcium deposits. Pantothenic acid plus a generous amount of the whole Vitamin B Complex can relieve the pain and resuscitate the adrenal glands, which may have become exhausted either before or during the disease. Lecithin can help the utilization of phosphorus which in turn helps calcium metabolism as well as the assimilation of food.

Exercises are invaluable, particularly those of Yoga, and of course it goes without saying that peace of mind is an essential. As with any disease Vitamin A must be generously supplied to help fight it. Two German investigators found that there was a factor in cream and molasses which relieved arthritis but both must be taken in very small quantities (about a level teaspoon of molasses in warm water or milk twice a day, and/or perhaps a teaspoon of raw untreated cream mixed with it). Exercise, fresh air, sunshine, fun and relaxation also help.

Beauty

The most endearing beauty lies behind the face although that is not the sort most women want. The first essential is to lose weight and the next is to enhance the skin. It is worth remembering that all vegetarians have beautiful skin, although this subject is dealt with separately later in this section. The hair and skin both need Vitamin A and a correct salt balance. The eyes particularly benefit from a fast (even for one day). Your expression comes from your mind (see the section on Happiness). Lecithin and Vitamin E are often called the beauty vitamins. Vitamin B Complex will help to give you a clear skin and brewers' yeast will keep it that way. Vitamin A softens the skin and gives it a youthful appearance.

Blood Sugar

Part of the lift from smoking a cigarette is caused by a rise in blood sugar, so it is from drinking alcohol, eating sweets or drinking coffee and tea. But immediately you stop doing these things the blood sugar drops below normal, so inevitably you reach for your vice again to make you feel good. The object of correct diet is to maintain the blood sugar at a constant level continually, so that you feel good all the time instead of just when indulging your vices (which I hope you will have given up.)

The symptoms of low blood sugar are all those of fatigue: lassitude, apathy, tension, nervousness, aimlessness, weakness, trembling, sweating, headaches. Correct diet is the way to cure these symptoms and therefore all refined carbohydrate must be eliminated: white sugar and anything made from it, alcohol and soft drinks, and to a lesser extent white flour and white rice. Whole grains and brown rice should be substituted, perhaps a little honey, fruit and even complete starch foods. Adequate protein and unsaturated fat are necessary for the correct metabolism of these, so is Vitamin B Complex. Vitamins C and E are both concerned with the oxygen supply, and therefore endurance, so they are vital to energy.

Bones

They are made of calcium, phosphorus and magnesium, so refer to these in the nutrition section. Without these minerals bones will not mend and later in life become brittle. Check on an adequate supply of calcium particularly in the diet. For bruised bones and for their surfaces take the appropriate mineral cell salts.

Bronchitis

This usually follows a common cold or flu. Stay in bed if feverish and saturate with Vitamin C. The bioflavonoids (Vitamin P) should be taken (in food and supplements), so should garlic for the fever and catarrh. Biochemic mineral cell salts can often reach the cause of the trouble and fasting can often completely cure. See notes for constipation.

Burns

Lasting scars can be prevented (if not too large), providing the body fluids and minerals are replaced immediately. Therefore blood transfusions are the first need with serious burns. Cold running water should be applied immediately which will cool and bring blood to the affected area. Since the stress of burns is acute, follow the instructions for stress. Take biochemic mineral cell salts. For sunburn use an ointment with para-amino-benzoic acid (a B vitamin) which will usually relieve it. Salt is always lost from the body after any form of burning (sunburn or otherwise), so a level teaspoon of sea salt in water will help to relieve the symptoms (see under Salt in the nutrition section). Vitamin C will help to detoxify the extensive poison caused by a burn. Vitamin B Complex will help with shock and repair. Vitamin A is always needed for anything to do with the skin. Adequate protein is needed to repair a serious burn, so is unsaturated fat and a nourishing diet. Burns are serious and should never be treated lightly.

Bruises

They are always the first sign of a Vitamin C deficiency and it is best to take the bioflavonoids as well. Vitamin E is always needed for blood vessels, also biochemic mineral cell salts Ferr Phos and Calc Fluor or a food source of iron to help strengthen the walls. Calcium may also be deficient. Bruises show that the capillaries are weak and this predisposes the body to infection and heart attacks. Increase your fruit and vegetable intake, add whole grain flour or wheat germ or its oil. Never ignore bruises. If you are healthy and your capillaries are strong you will seldom have them.

Cancer

Biochemic mineral cell salts have been used in its treatment, so has raw food therapy. Both are intended to achieve the same object, namely the health of the cells. Potassium plays an important part in the biochemic method because sodium has usually replaced potassium inside the cells. Raw food ensures healthy capillaries which guarantees proper nutrition to the cells and the elimination of their poisonous wastes. Cancer is a disease of the cells.

For references read *Raw Food Treatment of Cancer* by Dr Kristine Nolfi (the late Danish physician), *The Prevention of Incurable Diseases* by Dr M. Bircher Benner, the Swiss dietician and doctor, *The Earth Heals Everything* (The Story of Biochemistry) by Justine Glass, *Cancer, How it can be Caused and How it can be Prevented* by J. Ellis Barker (who also wrote another book about it). These books are all published in Europe and on sale in England.

Cataracts

Since the eyes are made up of the same physical matter as the rest of the body, cataracts have been improved by correct diet. Deposits of inorganic substances are obviously serious and this is where biochemic mineral cell salts can help. A raw food diet and fasting have also worked wonders. In old age the blood supply to the eyes is often reduced, so stimulate that by douching them with cold water. Alternatively tightly close them for a few moments and then open or cup them as suggested in *Perfect Sight Without Glasses* by W. H. Bates or *Better Sight Without Glasses* by Gaylord Hauser. The Yoga exercise of standing on your head can also help.

Change of Life (Menopause)

Vitamin E can help to counteract the unpleasant effects of the change of life. The calcium/magnesium balance is also important. Your diet should ideally consist of at least two-thirds of raw food. Have as much fresh air, relaxation and sunshine as possible. The mind plays a vitally important part in this condition, so see the section on happiness.

Chilblains

These are a problem of the circulation so Vitamin E and or Wheat Germ Oil are vital, plus Lecithin. Biochemic cell salts (Calc Phos and others) may help.

Colds

I am sure it is true to say that colds do not come without the right emotional circumstances. However, stress of any kind can unbalance the body chemistry and start the chain of circumstances which lead to a cold. Never neglect a cold when it has arrived and stay indoors, or even better in bed if you have a temperature. Immediately saturate the tissues with Vitamin C which will lessen the period of illness and make you feel better by eliminating the poisons. The biochemic cell salts Ferr Phos, Kali Mur and others work wonders. Ensure you have garlic with meals or in capsules. Take additional Vitamin A and B Complex. Drink fresh lemon barley water with some honey to which can be added Vitamin C. Take a little salt and water in the very early stages when eyes and nose are running but stop if cold develops. Gargle with salt and water or Vademecum or your own favourite brand. Ensure regular bowel movements (see constipation). For catarrh see Catarrh.

Alternatively a two-day fast on fruit juice will often completely eliminate a cold providing you stay in bed. Never suppress a cold. Nature cure regards it as a healing crisis (a natural elimination of poisons). Frequent cold-getters should have lots of fresh air and build up their constitution with cold baths and outdoor exercise, sleep with bedroom windows open and take a course of biochemic cell salts to build up strength.

Cold Sores

The biochemic cell salt Nat Mur will often dry cold sores out, or sometimes a little salt applied externally. Otherwise Vitamin B Complex can be used if they are caused by a lack of that.

Constipation

Since this is the cause of so many diseases it must be dealt with immediately. Prunes or dried figs are the pleasantest and easiest cure. Alternatively a bare level teaspoon of salt and water with 500 mg of potassium chloride will almost certainly do the trick. Both of these are only temporary cures, the long-term solution lies in correct eating. Lots of fresh fruit and vegetables will provide the bulk and the liquid necessary for an easy bowel movement. Vitamin B Complex is especially important (brewers' yeast). Without exercise you may remain constipated. Faulty liver can also be a cause (see Liver Troubles).

Convalescence

Follow instructions for anaemia because that is the way to rebuild strength and energy. Biochemic cell salts Calc Phos and Ferr Phos are needed. Take as much raw food as possible and of course all the vitamins. Exercise in the fresh air is vital and some sunshine and swimming. Relax and enjoy yourself.

Cramp

Leg cramp is sometimes caused by salt deficiency, otherwise it indicates heart trouble and needs Vitamin E. Salt deficiency can be brought on by diarrhoea, vomiting, excessive sweating or sunbathing, extreme cold or violent exercise. Menstrual cramp needs biochemic cell salt Calc Phos, other sorts need Mag Phos.

Dandruff

This is caused from inside the body: possibly it is due to a salt deficiency. The biochemic cell salt Kali Mur or Vitamin A may help. No amount of outside lotions will help, except to prevent the flakes from falling. Consult a biochemic handbook.

Depression

This can be physical as well as mental. Since the first stage of stress eliminates salt from the body, this can correct that sort of low spirits resulting from unrefreshing sleep. Weakness, tiredness, insomnia, emotions and imagination can also cause depression. All the biochemic cell salts for nerves should be taken. Vitamin B Complex is the nerve vitamin. Improve your diet for lasting results.

Diabetes

Many diabetics have been greatly assisted by Vitamin E. Follow the instructions for this vitamin to find the right dose. Since it is a degenerative disease, diet is the only permanent treatment. Avoid all unbalanced carbohydrate such as white sugar, alcohol, white flour and white rice and substitute whole wheat and brown rice. Give up sugar. Take Wheat Germ Oil as well as Vitamin E and include Vitamin B Complex plus brewers' yeast. The deficient biochemic cell salts are important too. Vitamin C is needed for weakened blood vessels (see BRUISES), lecithin will help the effectiveness of Vitamin E and prevent the characteristic cholesterol deposits. Raw food eating could easily make the difference between success and failure. Obviously with this disease all diet, including vitamins, should be supervized by a doctor.

Diarrhoea

This is a surplus of water in the bowel and natures way of eliminating poisons or toxins from the system, unless it is a mineral imbalance which has the same effect. Charcoal is by far the most effective immediate measure, followed by the correct biochemic cell salts. Since garlic is the best intestinal antiseptic take this (raw or in capsules). Salt and potassium deficiencies will almost certainly be present and must be remedied. Many of the important vitamins and minerals as well as intestinal flora will have been washed away, so a more than adequate diet is vital, and large enough meals to ensure at least some absorption. Take additional vitamins and minerals and some honey to give immediate energy. Complete foods like eggs, milk and liver are important, also whole grains and enough unsaturated fatty acids to slow down digestion. Vegetables and fruit will do no harm if they can be retained. Do not try to prevent diarrhoea artificially as the body has a reason for behaving as it does.

Emotions

These come from the mind, so read the section on happiness. Since nerves play an important part in emotions take Vitamin B Complex and the biochemic cell salt remedies. Magnesium is nature's tranquillizer and calcium is a tonic for the nerves. Speak about your troubles or write them down, but never let them fester. Since one of the secrets of happiness is to control your emotions, you must learn this exercise.

Energy

This is mentally generated as well as physically. Oxygen revitalizes (Vitamins C and E and iron) so does happiness. Vitamin B Complex is the principal energy maker (brewers' yeast). Vitamin E conserves oxygen and Vitamin C produces endurance. Honey (in moderation) provides the best kind of sugar. Fruit and vegetables supply the food kind of raw materials. Fresh air, exercise, relaxation, games, fun and sound sleep also provide energy. See Blood Sugar for constant energy supply.

Eyes

Bad eyesight can be improved, but not with glasses. Since it is the muscles behind the eyes which control your sight, unless it was defective at birth, these are what need attention. Exercises are essential to give them tone (read Hauser's or Bates' books). Vitamin A is the eye vitamin, for night-blindness or sensitivity to bright lights, Vitamin B Complex (B_2) for clearer vision, Vitamin C and bioflavinoids for capillaries on which eyesight depends. Vitamin E and biochemic cell salts help blood circulation to the eyes. Watering eyes, weakness and bags under them is usually due to salt deficiency. Fasting turns dim-looking eyes into headlights and sometimes keeps them that way. Correct eating is the long-term cure.

Flu

It attacks even the healthiest so do not dismay. Go to bed immediately and do not get up till your temperature is normal. Take biochemic cell salts immediately. On no account take drugs as this will drive the illness further into the body. Fasting for two or three days is the quickest cure, and when you start to eat again select the most nourishing diet and follow instructions for convalescents. Vitamin C saturation should reduce temperature but it may be necessary to take it intravenously with calcium. Take Vitamin A to fight the infection and Vitamin B Complex to help the stress. Fresh raw fruit and vegetables will help rebuild your strength. Be careful immediately after flu, otherwise it may return. Do not be strenuous as this may affect the heart. Convalesce for at least a week because the after-effects of flu can be serious, even crippling.

Fevers

See for FLU.

Glands

They are vital to normal emotions and the healthy working of the body and mind. Your sex life depends on them. The biochemic mineral cell salt Calc Fluor and others are important (they can even soften hardened glands. For the prostate and sex glands, pumpkin seeds (for their zinc) are invaluable. For all glands, unsaturated fatty acids from nuts and seeds or vegetable oils are essential raw materials. Vitamin E is vital for the thyroid, pituitary and sex glands, as well as the pancreas, liver, kidneys and most of the others, as it will stimulate their secretions. Vitamin A softens mucous linings including those of the glands. Vitamins B and C are needed for stress and those particular gland secretions as well as many others. Your health depends on your glandular secretions and correct eating maintains their health, but the mind controls most of them so you must learn control (see Happiness section).

Gout

Vitamin C saturation can be extremely effective. Raw fruit and vegetables help neutralize acids, so do the correct mineral cell salts. Drink lots of juices or any other liquid to help eliminate uric acid crystals. Alkaline foods like milk may help. Avoid acid-forming food, in particular incomplete protein. Since stress of any kind can cause an attack, avoid it and read instructions for stress. Diet is the lasting cure.

Gums

Bleeding gums are the first sign of Vitamin C deficiency as well as degenerative changes, so check on your general health. Take Vitamin B Complex also and change your diet. If diseased gums are neglected you will be in serious trouble. The mineral cell salt Calc Fluor is also useful for loosened teeth.

Hang-Nails

These are usually caused by a salt deficiency which mineral cell salt Nat Mur or sea salt will correct. Protein and calcium are also needed for nails.

Headaches

There are many different kinds, so first you must establish the cause. Some possibilities are: allergies, acidity, anaemia, emotions, high blood pressure, lack of energy, infrequent meals, iron deficiency, kidney damage, low blood sugar, change of life, menstruation, eye troubles, stress, toxicity, water retention, Vitamin B deficiency, colds, catarrh, indigestion, biliousness, nervous disorders, local infections, constipation, as well as many others. Therefore see specific disease, otherwise here are some suggestions:

1. *For congestive types*: lie down and relax for a few minutes (in a Yoga position if possible). Take mineral cell salt Ferr Phos.
2. *For toxic types*: Vitamin C saturation immediately. Lie down and rest for a while.
3. *For nervous types*: Vitamin B Complex and the correct mineral cell salts.

Heart

Most of the serious heart troubles come from blocked blood vessels, therefore Vitamin E and lecithin are first aid, but degenerative changes are the basic cause, therefore nutrition is the best long-term therapy. All the vitamins and all the minerals play a part. Do not over-eat, avoid white sugar and anything made from it and do not take too much sugary food particularly incomplete starch such as white flour and white rice. Strong coffee or tea are bad, so is alcohol, animal fat, cholesterol, stress, over-weight, excitement or over-exertion, They are all potential killers if the heart is in trouble.

Have plenty of relaxation, develop peace of mind, take regular exercise (particularly swimming), lots of fresh air and deep breathing, sunshine, develop a philosophy, ensure sound sleep and learn how to eat properly (see About Nutrition). Fasting (with great care) is probably the most certain way of making a lasting cure, providing your diet afterwards is properly planned. You can take many short fasts or several long ones (it rather depends on your condition and the available advice).

Indigestion

This is frequently a form of degenerative disease and therefore depends on improved health. A disturbed mind can cause indigestion. Goats' milk, untreated honey and raw fruit are the most easily assimilated. The enzymes in raw food are essential to good digestion, so are minerals. Charcoal has helped many people with acid indigestion and is always useful. Since digestion is a biochemic process, the correct biochemic mineral cell salts can be invaluable, so can peace of mind while eating and rest afterwards, chewing properly and eating slowly. An excess of salt speeds the digestion too much and too little delays it for too long. Indigestion takes time to cure so be patient. Never take bicarbonate of soda or antacids.

Insomnia

Sleep takes place in the mind and therefore the nervous system dominates it. Worry about not sleeping is usually more harmful than lack of sleep. If this is caused by heart trouble, attend to that immediately. Physical exhaustion induces sleep, so does fresh air, relaxation of any sort and peace of mind. (see section on Happiness). An over-active brain is sometimes the cause of insomnia, so unwind before going to bed by taking a short walk or bathing, perhaps eating something, reading a novel or doing yoga exercises. Indigestion, worry, anxiety, overwork or stress should be avoided. Vitamin B Complex and all other nerve foods and minerals can help. Sleeping pills do not eliminate the cause of insomnia and are dangerous to health. The mineral cell salt Kali Phos works like a sleeping pill with me.

Jaundice

This complaint can ruin the rest of your life if not completely cured, so have a long convalescence afterwards and learn to treat your liver through your mouth. Change your diet immediately and stick to it as long as you live. Give up alcohol, animal fat, white sugar and all semi-foods. Take large doses of Vitamin B Complex, saturate with Vitamin C and continue these for a long time. Vitamin E (plus wheat germ oil) is of great assistance and Vitamin A from correct food is a must. Do not overeat, keep the sugar intake moderate (fruit only), perhaps add some honey and have some regular exercise when you are recovered.

Take mineral cell salts Nat Sulph, Kali Mur, Nat Phos, Calc Sulph, which will help to stimulate and repair the liver. Ensure adequate first class protein which is necessary to regenerate the liver (two-thirds can be destroyed but will grow again with adequate protein). Raw food eating ensures a swift and complete recovery but you must never return to your old eating habits or to alcohol after you are well. A little honey helps to supply the missing energy (but not too much). Lots of rest is needed, so are relaxation, fresh air, sunshine, swimming, games and fun. It takes a long time to recover from liver troubles and only your own body can do that work.

All organs of elimination must be kept active because accumulated toxins lengthen the disease. Complete recovery is vital to your health and the enjoyment of life afterwards, so never treat jaundice lightly. Take great care during and after the disease. Raw food eating is your best medicine. Avoid fish soup, left-overs or any other food which might be toxic. Since the homeopathic principle that like cures like is true, frequently eat liver because it has all the nutriments your liver needs (a little is just as good as a lot but take it regularly and daily while you are ill). Alternatively take desicated liver tablets.

Joints

Vitamins C and B Complex should help to keep them lubricated but biochemic mineral cell salts are needed too. For further information see Arthritis.

Kidneys

Like the liver, these can only be approached through the mouth. Nutrition is the best medicine, never surgery Immediately saturate with Vitamin C to relieve them of eliminating some of the poisons and take the correct mineral cell salts. Avoid acid-forming foods like meat, eggs, cheese, grains, white flour, white sugar or anything made from it and incomplete proteins. Reduce your total protein intake to 1 gram per kilogram of body weight, using brewers' yeast, soya beans, nuts, seeds and green vegetables as your only source. Beetroot is helpful and asparagus acts as a diuretic.

Lips

Whether they be cracked, peeling, have vertical lines, are blueish-red, have lines at corner of mouth, are dry, sore or in any other way abnormal, the cause is nutritional. No amount of salves will help. Cracked lips are often caused by salt deficiency. Vertical lines and disappearing upper lips indicate a lack of Vitamin B Complex, so do cracks at the corners, sore lips and mouth. Enough Vitamin A and vegetable oil are also essential.

Mental Health

This also comes from bodily health and a good bloodstream. Otherwise read section on Happiness.

Memory

This is a problem of the aged but can be helped by the correct mineral cell salt as well as diet and Yoga exercises. Circulation is one cause of failing memory and nerve impulses another, so see for heart troubles and nerves. Memory can be greatly improved by making the brain remember. Like muscles, the brain gets out of training and then softens and degenerates. People who cannot read or write often have fantastic memories.

Metabolism

This is the never-ceasing activity of all the cells of the body, and therefore essentially biochemistry which is the chemistry of the cells of living matter. Obviously mineral cell salts are the vital need but correct nutrition is the long-term answer. Metabolism is the conversion of food into living tissue which includes digestion, assimilation, repair, heat and energy. Minerals, vitamins, enzymes, protein, fat and carbohydrate all play their part, so does the thyroid gland which dictates your rate of metabolism and therefore the rate of energy production. Healthy cells from eating raw food also mean perfect metabolism. Impaired metabolism is a degenerative change which takes time and correct eating to put right. Eliminate any harmful habits.

Mumps

This can be tremendously helped and even cured with massive doses of Vitamin C, but the doses must be enormous. Mineral cell salts are also a must.

Muscles

The heart is a muscle like any other and needs oxygen (good red blood), a constant energy supply (see Energy), protein for maintenance, calcium and magnesium for correct rhythm, adequate Vitamin E and B Complex, healthy nerves (see Nerves), enough salt but not too much, regular exercise, adequate rest, unsaturated fats and an adequate diet. Muscles can literally be built by continuous use. Equally they can degenerate through lack of use.

Nails

Protein and calcium are their principal food. Take mineral cell salts for crippled nails. Check calcium absorption and amino acid balance (see under Protein in About Nutrition). Vertical lines mean kidney troubles so should be taken seriously. Horizontal ones indicate calcium problems.

Nerves

Disturbances of the nerves can be mental or physical in origin and the most difficult to cure are the mental sort. Mind control is the key, and that means studying Yoga or Buddhism or consulting an Indian guru. On the physical side there is much one can do: Vitamin B Complex is the immediate first aid, next come calcium and magnesium, unsaturated fats (from vegetable oils) to protect them, lecithin which is part of their structure, biochemic mineral cell salts from which they are also partly made, Vitamin E which is vital for preventing and even curing neuro-muscular diseases. No glutein for multiple sclerosis or muscular dystrophy patients.

Rest and relaxation are essential, a change of scenery, regular exercise in the fresh air and some sunshine can also often work wonders. An open-air life rather than an intellectual one is the best medicine till all is well. Wrong nutrition can cause nerve deterioration (refined carbohydrate causes Vitamin B Complex deficiencies) so correct your diet. Nerves are physical and therefore are fed by the bloodstream so do not overlook this fact.

Neuritis

Everything I have said about nerves applies here. Your first aid is Vitamin B Complex and all the foods containing it. Mineral cell salts come next because some of them can relieve the pain. Rest in bed and eat simple nourishing meals. Saturate with Vitamin C to eliminate toxins caused by it. For the extreme stress of pain see Stress.

Pain

Calcium can help to decrease the sensitivity to pain. Mineral cell salts can help with certain specific pains. See notes on Stress. Good nutrition helps fight against it. Essentially you must find its cause and put that right. Take Vitamin B Complex for the nerves and Vitamin E for nerve strength. Never give in to pain. Your mind is your greatest ally. Find a distraction and concentrate on that.

Piles

These can not only be corrected immediately but also cured for ever. Suppositories sometimes work immediately as a temporary measure. The real cure is rutin (part of Vitamin C Complex) also called the bioflavonoids (see under Health Food Section) which the Swiss have analysed and manufacture synthetically (much stronger) under the name Venoruton P_4. The ointment and drops or capsules should both be used. Take Vitamin C also either as ascorbic acid, rose hips or acerola berries, as well as in fruit. Wheat germ oil is the best food supplement and can be combined with Vitamin E for better effect. Iron is also needed to strengthen the walls of the blood vessels, so eat some iron-rich foods. Check for salt deficiency symptoms. Take mineral cell salt Calc Fluor for a longish period, which will help give back the missing elasticity. If you are constipated it is vital to remedy that (see Constipation).

Poisoning

The first aid is always the same no matter what the cause: whether it is food, metal, drugs, insects, snakes, alcohol or autointoxication. Saturate with Vitamin C and if life is at stake take it intravenously with calcium. To prevent liver damage take Vitamin E and sufficient protein, plus Vitamin B Complex (fed through the skin if vomiting) for the stress. Pump out the poison from the stomach if possible.

Prostate Gland

Zinc is the vital need here and the easiest source is pumpkin seeds. Next most important is unsaturated fatty acid (vegetable oils) which is the raw material the gland needs. The mineral cell salt Calc Fluor will help to normalize if enlarged or hardened. Vitamin C saturation is needed if inflamed and to help eliminate accumulated poisons there. See more about this problem in section on Sex.

Respiration

Problems here should first be dealt with by proper breathing in clean fresh air. Garlic has cured many catarrhal troubles in the lungs and Vitamin C can help to eliminate the toxins congested there. Take Vitamin A for the mucous linings of which the lungs and bronchial tube are made. Improve the diet. Also see under Allergies.

Rheumatism

This is a degenerative disease in so far as it is often caused by an accumulation of toxins or acids from wrong eating, emotional troubles, suppressive treatment of disease, continued stress, poor elimination, ulcerated teeth or some other suppurating infection. Had the body eliminated these poisons, rheumatism might not have occurred. The best way to eliminate these deep-seated toxins is to have a long fast and then follow a correct diet. Use Vitamin C saturation to help eliminate them, Vitamin E to help the circulation to that part, Vitamin B Complex for the stress involved, also take biochemic mineral cell salts: Nat Phos for acidity, Calc Fluor for enlarged joints, plus others which can be most helpful. Avoid acid-forming foods and follow a very complete diet to ensure an adequate supply of vitamins and minerals. Do not eat excessive protein, as all protein metabolism causes acids and excess nitrogen needs eliminating by the kidneys. Exercise is important, particularly swimming.

Scars

They need not be permanent and even old ones can be greatly improved if not too large. Vitamin E has the power to melt scar tissue both inside and outside the body. Pierce a capsule and rub over the scar, also take internally. This applies to stretch marks from childbirth or being over-weight. Vitamin A is always needed for skin troubles. Raw food eating produces the most beautiful soft, transparent, umblemished skin.

Sex

See more about this in the section on Sex, but remember that the physical side of sex depends on a healthy body and that the mental side is just as important, which can be affected by inhibitions, ignorances, social taboos, fears, boredom and annoyances. Vitamin E is the sex vitamin, but large doses of Vitamin C can also stimulate the sexual urge. The mineral cell salts Calc Fluor and others will help glandular function which is all-important. Also see under Glands. The vital foods are: wheat germ oil, nuts and seeds, kelp, honey, lecithin, fresh fruit and vegetables, vegetable oils.

Shyness

This can be greatly helped by improved nutrition, as it can also by mineral cell salt Kali Phos. Escape from any overbearing influence. Take the B vitamin pantothenic acid.

Sinus Problems

Vitamin C saturation is always the first aid and can often cure (particularly intravenous injections). Vitamin A is important for the mucous linings. Some Yoga exercises, particularly standing on your head, can be a great help. Deep breathing is essential. Take biochemic mineral cell salt Calc Fluor for lasting effects and others for the mucous. See also under Allergies.

Skin

Skin troubles are usually caused by one of the following: 1. Local irritants (dirt, foreign bodies, etc). 2. Toxic conditions or allergies from any cause. 3. Constitutional (a diseased condition inside the body).

Cleanliness is most important for irritants, Vitamin C saturation for toxic and allergic conditions, Vitamin A and B Complex for constitutional troubles. Improve the diet and take mineral cell salts. Vegetarians always have beautiful skins. Raw food diet is a certain cure. Fresh air and cold running water play their part as do lecithin (the beauty vitamin), Vitamin E (for soft skins), brewers' yeast (for clear skins), and several of the mineral cell salts. The oils of the skin should never be washed away with soap. Dirt can never accumulate on naturally oily skin and can anyway be washed off with a little water.

Stress

This is anything which harms the body or damages, breaks down or destroys the cells: for example overwork, fear, excesses of all kinds, temperamental and environmental difficulties, surgery, infections, poor diet, exhaustion, extreme cold or heat, worry.

Dr Hans Selye of Montreal revolutionized medical thinking by proving that the body reacts to every kind of stress in the same way. It follows therefore that if we know how to deal with stress we are a long way to curing disease and preventing it. The anti-stress foods I have already specified under Special Foods. To these must be added Vitamins C, E and B Complex as first aids. Next comes Vitamin A for any infection. Adequate protein and unsaturated fatty acid (vegetable oils) are needed because stress uses them in large quantities.

The danger of continued stress is that it will exhaust the adrenal glands, but if pantothenic acid (part of B Complex) is taken regularly (perhaps 500 mgs or more daily) this can be prevented. Even if the adrenal glands have become exhausted they can be resuscitated with pantothenic acid. Rest is essential to allow recovery and obviously avoidance of stress is also vital. Do not forget that the first stage of stress eliminates salt from the body, so a little salt and water can counteract this (ie a runny nose from chills or cold), but after that salt is retained, so avoid taking it. Diet alone can build resistance to stress.

Sunstroke

Whatever the degree of sunstroke, reduce the body temperature with cold water and take some salt and water for the first stage of stress. Vitamin C saturation will help eliminate any poisons caused by it. For burns see under Burns.

Teeth

Soft and rotting teeth are a sure sign of degenerative changes taking place inside the body and therefore the result of a faulty diet. White sugar and its products are the worst offenders here because of the deficiencies they cause. Mineral cell salts Calc Phos and Calc Fluor can help greatly, so can an improved diet. Good teeth and good nutrition go together, and rotting teeth and a rotting body are synonymous. Diet is your most important medicine. Ulcerated teeth can be cured by Silica, Calc Sulph, Calc Fluor and Kali Mur. There is no need to have the teeth out.

Thirst

This usually means that the body is trying to eliminate an excess of salt or sugar or that not enough water is being retained in the intestines for reabsorption, therefore that the diet is wrong. The body is built to retain enough water for all its needs of cooling, lubrication and otherwise, providing you eat properly (I have drunk little water for ten years. I get it from food). If there is not enough salt in the body the water already there is inert and improperly utilized and distributed. People who eat excessive carbohydrate or fat of any kind are always thirsty and retain excessive water which makes them look fat. By drinking too much water they then wash away the water-soluble vitamins, many minerals, protein and other valuable nutrients. If you are continually thirsty something is wrong, probably your diet. Raw food eating ensures a proper sodium/potassium balance and thus a correct water distribution.

Thyroid Gland

This gland dictates your rate of metabolism and is therefore vital for your energy production. It gives you zest for work and play, influences how fat or how thin you are and can be the cause of heart troubles if not working properly. Goitre is the most common symptom of a malfunctioning thyroid gland, but you can also have an over-active or an under-active one. In all cases the immediate need is iodine (kelp or other forms of seaweed) which can prevent goitre and normalize malfunction. Vitamin E is needed for the absorption of iodine and Vitamin A for the production of thyroxin (the thyroid hormone). Vitamins C and B Complex also play their part. Take biochemic mineral cell salts if the gland has hardened (see Glands). Time is all-important for recovery and quick results cannot be expected. Never have the thyroid surgically removed unless it is killing you.

Tongue

This is very often the clue to many troubles inside the body which is why doctors always look at it, so should you. It should be an even pink colour, smooth not shiny, without cracks, fissures or indentations. When Vitamin B Complex is deficient the taste buds clump together forming grooves or ridges, or it may become purplish, smooth and shiny, brilliant red, enlarged and beefy. Coated tongues often indicate digestive or eliminative problems, so Vitamin C and garlic can help. Mineral cell salt Calc Fluor can help if cracks persist and others for different kinds of coating. If you are not feeling well the first thing to do is consult your tongue. Nutrition books will help you to read the symptoms.

Twitching

Trembling, stammering, ticks and twitching can usually be cured by magnesium (biochemic or otherwise) and Vitamin B Complex, although they do not always work. Even St Vitus's Dance and Parkinson's disease sometimes respond if tackled early enough. Also take all biochemic mineral cell salts for nerves and follow instructions for Nerves.

Ulcers

Whether inside or outside the body the healing of ulcers requires the same treatment. Vitamin C is always needed for healing any wound, so is the mineral cell salt Calc Sulph. Vitamin E must be taken to prevent scar tissue, Vitamin A to protect the mucous lining of the stomach, Vitamin B Complex for the stress which sometimes causes the stomach ulcers, also follow instructions for stress. Excess stomach acid can usually be neutralized by mineral cell salt Nat Phos. Take rutin (bioflavonoids) or Venoruton P_4 to help the healing (it works with Vitamin C).

Ensure that the diet is 100% nutritious. Eliminate the mental stress which usually causes ulcers, otherwise you are wasting your time trying to treat them. Enjoy yourself, go out and have fun in the fresh air and sunshine. See there is enough fat in your diet from nuts, seeds, soya beans and vegetable oils. If the fibres of raw food irritate, purée them but do not stop taking them. Alternatively make soups from bones and vegetables, soya and other beans. Follow all the instructions for stress.

Varicose Veins

Piles (haemorrhoids) are the same complaint in the rectum. Standers, sitters and pregnant women are the worst affected, but the cause, prevention and cure are nutritional, although constipation may aggravate the symptoms. Vitamin C and rutin (bioflavonoids or Venoruton P_4) are the first needs. Next Vitamin E (preferably with wheat germ oil) helps prevent and dissolve any blood clots and strengthens the walls of the blood vessels. Mineral cell salts Calc Fluor and Ferr Phos are of great assistance. Check instructions for piles. Avoid all stimulants such as coffee, tea, alcohol and smoking. Do not eat white sugar, white flour or any semi-foods which cause deficiencies, and take lots of fruit and vegetables. A raw food diet is the most certain cure, given time. Surgery is painful and not always successful. Anyway it does not cure the cause of varicose veins so your condition elsewhere in the body remains serious.

Water Retention

Most over-weight people are just water-logged. Any condition where too much water has accumulated is serious and must be tackled immediately. Eating excessive carbohydrate or fat causes water retention, so does adrenal exhaustion, cortisone, stress, an excessive salt intake, kidney and liver troubles and some allergies. First you must correct your sodium/potassium balance which is not easy to do and takes time (follow instructions for salt), but raw food eating is the best way. Vitamins C and E both act as diuretics (de-waterers). Vitamin A helps the kidneys. Protein and calcium are essential for urine collection. The mineral cell salts Nat Phos, Nat Mur and Nat Sulph control the quantity, distribution and metabolic byproduct of water in the body. If the cause is adrenal glands see for Stress.

Warts

These need not permanently disfigure. The mineral cell salt Kali Mur alone usually cures. Vitamin E used externally and internally can also help. Vitamin A is the skin vitamin.

4. About Happiness

ABOUT HAPPINESS

Unhappiness	113
Happiness	116
The Recipe	120
The Ingredients	
Health	126
Appreciation	127
Peace of Mind	129
Security	132
Environment	133
State of Mind	134
The Ego	138
Affections	139
Unhappiness	140
Sensitivity	142
A Happy Ending	143

A WAY

To be at peace and never touch this earth,
   To be at war and rule the universe,
We have a choice or so it seems,
   For those not born already yoked,
To seek our happiness unbound.

   So even those not struggling o'er the battlefields of life,
Like those above or on an earthly plain of strife,
   Can still be happy if they know the way
To choose a path direct and straight
   And never stray.

The choice is legion like the roads of life,
   The journey hard, continually a fight,
For only we can win so great a prize,
   With courage, strength and purpose, knowing how,
A way of living, giving, seeking, sought.

UNHAPPINESS

IN *About Nutrition* I explained how to be healthy by eating correctly and in *About Diseases* how to cure illness by the same method. Now I must tackle the third aspect of health, namely the mind, without which the whole is not complete, for each is dependent on the other and all are complementary. You may wonder why I have called this section ABOUT HAPPINESS and not ABOUT THE MIND. The reason is because my subject is an end-product of the mind and not its intricate workings, in other words this is about philosophy and not psychology, and happiness should be the principal pursuit of philosophy.

The sensation of unhappiness, like that of happiness, takes place in the mind; it is how we register that something is wrong with our lives, either in our bodies or our emotions, in our environment or elsewhere. We cannot live for long in such a state because apart from anything else the laws of nature object. We become ill or we die or we kill ourselves, but we never go on living in misery if we can possibly avoid it. Of course it is a question of degree, we can learn to adjust, but we cannot go on living with any appreciable degree of unhappiness, we have to cure it or life is not worth living.

Happiness is not something to be toyed with lightly, it is a whole state of mind as well as peace of mind, it is security and environment, our egos are involved so are our affections, it is health and an appreciation of the value of living, a sensitivity which makes us one with our true selves, the infinite or if you prefer to call it your God.

I have come across such happiness once in my life, when I went to discuss the Hindu religion with a guru at Banaras in India. Although I could be accused of having imagined it, I really felt that effervescent freedom of mind which only comes when all is well within, which also means that all is well without. That is intellectual, physical and spiritual perfection, something which has to be acquired the hard way, but when it is yours, there can be no greater prize on earth, if indeed it is an earthly possession.

What I have to offer you here are a few common-sense

facts about everyday living, not an intellectual exercise which you cannot understand, because like all other great things in life, I believe there is a simple method of attaining happiness. If the method were complicated I should suspect it of being wrong, for man is meant to be happy not unhappy, therefore it must be within his grasp. But although the way to acquire it may be simple, I am afraid the actual possession of happiness is not so easy, for books alone can only take you part of the way, the rest must be learnt by you, unless you are instructed. However when you consider the value of your prize at the end, it is not unreasonable that you should have to labour to achieve it.

The basis of health and happiness is what we put into the orifices of our head, consciously and subconsciously, yet so few people seem to be aware of this fact. What we eat and breathe and see and hear dictates our state of mind and body, there is no other alternative unless some physical accident causes distress, but even that is registered in the head. Most of this we have control over, although some of it is given us by the environment in which we dwell, therefore we must become conscious of what makes us well and what makes us happy. From that knowledge we can then choose our own path and make ourselves responsible for our own state of mind and body. That knowledge I will try to give you here, at least about the mind, the rest you can find in *About Nutrition* and *About Diseases*.

But let us be quite clear before we start that what is at stake is your way of life, no less. It is not simply a question of understanding exactly how you should eat for health (which you can find out from *About Nutrition*) and of analysing the exact constituents of happiness, then putting them all into practice. Some will be capable of it, others not and will therefore have to be aided by religion, politics or the laws and customs of their own family, clan or neighbourhood. The most I can do is give you the facts, the rest is entirely up to you.

The formula was originally established many thousands of years ago by the first Yogis and little has changed as far as the human body and mind are concerned since those days. We know more about why various foods make us healthy or not and we know more about the exact workings of the brain, but more people are sick and dying at an early age and there is more neurosis and lack of peace of mind than ever before.

What is wrong? How can we be putting men on the moon and yet rotting inside our minds as well as our bodies? Perhaps the whole function and life-cycle of man has been changed, perhaps we have at last discovered the small value of human life and its uselessness and through our scientific advance are equating the imbalance? Be that as it may, if one is in danger of losing one thing, usually an alternative springs from nature to try and redress the balance. That alternative must surely be the cause of health, embodying as it does the essence of nutrition as well as the elementary facts for achieving happiness.

But certain facts of life have changed since the days when Yoga was evolved, one of which is the relative smallness of the world today. No longer is Europe filled with warring tribes or even warring countries, it is now nearly one country, not as yet united by one currency or one language, even one philosophy or way of life, but those must come. Perhaps there is something we can all strive for and not fight about, namely the health and happiness of the people of the world.

But I am diverging from what I really have to say. As the world shrinks and the barriers come down, as knowledge is spread and maybe food as well, what is old-fashioned and out-of-date must be dispensed with. Surely from this will come a unified understanding of our responsibilities and the purpose of us all, something which has been sadly lacking till this date. Perhaps we shall find the whole embodiment of health is a basic individual right, that a properly balanced diet and a knowledge of the laws of living and nutrition can be the heritage of us all. Yoga was the first such attempt, now that knowledge has been diversified into the hands of nutritionists and philosophers, but the information is all there, available to us all. I hope this makes it clear how fundamental is the subject about which I am writing now and have written before in *About Nutrition* and *About Diseases*.

HAPPINESS

As I have been preparing my notes for this book I have been living very close to someone who is being persecuted and I have watched the manifestations very carefully, for they have helped me enormously in sorting out my ideas. To persecute someone effectively you must attack their mind, although in the last resort the body is also assaulted through lack of sleep, even through disease when that is at all possible. The aim is to deny the person happiness and to make their life not worth living, so it is a good object lesson for me to use here.

The first important point to ram home to a person being persecuted is that he *is* in fact being persecuted, to get into his conscious and subconscious mind the fact that anything which goes wrong in his life is due to his persecutors. Otherwise he might shrug off such misadventures as bad luck and therefore accept them, which would be fatal, for then his peace of mind would not have been disturbed and he would have been able to go on living quite happily. So that is clearly the first and most important aspect of happiness, that it is basically peace of mind.

Next it is necessary to make sure he is never able to appreciate anything, whether it be the beauty of a sunset or the magnificence of a view without interruption, either from the roar of an open exhaust, the screech of a motor-cycle or some other annoyance. For however strong-minded the person may be, he is bound to react adversely in such circumstances and the moment of beauty is lost for ever. In this way all other forms of pleasure can be denied him, for appreciation is thus negated and pleasure needs to be appreciated.

His security must also be disturbed because to live in fear wreaks havoc in the mind and body and in the end destroys them both. His ego comes next, for that is something very close to him and to be brought down in one's own eyes is cause enough for some to murder, wage vendettas, or even wars until the slight is vindicated. For the weaker-minded, persecution upsets their state of mind, not just temporarily but over a continuing period which causes illness. For resentment, worry, anger and an outraged mind all react upon the glands which then pour out an endless stream of hatred in the body. This poisons the system, causing ulcers, heart disease, arthritis and a thousand other psychosomatic complaints. If the person has great self-control and his understanding of the workings of the world is complete, then it may be possible for him to withstand the urge to seek oblivion from his troubles by becoming ill.

If friends, acquaintances and a social life are correctly included under environment, then to deny a person these is to disrupt his environment and that too is persecution, for without them the landscape is bleak and the view monotonous. Solitary confinement has been used throughout the ages as the most demoralizing form of punishment, reducing as it does one's environment to four walls and possibly a grille.

Affections come next, under which one must include sex for it is the strongest of them all, but laughter, relaxation, pleasure, fun, being wanted and cared for are more lasting. If these are denied, then a deadening sense of frustration can be induced which eventually can disfigure the face and warp the mind of those with talent, brains and drive. To deny the satisfaction of fulfilment comes high on the persecutor's list because he can thereby induce a sense of failure.

Lastly, if all else fails, or even as all else is being employed, the denial of sleep can wreak the greatest havoc, even kill or impair for life. Coupled to this comes any form of physical attack, to help weaken the body, and thus the mind. For health, no matter how one may deny the fact, is part and parcel of a happy life. In sickness life is hardly worth the effort to go on and in the end of course you do not.

So, if any of my readers have anything they want to force down someone else's throat, there is the blueprint of how to go about it. In reverse it is also the way to find happiness (with the addition of sensitivity) and that is my reason for going into such details here, for out of our own experience we learn and that way our lessons stick.

The happiness of others is not, unfortunately, a matter which greatly concerns the majority of the world. Politicians pay lip-service to it to gain your vote, businessmen are concerned with it so far as it affects production or the efficiency of their firms, husbands want their wives to be happy because it relates to their own welfare, but the tramp in the street would kill his fellow tramp for his crust of bread. Let the happiness of the rest of the world be our own happiness as well, for the two are connected.

What your country is you become, at least to a very large degree. It overrides your race, religion and upbringing, for the climate and the customs embrace your whole way of life and train of thought. Your house, both metaphorically and literally becomes like all the other houses, at least in style. How much more important does it thus become to see our world is full of flowers, for what is outside rubs off and becomes a part of us. For our mind, like a computer, starts accumulating the day we are born and gradually becomes our whole personality, ourselves, our country.

From what I have so far said one could liken happiness to a delicious cake, which requires many ingredients for the making. Basically peace of mind is the most important ingredient but all the rest are also necessary. Without the security which comes from the unconscious happiness of family life and a mother's love we miss an appetizing ingredient in our cake of life. The same is true of health, of our basic appreciation of life and all that it contains, our environment and our egos, our state of mind and affections. Without the search for sensitivity, life is a bare existence, hardly worth the effort of getting up in the morning.

So happiness, like life, can never be just one thing, but many. Also happiness is something animate, therefore it must live and nothing which lives can ever be too perfectly combined, for as the biochemists would agree, in the perfect union all motion ceases and what was animate becomes inanimate or dead. In the same way one cannot keep happiness as people now expect in their stupidity to keep their food, for when anything which was alive becomes dead, it immediately begins to rot and lose its substance. Therefore if you cannot be bothered to live you will die, for it is the effort of life which keeps us alive.

Happiness is often used as a measure of whether people have a right to go on living for we say: 'He is still enjoying life.' Personally I prefer to regard happiness as the whole art of living, so I put it on a pedestal as the criterion of a way of life. For those who do not have the time, the wit or the material means, happiness must be given to them, or rather they must be assured the ingredients and that is not beyond the means of any state.

Ignorance may still be bliss, but who is ignorant any more with radio and TV, books, papers and all the other means of communication? More pity for the world that that is so, but equally nothing is more dangerous than a little knowledge or more unsettling to peace of mind and therefore happiness. At one time, people, like animals, were concerned about nothing else except their need to eat, their constant supply of food, their lives and those around them. Now our mode of life has changed and all these things are or should be guaranteed us by a benevolent society, so we naturally accept them as our right.

The danger is that the hand which feeds us shall demand too high a price, for then we could indeed return to slavery in a very short space of time. Already the Communists are demanding the ultimate, for Castro admits to having killed 3,500 of his own people in Cuba and having imprisoned 20,000 more and Mao has killed 46,000 scholars. Multiply those figures by a few hundred or even more and you have the happy picture of Communism in Russia and in the Iron Curtain countries.

Doubtless in the free world power is still retained by force, but at least there is some freedom for the individual and life is seldom taken or people imprisoned for political reasons, only in extremes like revolution. So there seems to be the crux, because we are talking about happiness and I do not believe slavery of any sort can ever be a happy state. People work for themselves, not for the greater glory of the state, so they need to be identified and given freedom of expression which alone produces its own reward.

Given the physical necessities which are now within our power to give, it only remains for an answer to be found to the riddle of the mind for happiness to be ours. And I think we already know that answer, if only it can be presented in some acceptable manner to people who have now graduated from tribal life and become perforce partly educated.

Lastly, if people could die happily too, then there would be even more tranquillity on the road of life, but perhaps it is enough to know that modern drugs ensure we reach the end painlessly and without a waste of time. Of course it would be better if we could refuse wheat like a rice-eating Indian once did in a famine, knowing perfectly well he would die as a result, but he was happy to do so because he believed he was returning his soul to eternity to be reborn in another man. But that may not be possible in these times, so we must learn not to be afraid of death and make terms with it at an early age.

As children we are happy except when we are not and those moments are very temporary, so it stands to reason that the facts of life which we learn as we go along are not particularly acceptable or pleasant. We should all make some sort of concerted effort to eliminate from society those offending facts and try to live our lives towards something better, for without a conscious effort this can never be accomplished. That is the challenge of our time, because it is now all possible with the means of mass communication, a greater technical know-how for physical progress and a more sympathetic attitude towards the people of the world. If we do not become aware of this fact and do something about it now we shall all suffer.

THE RECIPE

In the days when Mrs Beaton held the kitchen floor in England, her famous cookery book was often jokingly supposed to recommend taking two or three bottles of champagne, three or four pints of cream, several pounds of butter plus innumerable other delicious ingredients which, before you ever started to blend together, you threw away, then reached for another lot. That is rather what this recipe does not recommend. Instead you take some seeds of grain and you use all of them, none is wasted. Then you gather your other ingredients fresh from your garden or store and use them immediately. It is hard work and probably means a departure from what you are used to, but the reward is more than worth the effort involved, anyway that is all part of the recipe.

Before beginning it is necessary to state that we are not born civilized. We have to acquire civilization on our journey through life, and that is a process of learning and education however indirect it may be. For life is an act, and whatever lines we learn we will perform on the stage of life, and our reactions will conform.

Therefore to make this great cake of happiness it is necessary to start the day we are born. Of course it can be made at any time by someone who is adept at the art and has some intelligence and character, but time and an early start are important to the full development of the product. So our grounding is important, whether it be sucking at our mother's breast instead of being fed from a can of condensed milk, or growing up in the reflection of her love and warmth instead of never knowing it.

It follows that happiness is a state of mind, but it can be greatly helped if we feel well and equally hindered if we feel ill. So first into the mixing bowl goes health, not rippling muscles or Atlas frames, but a strong heart and efficient glands, a solid frame and a reliable network of nerves and blood vessels. This I have likened to the butter in the mixture of the cake. Much of health is what you eat, but some of it is the workings of the mind and learning a few elementary principles of a way of life.

From our family in youth we expect and receive food and shelter and they also try to give us health. Since I am assuming in this book that the world has now progressed far enough to be able to guarantee us all those same commodities, then it is also within our power to ensure the health of the world as well. Because even with only a daily handful of grain plus some other food, the world could be healthy, provided the grain was milled and eaten in its entirety and the other rules about whole food applied to the rest of what we eat. If that was done and the basic principles of how to eat and behave were passed on by means of the mass communication media, none should lack the most pleasing of our natural gifts, that of health.

Next into the bowl goes peace of mind, by far the largest ingredient necessary for a good cake, in fact it is even possible to make a sort of cake with this alone. People can die happy, they can even be happy in prison and in many other states of unbelievable distress, discomfort and danger, providing they have peace of mind. Without that peace, no matter what their condition they are not likely to be happy. But how does one acquire it? That is a question millions of people seem to be asking just now, and many of them come from the rich and progressive New World. To answer that I must go into greater detail which I will do later in the book. For the moment it is enough to say that peace of mind is the basis of our cake and most of the other ingredients have a bearing on it.

Another important part in the making is the mixing and this I have likened to appreciation. Nothing that we do or see or hear has any meaning or happiness without it. It is something over which we do not have complete control, for too much of anything will spoil this most valuable attribute to the art of living, as will too little. But to choose exactly the right amount, to have awareness and time also, help appreciation and for these reasons we can usually acquire this delicate and rewarding sense. With appreciation, inconstant happiness can be made more constant, and the simplest parts of our daily life be given pleasure and enhanced in value. So appreciation comes high on our list, because with it something can be made out of nothing and that is a valuable secret in life for rich or poor.

Security comes next on the list because it is also something basic to our cake and helps to give it solid form and foundation. Some of it is given in our childhood, some should also be given by society, the rest we have to work for and discover in our daily life. It is as essential to happiness as peace of mind, but since it is also a part of it I have added it here. Those with the strength and the will can find it in most states of life and from many circumstances, but few have the courage for this or the faith it needs.

From there we reach for the most versatile of the ingredients, state of mind, which is the brandy, rum or other flavouring. The sight of death or laughter or even a pretty face can all change our state of mind, as also can an enormous cheque or gigantic bill. It is the difference between walking up the steps to find the body of your wife in a coffin at the top or seeing her waiting in her wedding dress. State of mind is fickle and short-lived, physical as well as mental, it can be treacherous and unreliable and if we are to be happy we must have some sort of control over it. It goes into our cake because we cannot prevent it from being there, even as a part of some other ingredient, but equally we can learn to minimize its effect and localize its influence. But more about that in its proper place.

Environment is nuts, raisins and other spicing in the cake

and over this we can exercise control. We can live in a pigsty or a neat and tidy, cheerful room, that much is at least within the limits of us all. Climate and beautiful scenery are wished upon us, unless we deliberately forsake them both to travel the world, which these days is perfectly possible. On the other hand environment tends to become a norm and so remains unnoticed in a crowd of other daily impressions, but even so it affects our lives.

Our egos have the most profound effect on our ability to be happy, for if we are always one degree down, always feeling slighted, life becomes a constant battle with ourselves. The sad thing about our egos is that to a large degree they are given us and if wrongly developed that niggling feeling can become a permanent accompaniment to our daily lives. But we all have egos, so I call this the baking of the cake.

Our affections are the icing and an excess can ruin the best of cakes. To make one without any icing can equally make it dull and uninteresting, anyway this type of cake is meant to have it and would not be complete without. But our enjoyment of the cake depends on how we treat our affections, because we must learn to control them, otherwise we shall find that they control us. Like everything that is part of us they have their place and it is important to find exactly where that is so as not to spoil things.

Unhappiness is also an ingredient in our cake, as a negative quantity, because unless any cause for unhappiness is eliminated in the making, the cake will not be right. As stones and dirt may find their way into any mixture through any ingredient, so can unhappiness. Sometimes it takes a lot of discovering, sometimes we cannot even see it ourselves and need outside help, but if it remains there it will ruin the cake. The causes are many and varied, conscious, subconscious and unconscious, but like dirt, stones or toxic material it can poison the whole system and ruin our lives as well as our happiness. So it is best to sift through all our ingredients and see that they are free from foreign matter and if necessary call in some help.

Last on the list comes sensitivity, the honey, molasses or sweetening. Last, because it is possible to make a cake without it, but what sort of cake I would not care to say. To my way of thinking it is the best part of the cake, but I know others who have made cakes without it. At this stage I must depart from the analogy of the cake because someone else's happiness cannot be savoured, it can only be imagined. Many people have been very wrong about other people's happiness, as well as unhappiness, even though some obvious outward tests should suffice.

The sort of sensitivity to which I refer is the whole secret of finding anything and everything you want in life, and should therefore equally be the secret to happiness, but to say just that is not enough, you must wait till later in the book. In my cake I should add generous quantities of this ingredient and I should ensure it was blended well throughout the mixture, for that way I could be certain of making a really delicious cake.

So there are most of the ingredients and the making is not too difficult, it follows the pattern of most other cakes. It is important to turn on the oven well in advance for our egos need a long time at a high temperature to be well and truly fixed in place. There is nothing more unsatisfactory than eating a cake which has not been properly cooked right through. The mixing is also important, because appreciation is the corner-stone of philosophy and philosophy is the search for wisdom and wisdom is foremost an attempt to be happy. For the best results I would suggest melting the butter in the basin first, then you know that health is well and truly embodied in the mixture, because it is such a help to the cake. After that comes the flour, sprinkled in slowly as there is so much of it and since it forms the basis of the cake. That is peace of mind.

Having now mixed the first important ingredients we must thoroughly blend the contents of the bowl until it is the right consistency before adding the frills to the cake. Nuts, raisins and the like come next as our environment, followed by the brandy, rum or other flavouring which is our state of mind. It is well to spend some time seeing that these are evenly distributed for they make a big difference to the taste, although perhaps not so much as the honey, molasses or sweetening, the sensitivity, if you should choose to use these delectable nectars. When the mixture has been shaped to your satisfaction, place it in the oven and leave it to bake for twenty-four hours, which is the full cycle in which we have to live and sleep each day of our lives.

When the cake is ready and has had time to cool, it must be iced with our affections, taking care to get the right thickness and perhaps creating some work of art on top. Now it only remains for the cake to mature in our blissful security for at least a year, then it is ready for eating on a day which is bleak and cold outside, so we can appreciate what we have made. If it does not taste good then, it never will and you would be best to throw it away and start again.

So there is the recipe. It is not complicated, it is like every other cake with a few exceptions. Read now what I have to say about the ingredients so as to make sure of buying the exact requirements, because imitation or synthetic products will not do and cannot possibly make a satisfactory cake. For something so important in our lives it is necessary to take a lot of time and care to achieve the best results, for the reward is long-lasting. Happiness should be for us all, so the ingredients should be available to each of us, as should the knowledge of how to make the cake. It is not a luxury, it is a necessity and the sooner everyone in the world comes to realize this fact, the sooner it will become a reality.

I cannot recommend too highly the recipe I have set out because I can see no other point in living than to be happy, the rest is vanity, a pointless struggle for a miserable end. If we call ourselves civilized, now is the time to prove it and what better way of doing so than to create a happy world for everyone to live in? If we cannot or are unwilling to do so, then we are no better than animals, squabbling and fighting about who has what, when there could be enough of everything for us all.

If I am branded an idealist for such utterances, then I am proud to bear what has become such a derogatory title, for if that is idealism and considered impractical, then the words of our language have become debased. This needs no desert island, no sheltered sanctuary, only the will of us all to achieve that end. Can you really look at your neighbour and deny him this right? Can you say that this is for you and not for him, knowing that it is within the reach of you both? Of course you cannot, you would not be human if you could. So let us get on with it, now.

HEALTH

Physical health does not take place in the mind but in the body, although the one influences the other, hence the need for this section. If you look at any work on Yoga you will find that before you are taught anything else, you learn to eat correctly, after that come the exercises, then the mental and spiritual aspects. The fact is that you cannot be really healthy unless you do eat correctly, which means eliminating all foods from your diet which are not whole. It is nearly as simple as that, for within reason any food which comes straight to your plate from the garden, field or animal is properly balanced for digestion and therefore assimilation and will do you only good. Of course it is better to know a little more than that, about not eating too much starch and balancing your protein foods with fruit and vegetables, but the essential point is whole food.

In *About Nutrition* I explained how to eat correctly for health, itemizing the vitamins, minerals, proteins and stressing what not to eat and what habits to avoid. In *About Diseases* I related food, vitamins, minerals (also Biochemistry) and natural cures to illness. From these two sections you should be able to become healthy and remain so, if you apply yourself to the subject with a will which is also necessary. I will now add some other points which I did not include there.

The health of your body is like the functioning of a symphony orchestra which needs beautiful music and expert musicians all playing in harmony. So does your body need not only the right food but also well-functioning internal organs. To acquire the latter one must not only eat correctly but have a proper grounding such as being breast-fed and having a satisfactory emotional life from a very early age, because the love of your mother and all the other family ties and emotions play their part in building emotional balance. Included in this should be a discipline and self-discipline which will hold your body and mind together in times of stress, for unless you can control yourself you will neither be healthy nor happy. This applies to sex as well as to drinking, to work and play, love and hate, fear and the rest of your emotional life.

Health also includes enough light and fresh air, exercise and relaxation, cleanliness and rest. A plant will die without sunlight, so will man, likewise can foul air kill. Lack of exercise causes innumerable physical troubles, as does insufficient relaxation. Rest is the greatest rejuvenator and repairer and cleanliness does something to our insides, both mental and physical. Health is a part of happiness and vice versa, they are as important to each other as husband and wife are part of the tree of life. That is all I have space to say here, but perhaps it serves to show how much a part of your way of life health should be, as indeed happiness. Everything in modern life works against it, speed, noise, tensions and the manner of marketing food, so counteract those by learning to eat correctly and by discovering how to be happy.

APPRECIATION

To begin with I must quote what I once wrote in a novel with the theme of appreciation: 'The sky was a clear, clear blue and he wondered why it meant nothing without the odd wisp of white cloud drifting across it, why the sun was so boring without the unfathomable depth of shade. He wondered if one could appreciate the true beauty of the sea without land or peace without war, life without death, play without work, light without darkness or love — — love without what? For Bob, So Ying, for us all the possession, contact with the object of our love.

'Does good need evil to be good, he asked himself, and is there no distinction otherwise? Does right need wrong to be right? And what is good and what is right? So to the desperate dialectic of opposing forces to which there seems no answer except the manner in which it is construed. Love without the realization of what we are without is nothing. Without a dagger through the heart we cannot feel the truest pains of love or know what life is really like to be in love. Thus is the clever woman she who digs her dagger deep within the breast of whom she loves and then withdraws without a trace or scar.

'So that is love. That is life. To think all that is necessary to give our world some meaning, if not we have no feeling and there is no point in our attempt to live or love. Forego it all and never taste the sweetness of real life, continue along the true, correct, conventional straight line, it is pointless unless crossed by another, endless, meaningless. No straight line can be graceful, it is inartistic, hard and angular, that is why the cobbled, uneven streets of Macau have beauty.'

There is hardly need for me to say more. Appreciation is the theme of the East, where the difference between life and death is a bowl of rice, where you learn to appreciate the simple pleasure of sitting under a tree drinking a cup of tea. For until you can draw happiness from the simplest things of life you cannot begin to appreciate living. As I wrote once before 'The more you take away from life (within reason) the more you in fact add to it.' Never to want anything is the same as the perfect union in chemistry, it is stagnation or death. In this spirit we should therefore accept what happens in our lives, for without the storm we should not appreciate the glorious day, the good times without the bad.

But I am afraid the perversity of human nature is such that those who are free want to be tied and those who are tied want to be free, so one must either understand that and accept it, or attempt to give it rein by indulging one's fancy within limits. In the same way one has to understand that suffering seems to be part of the human character, the forge on which it is made.

The only commodity one can partly adapt to one's own use is that of time, and the more you are able to do so the greater will be your sense of appreciation. If time dominates you, then you will never be able to appreciate anything, if you are the master then appreciation is also nearly yours. Mostly it is a mental exercise in relative importance, but also it is being able to organize available time so that you always have it when you want it.

Lastly appreciation is change and movement, for when you get away from something you see it in a different light. This is something we can influence ourselves and should do so as often as possible, whether it be going away for the weekend, fasting for a day or two, meeting new people, discussing new ideas or seeing new things. It needs effort to get out of a rut, but how much more comfortable is that rut when you get back into it! So that is all I can say here about appreciation. With a little practice and some awareness it will help to brighten your life, even add another dimension to it and make you happier.

PEACE OF MIND

Peace of mind is the foundation of happiness, for without it you will have none. We are born with it, therefore it stands to reason that we disturb it or even lose it on our way through life. Since it is a norm we should be able to regain it by resolving the causes of that disturbance by a process of reason, confession or faith. For those with a religion the problem is easier because they are able to dump their troubles in the lap of their God. Those without must learn to discuss their worries with their friends or if they cannot do that, to write them down, which very often has the same effect, even though the words are never read by another's eyes. If none of this is done, then it is necessary not only to understand but to find a solution for whatever ails you and that is not always easy, even though the answer need only be a mental one and not put into effect.

But peace of mind is not simply composed of negative qualities such as problems or worries, it also contains parts of other ingredients. For example, it would be difficult to have peace of mind without security, yet the security might only be that which you yourself have created by your own courage and understanding. Likewise it is also partly state of mind and environment, your ego and affections, no unhappiness and sensitivity. That is why this peace is so important to happiness. But the fact remains that people are happy till their peace is destroyed, so let us investigate the matter further.

As a start I find one writer who says: 'Thou shalt have it only when thou hast ceased to desire it.' How true of so many other things as well, although in this case the writer means that when you forget about yourself, peace shall be yours. Next comes the fact that when the way is barred there is usually peace of mind. This is simply acceptance, something which is forced on the Indians by their caste system and on others in different ways, but it can also be achieved by the knowledge that it is necessary to live at peace with yourself and the rest of the world and therefore accepting the circumstances.

The mind, like the body, gathers poisons and in the same way these must be eliminated or the person becomes ill. This is true whether the poison is conscience or worry, problems or frustrations, fear, hate, doubt or any of the other negative emotions. Elimination from the mind means not thinking about the offending matter, and the way not to think about something is to find a solution to it or to understand its lack of importance. This can be done by yourself if you are wise enough and strong enough, by discussing it with another person and so resolving it, or in the case of religion by giving it to your God and having the faith that it will be answered. Of course another way is not to allow any poisons to accumulate in your mind, but that is easier said than done. However let us inspect some of the causes and see.

Conscience comes first, which is your own shame at wrongdoing. It is all very easy to say do not do what you think is wrong or alternatively eliminate your conscience, but for most people those two things are not possible, therefore you must live within their bounds.

Worry comes next, which is often selfishness, because if you are of no importance neither are your worries. But that is easy to say and difficult to do, so one's worries must be aired to one's wisest friend or someone who can help put them right. There is no other way unless you can answer them yourself, in which case they are no longer worries.

Festering memories are more difficult because they go deep into the subconscious, but somehow they must be dragged from those depths and placed in the sun. This again requires a process of speaking about them if you know what they are, otherwise talk about your life to someone else and that may disclose the sore. In the future, always chat about your disappointments and frustrations, your fears and hates, your desires and loves, that way they will never take root and start festering.

Doubts can partly be destroyed by the confidence which comes from knowledge, but if you are not in that fortunate position then you must be firm in your own beliefs and stick to them, for nothing can destroy your peace of mind more quickly or more certainly. The strong and the stupid never doubt, the intelligent and the weak suffer torture.

Fear – or your reaction to it – is partly physical but also it is selfishness and lack of understanding. The cure for it lies through those three channels and in your own strength to combat it. But that is an over-simplification, for there may not be a cure. Either way, never live in fear, eliminate it or get away from it.

All one's negative emotions are great destroyers of peace of mind, whether they be hate or envy, greed, lust or meanness. Somehow they must be controlled, either by an understanding of their worthlessness or by a reformation of your own character, if that is possible. In all events, if you can prevent them from seeding in your mind you have negated their effect, which is all that matters.

Hope can be a great life-saver for your peace of mind and this is tied to sensitivity which is your conscience and your faith, but more about this when I come to sensitivity. Otherwise you can do a lot by convincing yourself, through autosuggestion, of a satisfactory outcome and very often your will to win will pull you through. In religion this would be called the power of prayer, but even outside it is an act of faith, a compelling power within yourself to make this happen.

Self-respect can also play a part in creating or destroying your peace of mind. If you are always on the point of shaving or washing-up or cleaning yourself or your house, you never have the satisfaction of seeing the rewarding result, it is a burden on your subconscious. That all comes from being on top of your job or not, whether it be daily living or your work or family responsibilities. The reward for being up-to-date is peace of mind, for if you are impotent, frustrated, incapable or inefficient you can be eaten up by these failures.

Modern living is regrettably angled to destroy one's peace of mind, for we are constantly told we need things which we could easily do without. But modern living would be hard to change and probably undesirable, so we must build a resistance to it and learn to be our own judges. This goes for all the pressures which are put on us by advertising, society, politics or any other medium setting out to exploit us.

Finally I come to religion which could have been a unity and a purpose, a security and a way of life, an end and a future, perhaps other things as well, but it seems to have failed us, so it is necessary for people to find their own peace of mind from an understanding of what it is.

SECURITY

Without some sort of security there would be very little peace of mind and therefore happiness. It is as important as that, though Han Suyin correctly spurns it as a banal thing, for too much is as bad as too little, to be too comfortable is stultifying to thought and new ideas and in the end likely to dry up any form of mental progress. But for the majority of people the little they do possess is a necessity and something which makes their life worth living, for it is something to come back to and to base themselves on if they are not capable of making that sort of fortress in their own heads.

But security, as also insecurity, begins in childhood from the love and affection of the mother and the family. It becomes a part of you as you grow up and while you remain a member of that unit. That is the confidence which you find in all really happy people and it is their tower of strength. The opposite is all too painfully obvious in those from broken homes, and those who do not know where they are going nor even have a starting point. So if you have children that is one sort of security you can give them and there is another also you can help them with.

This sort springs from the same source, as does all security. It is the knowledge of right and wrong, of good and bad, your whole set of values, a pattern which usually originates within the family. Without it you are like a drug addict after a debauch, empty, demoralized and brain-washed until you have another shot. If your family cannot give you this (not the other shot but the security), then your community must, or your religion or whatever other institution moulds your ways, for without those values you are no more than a common criminal, devoid of the knowledge of right and wrong.

Of course security also comes from having enough money and the knowledge of what and whom you can buy with it, but that is still a mental exercise, for the base of security is in your brain. It therefore stands to reason that you can acquire it by your own ability, from your own confidence to do and to act and this type should last until your dying day. But it is not for everyone, most people have to rely upon the power and goodwill of an organization on which to pin their faith and sacrifice their individuality and from which in return they receive security.

When you are old you need the same as when you were young, some warmth, some food and shelter, even a little love if that is at all possible. Should you still have a philosophy, acquired during the course of your life, born from understanding and matured by wisdom and a process of thought, then you are indeed lucky, for that too is security, although old age can sometimes play tricks with the mind.

If only one could get inside people's heads and find out what they pray for, that too would be security. Most of it I fear is selfish, but then nearly everything is, so one should not be condemned for that. Security boils down to the knowledge of being able to get what you want, whether it be curing your ills, mental and physical, having enough to eat, a roof over your head or simply being looked after. For most people it is necessary to find that outside themselves, for they do not have the courage, the ability or the means to acquire it mentally.

ENVIRONMENT

Environment consists of all those external elements in our lives which affect us daily, atmosphere, climate, scenery, houses, beauty, manners, habits and customs. It is also the fact that the face of the ruled bears witness to the characters of their rulers. Some of our environment we control, the rest is beyond our reach so we must therefore escape it if we cannot bear to live with it.

Our own home comes first on the list because it is most frequently with us, although the conditions under which we work have now attained nearly that same degree of importance. Our whole mental outlook depends on our home and how we live in it. Lots of light and air are commodities some people do not see the need for, yet they profoundly influence our health, both mental and physical. Furniture, pictures and *objets d'art* are also part of environment, although usually we love them because they are ours, rather than treasure them because they are priceless.

Outside is our garden and you cannot have a beautiful garden without flowers, as indeed with life, so manners are important, as are all the other thoughtful deeds of daily life. You either accept your view or move away from it, as with your work and the conditions which it offers. The same with local government and what they have created for you in the way of drains and services, parks and public places, pavements, roads and the whole exterior of your town or village. Local customs, conventions and way of life also affect us, so that what our community is makes a big difference to our environment. This also applies to noise and all the other modern irritants, from rush and hurry to the many other tensions.

One's environment must also include the people round one, whether they be family or friends, workmates or the general public, so the sort of manners and characters they have matter to you. At the basis of manners is respect, in all its senses. Man's behaviour to man is the essence of civilization, in fact that is the meaning of the word, so if civilization breaks down, as seems to be happening at the moment, we are all the losers and no one gains.

Today we have at last become aware that industry is spoiling part of the public environment and we are attempting to put that right. If we could also become aware of how we can improve our own environment and that of those around us, we should be more than playing our part in making the world a happier place in which to live.

STATE OF MIND

Since I have already dealt with peace of mind separately, which is the most important part of state of mind (*vis-à-vis* health), this only leaves the more controllable aspects for me to deal with here. This is where Yoga comes in handy, for that is its whole object, to enable you to subject completely your mind to your will. The classic example so often stated is where the Yogi is able to make a blister in the palm of his hand by the power of his own concentration. Within limits, that is what you too should be able to do with your mind, control it completely.

Of course one's mind is one's kingdom in which one lives, therefore it is most important to take a lot of trouble with it. If you are in control of the situation you can keep the door barred to harmful thoughts, as the Christian Scientists set out to do, by not allowing them to take hold and this will prevent a great deal of physical damage to your body. If you are not in control, the slightest anxiety or disturbance will start the rot. You must learn to direct your thinking, in other words stop offending thoughts taking seed. It is easier said than done, but there is no other way of stopping your mind triggering your endocrinal glands and other bodily impulses and so starting a series of bodily reactions.

Conversely, one should equally be able to induce a happy state of mind or a curative one, although this rather depends on your philosophy and how far developed it is. But what can be consciously induced can also be subconsciously or unconsciously taken away, unless you really are master of the situation, therefore discipline is needed. Discipline is also the clue to the whole working of the mind, so this is your starting point if you are to acquire a happy state of mind.

The essence of discipline is instant response to your word of command and that comes from practice and training. Thus your state of mind depends on how you are trained or train yourself, so you can learn to become your own master and create your own state of mind. The secret of this has been written in many places, but perhaps the most comprehensive instruction comes in Yoga, because it gives you the whole picture and how to achieve it, although Buddhism is as good. For those who have acquired the art, they find no other method so effective for relaxation, for a happy state of mind and a contented body. I have found the same myself.

Having said this I have said everything, but you must also understand state of mind if you are to conquer it. There are at least three levels of thought, conscious, subconscious and unconscious. Conscious thought is obvious. Subconscious is any thought not too deeply buried which comes in for attention, as frequently happens while one is working or where you associate ideas just below the surface with some visible object, like something in a shop window. Unconscious thought is what takes place when we are asleep and the reason why we know the answer in the morning, when we did not know it the night before. The practice of Yoga teaches you to subject all these types of thought to your own will, then you can really begin to live and be happy.

In the meantime it is as well to start by controlling your reactions to sudden noise, to pain of any sort, fear, greed, hunger, lust, anger, distress and all the other daily impulses which pass through your brain. With practice you will find you can gradually subject your reactions to gain a more tranquil frame of mind. From there no limits should restrict you, but you must always be conscious of your thinking and of your reactions.

The opposite is also true, in other words the accumulation of your uncontrolled reactions to stress (which is tension) can also be controlled. This is largely done by relaxation which is part of the cycle of our nerves, contraction and relaxation, for if they only contract we have cramp and that is not so different from tension. This is another of the objects of Yoga and something we can make a start on ourselves by learning how to do it, for it is not only achieved by fun and games, diversions and hobbies. It is also learning to let go and that can as easily be accomplished by a walk in the country or lying flat on your back in the sun. For emotional relief it is usually necessary to have a physical outlet, such as tears or laughter, strenuous exercise or even sex, before the tension is dissipated, so let your tension run out of your body through some physical contact or activity. It can also be achieved through meditation (Zen), once you have learnt that art.

State of mind is also dictated by occupation, either physical or mental, whether it be work or play, so that thoughts of self and one's problems cannot come to mind. That is how boredom and vice are cured, how nervous diseases are brought under control and how some lunatics are distracted from their lunacy. If those people could control their own minds none of that would be necessary, but for some reason they have failed, so they wander in varying degrees. Lastly the busiest people are very often the happiest, if only for the reason that their minds are totally occupied.

Food also has something to do with state of mind, not just because the brain is physical, but because a full stomach or being properly nourished satisfies a need and satiates other emotions. Businessmen know this with their business lunches, although usually that is not all food! Perhaps that is partly why grain is called the staff of life, because it takes so long to digest that the feeling of satisfaction lasts longer. In any event sufficient food is conducive to a happy state of mind and insufficient is a cause of distress.

But the important thing is to learn to enjoy the journey of life, for one never in fact arrives except at death. Women are particularly good at this because they live for the occasion, although I sometimes wonder what they do in between times! Rather in the same way the Chinese say, the contented man though poor is happy, the discontented man though rich is sad. If one's state of mind is right, the circumstances of one's life can be subjected to it and that is an essential of happy living.

Finally it is worth remembering the enormous power of the mind, as an influence over one's own self and over outside events. It is possible to make events happen, as it is also possible to change your own personality, even appearance, if you really want to, but the will must be strong. For do not forget what I wrote in *About Nutrition*: 'You can die as well from the lack of the will to live as you can from lack of food, yet your state of mind can keep you going beyond the limits of physical endurance.'

If you think about something hard enough and create that state of mind, the reaction to those thoughts takes place in the body. Even talking about food makes most mouths water, and the sight or even thought of a pretty girl has some physical effect on men. Unfortunately this fact is also true of harmful subconscious and unconscious thoughts, and therefore of all psychosomatic disease. So be careful what you put into your mind and what you think about but above all learn to control your mind. Happiness will come from it.

THE EGO

The ego is the I, the self-important part of self and yet something over which we have surprisingly little control. Of course if we were able to humble ourselves and realize our complete lack of importance, we could bend our ego enough to make us happy, but that is easier to say than do. Those who grow to manhood without this discipline being imbued or nurtured in their childhood, will shy at anything better than themselves, because they feel inferior. They are as miserable as if they were going through life blind or deformed, because never can they be the equal of the rest of the world and yet that is the only thing they want.

But the ego is a strange commodity. Artists, writers and creative people usually have inflated ones, constantly blown up by themselves and others, like those of politicians. Ego is a respect and a self-respect, manners and confidence, the whole world in which we have to live, because it is our selfish reaction to ourselves.

That much is on the negative side, but there is also reward for the ego from success or achievement, from creating or accomplishing the impossible, congratulations and words of praise. It is even the goodness in the heart of the nurse who is able to help her patient, the ability of the shop assistant to serve his customer, the soldier and his cause, the street sweeper and his public. This type of ego we all need, it keeps us going. It is our defence against the inequality of the world and its unfairness. So never lose a chance to boost another person's ego, the habit might be catching.

The ego's relation to happiness is therefore two-fold. On the positive side I suppose we should never expect even a murmur of approval. On the negative side we should be grateful we are so highly placed in the eyes of others as ourselves, no matter what our position, function or background. If only we could rub the noses of our egos in the dust and trample on them occasionally, we might stand a better chance of being happy. Beastly for our egos and damaging, but better to do it ourselves than let life do it for us. If only, as in the cake, our egos had been firmly baked into place in the beginning we should never have trouble with them later on, so make sure your children's are.

AFFECTIONS

Affections are really no more than emotions and the dictionary definition of emotion is: 'Agitation of mind, feeling; excited mental state.' So we are back to the mind again and a very important part too, because that is where our pleasure takes place. Our affections are such things as love and laughter, excitement and sex, friendship and marriage, enjoyment and all sorts of pleasure. They are also hate and fear, pride and vanity, loneliness and self-pity, a need to be wanted and cared for. Emotions can be controlled and it is vital to our happiness and well-being that they are, but equally we cannot be complete unless we have a balanced emotional life, which means fulfilling them.

In Yoga one is taught to make oneself 'free from the lures and pleasures of this life', but having done so you are not necessarily expected to cut them out of your life, only ensure you are not enslaved by them. Most of the other emotions you cannot be free from, but equally you need not be enslaved by them either, which means controlling them. For example at a certain age sex is a necessity and part of the natural cycle of life, it was never meant to be swept under the carpet as something dirty or wrong. It is part of man's fulfilment and satisfaction in life, his expression of love for his wife or mistress, but like the other emotions it needs controlling for our own happiness and well-being.

An excess of any emotion is harmful, for gradually it ceases to give pleasure and in the end gives pain. That is why we talk about a properly balanced emotional life, because it is a balance in which the more emotions are involved the better they are integrated, resulting in greater happiness and mental and physical health, For emotions need to be expressed, not bottled up, otherwise we become frustrated and that is torture of the self-inflicted kind. But too much good food makes us sick, as does too much sex, excitement, fear, self-pity or loneliness, so Buddha was right when he preached the middle path, because it does produce a happy balance.

Our emotions work on our body principally through the endocrine glands and our nerves are affected as a result. That is how we become ill from emotional troubles, because we exhaust our glands or nerves or anything affected by them. The well-disciplined and the self-disciplined seldom have these troubles, they are able to control their emotions within reason. The properly nourished are also partly resistant because they can supply their glands, nerves and other organs with their daily needs, ensure that damage is repaired and eliminate the toxic poisons created by excess. So discipline and food both play their part in keeping that balance which becomes a happy state of mind and a healthy body.

But some are more emotional than others; we are not all the same. Partly this is due to climate, partly to our genetic self, our food and the whole manner in which we were brought up and therefore taught. Some need a lot of love, others do not, as there are those who are naturally affectionate and those who are cold. We all need different treatment. Likewise there are those who cannot find the love they seek, who are not cared for, who cannot find the sexual release for which they crave, as there are those who are lonely or excitable, fearful or full of hate. For those, there used to be religion, but what will happen when that has gone completely?

Doctor's waiting-rooms are full of people suffering from emotional troubles, which are manifest by some sort of illness, real or imaginary. They are given drugs which suppress the symptoms of pain and gradually nature helps them to recover. Had they been able to discipline their minds and bodies they would never have become ill in the first place, providing they ate reasonably correctly. This hardiness, for that is what it is, has nearly died out and we are becoming a world of mental cripples and physical weaklings.

UNHAPPINESS

It should hardly be necessary to include this here because it is so obvious, but people forget how important it is to eliminate any cause of unhappiness before they can be happy, or healthy for that matter. Partly it is this business of festering sores which can either be conscious annoyances like a nagging wife or dissatisfaction at work, or some daily occurrence which takes the pleasure out of life. Partly the trouble could be subconscious, like something that you have burdened your conscience with, a gambling debt, excessive drinking or any other bad habit. Lastly the cause of unhappiness could be unconscious, due to no love in childhood, unpopularity at school or continuous slights in youth.

Now I realize it is a sweeping statement to say eliminate any cause of unhappiness, when even psychologists find it hard to unravel the tangle of another person's mind, and trained social workers, priests and the like are equally at a loss. But it is something you must try and do, and do successfully. The best way is to talk about your life or even to write it down. This way you will unload the burden from your mind and you may discover which of many things was causing the trouble. Having done this, keep your life an open book and discuss your doings and undoings all the time with whoever is close at hand, then nothing will fester in your mind and cause disease.

There is nothing like an open mind for physical and mental health, for this means letting things in as well as out, and both are necessary for the cycle of life. We eat food which we then digest, but we must also eliminate the wastes, otherwise we become ill. The same applies to the mind: we need reactions going in all the time but we must also eliminate the painful or indigestible ones.

But for some people to keep an open mind is very difficult, because they lack the ability to communicate. That is the cause of millions of broken marriages and family strife, because invisible strings hold back the words of love or fear, hate, anger, distress or hurt. They cannot bring themselves to open the difficult conversation and so they are never able to unburden their minds. Eventually the pain can be borne no longer and the person becomes ill. So if you are a father, help your wife and family to talk about their lives and make them tell you any causes for unhappiness. Once the ice is broken it will be easy to go on.

Those who have a religion and are true to it are taught to confess their sins and that has the same effect, but fewer people go to church these days and even fewer confess their sins. Whether you have a religion or not, your own criminal or merely anti-social activities can still cause you anguish. For example, I do not suppose people who steal are happy about it, or those who lie or kill, the drunkards, libertines or other social outcasts.

One has to learn a set of rules in life, not just for your own happiness but for that of the community as well, so it is right you should be acquainted with these rules from the start and put them into practice straight away. Then your causes of unhappiness are likely to be less and your chances of happiness greater. So learn to recognize your causes of unhappiness and eliminate them from your life before they cause trouble. Only you can do this.

SENSITIVITY

You cannot feel anything by pressing your finger hard down on the surface, you must rub it gently along the top. The same is true of the mind, for if it is knotted like a ball of muscle, nothing will come through. Equally you have to be aware, otherwise you feel nothing either, however gently you stroke the surface of the world. Both of these need practice, for you have to become conscious of what you are doing and aware of where you are going. By this I mean what I once wrote about the artist: 'The hand that guides it (the brush) has another source of power as well.' That is sensitivity.

It is many things and it is everything. It is the artist's line and colour, composition and effect. It is the writer's selection of words and ideas and the way they are strung together. It is finding what you want when you need it and being in the right place when you should be. It is an addition to thought but never a substitution for it, although it should lead one to the right decision. It is being aware as well as intuition and perception, it is knowing without being told. It is relaxing so you can find the right answer and not forcing a wrong set of circumstances on yourself. It is receiving as well as giving out, a sense of what is right as well as what is wrong.

It is instinct, yet it is acquired, it is sought and found, but only by trial and error, hard work and some tears. It is love and charity, gentleness and an understanding. It is knowing we are right and being confident to follow it through. It is courage and strength, a will and a purpose, a negation of doubt, a star in a cloudless sky. If you seek it you shall find it. If you want it then it shall be yours, but only if you really want it. Some find it in their search for a God, others because it is their whole point in living, in fact it is their God, but it is there for us all for our humble admission.

A HAPPY ENDING

What else can I say in conclusion that I have not already said, except to wish you all enormous happiness. Please read what I have said carefully and then re-read it. When you are quite clear what it is all about, try and put it into practice.

If you keep in mind the ten ingredients and remember what they are composed of, you will be progressing a long way. After a period of time it may be necessary to read this section again to check your achievement. If you find you are not getting anywhere on your own, bring in a friend or member of the family and discuss it with them.

Then, if you want to make some comparisons, have a look around the world or even your own neighbourhood and see if you can spot who is happy, and who is not. Then try and work out why. After all criminals are sometimes used to cure criminals of their anti-social habits, and alcoholics, alcoholics. If you see the stupidity and mistakes of others, you can very often prevent your own, because all you are really doing is getting outside yourself and seeing your own shortcomings in perspective.

A look around the world is also helpful, providing you have had the advantage of sufficient travel to be able to make the necessary comparisons, because some nations and communities are obviously much happier than others. You will have to delve quite deeply, but the evidence is there before your very eyes and one's eyes do not often deceive one. The world is more than ever what you see it to be; people's faces portray their characters if you have the ability and wisdom to read them. So look closely at the world, then analyse why one nation is happy and another not.

You will have to go into this carefully, and find out about their eating and cooking habits, about their philosophy and religion, the geography of their country and the history of their race, their way of life and their aspirations. Somewhere along the line you will find a solid core of happiness which emerges from a central cause. It will not necessarily be the ones who have arrived who will impress you, but probably those who realize they will never arrive and therefore continue the journey.

Those who sink their all into the cause of their own family and people will almost certainly be the ones who will come out on top. They have negated themselves and subjected their ego to something greater than themselves, so any happiness they may achieve will be multiplied. By not setting out to seek their own happiness, but the welfare of those nearest and dearest to them, their own people and country, they will justly receive their reward, happiness.

So perhaps I ought to repeat what I quoted before: 'When thou shalt no longer seek happiness, it shall be yours,' because so great a prize is not meant for those who selfishly want it only for themselves or who want to buy it, but for those who give enough of themselves to have it as their reward. So go away and leave yourself behind, ask the world how it will have you serve it best and when you come back, battered and weary from your efforts, you will find a different person from the one you left behind.

Apart from this there are a few individuals left, thinkers and philosophers, intellectuals and artists who will need to find their way on their own, possibly because they are driven by circumstances or lack of opportunity. Their trail is longer and harder and not necessarily successful, but they cannot escape the force which drives them on.

So do not expect happiness to fall into your lap and do not grovel on your knees for it, but know what it is you want and you will find it. Happiness is for the garbage collector and the street sweeper as much as for the king or the president and is equally attainable, for it is a state of mind, although the physical aspects are still vital. If we disregard the need for happiness in the rest of the world, it will surely turn sour on us and that will accomplish nothing for anyone.

Nations are led along the paths they will follow, the people have no choice. For that reason they should not be expected to bear the worries of government or of rights and wrongs, but be given their values and their basic needs, then allowed to live happy, carefree lives. But because government is not for everyone, parliaments should be elected from the lowest common denominator of a country's subdivision, free from party politics, creed or race and re-elected at frequent intervals to ensure its proper functioning. In that way perhaps the happiness of the people would be ensured, although I fear that those who are only concerned with their own happiness would prevent such measures ever being carried through.

By starting elections in the smallest community, you would ensure (by a system of escalation through the various local councils), that the National Parliament was full of able men properly representing their country, rather like Norway's system. Unfortunately party politics has become a most offensive dictatorship, because unlike any other dictatorship it can never be disposed of. There are no two ways of governing, only one and that is for the best interests of the people in that country.

I can think of no other pattern for the future happiness of us all, because we all need help, and this would ensure it is given. Modern means of communication and industrial organization put too much power in the hands of governments, yet we are still working on an old-fashioned system of election and political organization. Our happiness is now so much more at stake and too much affected not to need reorganization, although I shall not be loved for saying so.

5. About Living Alone

AND
PLANNING A DIET

ABOUT LIVING ALONE AND PLANNING A DIET

If You Do Not Live You Die	151
Living	154
Living Alone	156
Food for Living	158
Selecting Food	160
Protein	161
Fat	161
Carbohydrate	162
Vitamins	162
Minerals	163
Enzymes	164
Anti-stress Factors	164
The Don'ts	164
Food Values	165
Cereals	165
Eggs	166
Dairy Produce	167
Pulses	168
Nuts and Seeds	169
Fruit and Vegetables	170
Brewers' Yeast	174
Organ Meats (Offal)	175
Meat and Fish	175
Honey	176
Sunshine, Fresh Air and Exercise	177
Water	177
Preparing Food	177
Raw Food	178
Cooked Food	179
Sprouted Seeds	179
Cereals	179
Eggs	180

- Dairy Produce ... 180
- Pulses ... 181
- Nuts and Seeds ... 182
- Fruit ... 182
- Vegetables ... 182
- Brewers' Yeast ... 183
- Organ Meats ... 183
- Meat ... 184
- Fish ... 184
- Honey ... 184
- Menus ... 184
  - My Diet ... 185
  - Your Diet ... 186
  - Sprouted Seeds ... 187
  - Cereals ... 187
  - Eggs ... 188
  - Dairy Produce ... 188
  - Pulses ... 188
  - Nuts and Seeds ... 189
  - Fruit and Vegetables ... 189
  - Brewers' Yeast ... 189
  - Organ Meats ... 190
  - Meat and Fish ... 190
  - Honey ... 190
  - Sunshine, Fresh Air and Exercise ... 191
  - Water ... 191
- Summary ... 191
- Nature's Medicines ... 192
- Living in the Mind ... 193

IF YOU DO NOT LIVE YOU DIE

I AM devoting this section not only to little old ladies about to put their heads into gas ovens, but also to the ever-increasing number of people who live alone, whether they be students or hitch-hikers, campers or travellers, divorcees or young marrieds, artists or writers, the old and retired, widows or widowers, bachelors or spinsters, pensioners from the services or from any other walk of life. In the days of the family unit there was never any problem because everyone was part of that great and indivisible unit. All the love and humanity, the care which only one human being can ever give to another, was manifest in such a way, because life does not consist entirely of material things and our only real security is our own family who love us and whose blood we share.

However there are some who do not have this or cannot, and times have changed. Everyone who can have the freedom of independence quite naturally wants it. This should present no problem, but it does because everything in life has to be learnt, whether it be running a house or a country, how to walk or read and write, and of course those who have been cared for all their lives take it for granted that they know how to care for themselves. But that is usually not the case, because it is one thing to watch someone else drive a car but quite another when you have to do it yourself. The same applies to eating.

As a writer on the subject of nutrition, I notice everywhere I go that people just eat whatever is put before them, they never think about *what* they are eating, only whether it tastes good or not, also perhaps whether they can afford it. What they should realize is, first, the only thing which does matter about food is what it consists of and, second, the cheapest food is very often the best for you. It has not been interfered with by food processors and therefore contains all the necessary vitamins, minerals and enzymes in their proper proportions to keep you healthy. So the first and most important matter I want to deal with in this section is to tell you how to select your food, how to prepare it and how much of it to eat. After that

I will tackle the art-of-living angle which is just as important for most people because they have never learnt how to cope with life on their own and lack the confidence and often the courage to do so.

No one in their right mind would think of setting a child loose in the world today completely alone, and if they did someone would most probably come along and care for it. Yet when we are first thrust upon the outside world, people expect us to know how to look after ourselves, but of course we don't. We think we do and we follow the pattern which we were brought up with, but we do it blindly, not really knowing why. That pattern probably never had any real meaning, but was simply carried on from one generation to another. That is how our eating habits are acquired, from our parents and from the world around us which puts the food before us which we buy.

So the first thing I am going to ask you to do is to think about what you are eating and to make a point of finding out what it consists of. Then you must learn how much of the various ingredients you need to keep you healthy. Lastly you must know how to buy and prepare that food, for there are lots of different ways of getting the best from what you have, and of choosing what is the most nutritious from amongst the rubbish. When you have done all that you will be able to keep yourselves healthy and that is important because you will then be strong and therefore better able to cope with life. If you are weak the battle is half-lost before you begin.

However it is also possible to be healthy and unhappy, to make a complete mess of one's everyday living for lack of the knowledge of how to go about it. This is true for the old as well as for the young, because people who live by themselves usually come to it from the security of community life and are therefore unpractised in the art of living alone. Make no mistake, it is an art, just as any other form of living is. A lot can be learnt from one's own mistakes, indeed that is often the best way of doing so, but it is painful, so perhaps I can give you the benefit of long experience.

Some people seem to be more prone to aloneness than others and I suppose it is circumstances which dictate that. For myself, I seem to have spent most of my life that way, but then perhaps I fit into Colin Wilson's description of an 'outsider', in which case this is my mould. Be that as it may, I have had to learn the hard way how to do it, how to live alone and enjoy it. I am not suggesting it is ideal or that it is commendable, I am not advocating it for society or encouraging people to live alone. But there are those however, and I am one, who have had it thrust upon them and in such circumstances one must do one's best or go under, it is a question of survival. Allow me therefore to tell you what I know and you can then judge for yourselves whether it is of use to you or not.

To begin with I would like to take you back to the first book I ever wrote called *Alone No More*, which was the story of someone's sudden awareness of the unbelievable misery which exists in the world because so many people are alone. He set out to investigate that misery and came across a vile and sordid world which he never realized existed. But the sad thing he found was that it wasn't so much the fault of those people as the society in which they lived. It was society's responsibility, yet it did nothing to relieve the situation, in fact its principal concern was to take advantage of them, to profit from their misery and weakness and use them for its own advantage. Of course you may well reply that that is the price they pay for living alone, but there are some who cannot help it and others who need a lone existence. So in the end he started an organization called ALONE NO MORE to try and help them and that is where he discovered the worst about lonely people.

But my object here is not to make a story out of loneliness, rather to try and help you alleviate your own so you can live a full and happy life. Thus *Alone No More* would be of little help, and anyway at that time I had not learnt how to be happy with nothing except what one creates for oneself. And that is the secret, what you yourself create, for it is like painting a picture or writing a book or producing any work of art, the art of living each and every day. *You* create it, it is your doing and if you don't, nothing will happen, in other words if you do not live you die. The only question therefore is how to live and that is a big one, but it is really what this section is all about, so I will try and explain.

LIVING

Life is defined by the Concise Oxford Dictionary as 'a state of ceaseless change and functional activity peculiar to organized matter and especially to the portion of it constituting an animal or plant before death'. Without food, water or air that ceaseless change could not continue to take place, nor could it without direction from the brain. Everyone therefore has the same task ahead of them each day, namely to find enough food to keep their body functioning and to pass the day profitably (in every sense of the word). For if we do not eat we eventually die and if our mind plays no active part in the day's proceedings that also degenerates until it is moribund. So those are our lifelines which must always be kept open if we wish to continue living. It is the effort of accomplishing this which is the spark that ignites the fire of life. Dispense with that effort and the lifelines cease to exist, so the fire eventually dies out.

But fortunately or unfortunately there are degrees of health, as there are also degrees of life, so we do not notice as we gradually degenerate because the process is so slow. Also one person may never be more than half-nourished, so it is hard to convince him there is a state beyond that. However for the sake of this book I must generalize, although I realize that one person's method and pattern of living is not necessarily suited to another. Even man and woman will follow different paths, as will the artist and labourer, the officer and the private soldier, the farmhand and the company director. However there are basic principles involved, both physical and mental, for nourishing the body as well as the mind, and it is there we must begin.

For our bodies we need vitamins, minerals, trace elements and enzymes, protein, carbohydrate and fat, water and fresh air, exercise and sunshine; in other words some food, water and exercise in the fresh air. My only stipulation is that the food must be whole as nature presents it to us and not as the manufacturer has spoiled it by refining it. Our minds are more complicated because unfortunately they accumulate all the rubbish which is put into them as well as the good stuff. Some are able to differentiate between sense and nonsense and some have the ability to think and reach conclusions, but since the process takes place from the time we are born, a lot has already entered before we have the ability to sort it out.

So living is therefore two-fold, physical and mental, but both rely upon health, each is interdependent and draws upon the bloodstream for its nourishment, so nutrition is the first consideration I must deal with here. After that can come the complications of the mind, such things as appreciation and peace of mind, security and environment, state of mind and the ego, affections and sensitivity, the elimination of any cause for unhappiness. Also included, of course, are the will to live and the spirit with which to do it, the strength and determination, the confidence which makes us meet the world on equal terms and enjoy it. All of this is living and a part of what we are seeking here.

Is there any more to life than that? It seems so simple when one dissects it and yet people make it such a burden, for they frequently expect too much and are not prepared to accept with pleasure what little they do in fact have. The enjoyment of life is registered in the mind, so if only one can condition it to be less demanding one might be much happier.

What I am trying to say is never spoil yourself or your children or anyone near to you or over whom you have any control, for then their set of values is destroyed as well as their enjoyment of living. That is why I said in *About Happiness*, that the more you take away from life the more in fact you add to it, for if you have nothing and expect nothing the slightest reward will seem the greatest pleasure. However that may be easier to write than put into practice, but nonetheless it's worth a try.

Thus it should follow that living under the hedgerows is the best way of enjoying life, but I don't suppose many would agree with me there. However if you can even develop that sort of state of mind without necessarily taking to the road, you would be doing yourself a good turn. For the act of life is really nothing more than a great big game, the only pity is that people take it seriously, because from that stems most of the misery in the world today. If only people could laugh at it all they would not only prove themselves to be sane, but also discover what a joke it really all is. With that let us leave the act of living before analysing it too far and move on to the subject of this section, living alone.

LIVING ALONE

Is living alone so different from living with other people, except that you have peace and quiet in which to read and write or do whatever else it is you want to do? Of course there is no nagging, no bitter hostility or contrariness, there are no objections when you decide to go somewhere, but equally there is no companionship, no warmth or love, no one to share your joys and sorrows. There are assets on both sides and perforce one adjusts to whichever is one's lot. But even so, living alone is not for the weak, it requires too much courage and strength, because if you do not stand on your own feet you do not stand at all. Neither is it for those who cannot think for themselves, because if you do not work it out yourself no one else will.

Those who live alone are thought to be lonely, but I wonder whether they really are. It is hard to look into another person's mind to discover such intimate details and outward signs do not necessarily give one the correct answer, anyway it also depends on several other factors: the first of which is age. When you are young you are constantly disturbed by sex and require an outlet for it, so naturally you seek a companion of the opposite sex, that goes without saying, assuming you are a normal person. But as one grows older one's material ambitions diminish as one learns to enjoy the pleasure of just living. Perhaps too, when one has accomplished much of what one wanted to do, the urgency of life is replaced by the satisfaction of living. In those circumstances it is easier to live alone happily.

Finances naturally play their part in living alone as they do everywhere else, because with enough money one can afford to do whatever one wants and thus cure one's loneliness and/or boredom. Friends are another important factor, particularly old ones, because they share so much of one's past that they cannot easily be replaced. Next comes the geography which surrounds one, the place where one lives, in the town or the country, and the climate which goes with it. In towns one is automatically subjected to a continual stream of reactions which the brain needs for survival, but in the country one can become isolated from them and have to make a journey to fulfil this need. And the climate in both places can make an enormous difference to one's outlook, because consciously or unconsciously one reacts to it and it affects one's emotions.

One's own past also has a bearing on one's peace of mind, particularly when living alone, because if you were spoilt by the luxuries and pleasures of life, it is more difficult to readjust if you are forced to forego them. But let's hope that this is not the case, for then you can continue on alone and perhaps even enjoy it all the more for having regained your independence. Which brings me to one's state of mind, for loneliness mostly is a state of mind. Those who have their minds well occupied are seldom lonely, but those with nothing to do or those who sit and think about themselves most certainly are, for loneliness can be self-induced by introspection and selfishness.

The last factor is one's state of health which mostly depends upon diet. I suppose there are some who have never felt really well in their lives, so it is hard to explain to them the pleasure to be derived from that feeling, and it is not just a passing emotion but something which can be always with you. It profoundly influences your way of thinking and your state of mind, your emotions and your enjoyment of work and play, your sleeping hours and how you feel on waking, your whole tranquillity and attitude to life. Nothing else has such a lasting effect on your daily life and it can be so easily yours. That therefore is my starting point.

But before beginning I must pose one more question. What is this business of having a cat or dog about the place, even a human being? Is it simply a sop for those who lead futile and empty lives or is it something akin to what the Americans are searching for with their 'Touching Clubs' (literally physical touching)? I suppose the outward-going affection for one's dog or cat releases something inside one, perhaps some tension, but a human being offers more than that, if only because he can answer back.

Perhaps the correct answer is that life does not take place

in the singular because human beings, like all animals, need the opposite of their sex to complete their life-cycle. By taking a partner we are therefore following our normal reaction to nature's world by fulfilling her design for us. Presumably we should not be normal if we did not seek that fulfilment, yet some must be without it and make do the best way they can.

No one in life has everything and if they did they would not be happy, because part of the enjoyment of living is striving for something. The house one lives in is never exactly right, there are always improvements one would make if one could afford to, yet we live in our houses as they are quite happily. That compromise must also be true of life, once we have accepted the fact that we can never have it all and cease to want it. Living alone is also a compromise and once we know that we can begin to be happy, much happier than before. However there is one thing over which we cannot compromise and that is food, because at least forty nutrients are necessary for our bodies to survive and without them we eventually fall sick and ultimately die.

So we must learn what those elements in food are, and where they are most easily obtained, and then ensure we have them daily. They do not necessarily come in the most expensive foods, in fact they can usually be found extremely cheaply in the natural foods of most countries in the world, but we must know what they are, how to prepare them and how much of them we need to keep healthy. That is our first and most elementary lesson in living, particularly in living alone, because we are the ones responsible for feeding ourselves, so our life is entirely in our own hands.

FOOD FOR LIVING

Now for a list of the various foods available to you, so you can see clearly what they are:

Cereals come first because they are cheap and grown in such huge quantities and form the basis of the majority of the world's diet. If taken whole and in moderation they can do you nothing but good, providing they are combined with other food at the same meal. This applies to all grain whether it is wheat, rye, barley, oats, millet, maize or brown rice.

Eggs are also good food and contain all the nutrients the body needs except for Vitamin C. For the not-so-young three or four a week is enough, but for the rest who take enough exercise it does not matter so much.

Milk and dairy products furnish all the necessary nutrients but are best taken in their natural state and not heated or processed, also not in excess.

Pulses of which soya beans deserve special mention because of their high nutritive value and because they are cheap, but being so concentrated they must be eaten sparingly. Lentils, peas, beans are also alright occasionally if correctly combined.

Vegetable Oils are a daily must but only two tablespoons: sunflower seed, safflower, olive, corn, soya, cottonseed oils are all good.

Nuts and Seeds taken daily will greatly improve your health. Almonds, brazils, cachou, hazel, pine kernels, pecans, sesame seeds, sunflower seeds, pumpkin seeds, walnuts.

Fruit and Vegetables are needed daily and as many as you can afford. Eat them fresh and uncooked for maximum vitamins, minerals and enzymes. Sweet potatoes are much more nutritious than the other kind.

Brewers' Yeast is another must for its Vitamin B, protein and minerals.

Honey is a bonus food for quick energy and a lifetime habit.

Dried Fruits such as figs, dates, prunes, apricots, sultanas, raisins are valuable for minerals but are concentrated foods and only ever a second best to the raw product. Anyway they are usually expensive.

Salt one bare level teaspoon (4 grams) is necessary each day under normal conditions (in and out of cooking), but only sea salt or biochemic salt.

Organ Meats (for non-vegetarians) such as liver, kidneys, heart, brains are all excellent sources of protein, minerals and vitamins.

Fish and Meat (for non-vegetarians) two or three times a week is enough.

Sunshine, Fresh Air and Exercise are essential for everyone every day of their lives for Vitamin D, oxygen and good circulation.

Never Eat processed fats, hydrogenated oils (solid ones) or too much animal fat (any sort) even pasteurized dairy products, white sugar or anything made from it, white flour or anything made from it, processed cheese or meat, fried food, excessive coffee, alcohol or cigarettes.

SELECTING FOOD

Those are most of the common foods available to you, now comes the question of how to select the ones you need. The following points may help you generally, after which I will describe the main food elements such as protein, carbohydrates, vitamins, minerals, etc., which should help you specifically:

1. Organize your protein intake first. See how you can best obtain 50–70 grams a day. This is the centre-piece of your diet and the principal test of whether it is adequate or not.
2. Divide your protein between your meals. Breakfast and lunch are best with just fruit at night, but that depends mostly on circumstances.
3. Balance your protein with some fruit at breakfast and some vegetables and fruit at lunch. Eat them all raw if possible and have as many as you can afford (within reason).
4. Ensure that green leaves are eaten daily, also 1 tablespoon of vegetable oil (or nuts and seeds), 4 grams of salt (but no more, in or out of cooking), and Vitamin B_{12} for vegetarians (a must for them).
5. If milk is included, have it as a separate meal, perhaps in the afternoon (unheated, unpasteurized and unhomogenized).
6. Vitamin and mineral supplements are best taken at breakfast to ensure they are not forgotten. The more of them you take the better your health is likely to be.
7. Eating too much is as bad as eating too little. It is necessary to strike a happy balance, because correct nutrition is a

balance of the right proportions of food elements. The answer to this lies mainly in selecting the right quantity and combination of protein, then ensuring it is properly balanced with raw fruit and vegetables. This way you should automatically get enough vitamins, minerals and trace elements, protein, carbohydrate and fat and ensure that the vital enzymes (from raw food) are there to utilize them.

Now let us consider in more detail the various elements in food:

PROTEIN

1. 50–70 grams (1½–2 oz) is usually considered more than enough in Europe, although the Americans prefer more.
2. The biological value of protein is more important than the quantity and this mostly depends on the correct combining of protein foods to achieve the best amino-acid balance.
3. Nitrogen from excess protein has to be eliminated and this over-works the kidneys. It also creates acids (poisons) in the body tissues which can be responsible for many rheumatic complaints, even flu and colds, unless eliminated. Incomplete proteins (from cereals and pulses) are the worst for this (unless combined).
4. Therefore vegetable proteins should never be eaten separately as they are often partly deficient in one or more amino acid, but they combine well to make a high biological value and are then more valuable than animal protein.
5. Protein is responsible for repair and maintenance work in your body, for growth, glandular secretions, nails, hair and muscles, amongst other things. So never neglect it. Later I will give you a list of some protein foods together with their values and combining qualities.

FAT

1. Like protein it is a basic part of the diet because without it energy cannot be produced from the carbohydrates we eat (except by utilizing our own body fat which happens during fasting).
2. Fat comes from both animal and vegetable sources, either in meat, fish, lard and dairy produce or as oil from nuts, seeds, olives, soya beans, etc.

3. In general solid fats and fat from animal sources (saturated fatty acids) are not good for one, whereas vegetable fats (unsaturated fatty acids) are essential to most body processes.
4. In cold weather you need about 25% of your total food as fat, but in hot weather only 15%. Justine Glass suggests $2\frac{1}{2}$ oz (70 grams) daily.
5. Excess of any sort of fat can also make you fat, partly by water retention.

CARBOHYDRATE

1. Is needed for energy. If we have to use body fat instead it creates acids which need eliminating, otherwise they cause disease.
2. Practically everything we eat turns into sugar in our bodies, all fruit and vegetables (as starch or fruit sugar), cereals and dairy produce (as starch or milk sugar), pulses and roots (mostly as starch).
3. Since carbohydrate of the wrong sort (white flour, white sugar and things made from them) is cheap, it is easy to eat too much and so become fat and unhealthy.
4. However if it is taken in the form of fruit and vegetables, an excess will do no harm and may not even make you fat. Likewise with raw dairy produce, pulses, roots or whole grains.
5. Processed carbohydrate such as white flour and white sugar and everything made from them will do you untold harm, because what has been taken from them in processing must be re-supplied by your body for proper digestion. This causes vitamin and mineral deficiencies of the worst sort, because they are a continual drain on the body.
6. If you take your carbohydrate as nature presents it to you, you will be healthy. If you take it any other way, you will almost certainly damage your health.
7. Honey is a good food in moderation, and possibly very small amounts of molasses.

VITAMINS

1. The word vitamin was invented to mean: 'That vital element in food, a deficiency of which makes the difference between

health and a state of disease.' In other words you cannot be healthy without them.

2. They are present in all *whole* RAW food but are usually processed out when canned, milled or otherwise interfered with.

3. If all your food was eaten as nature presents it to you, there would be no need to worry about deficiencies of any sort.

4. If you are ill, to any degree, you will need to take vitamin supplements. After you are 40 it is advisable to take them anyway, unless you are extremely healthy and have an unusually complete diet.

5. Vitamins in drug doses (very strong) are necessary if you are ill. For more information read About Diseases.

6. Vegans (vegetarians who do not eat eggs or dairy produce) must take Vitamin B_{12} regularly otherwise their health ultimately breaks down and they may get pernicious anaemia. Vitamin D also does not appear naturally in their diet unless they get enough sunshine, so supplements may be necessary.

MINERALS

Are as vital as vitamins and sometimes more difficult to obtain from food alone.

1. Calcium and phosphorus are used in the largest quantities and usually come together in food. Watch for in your diet.

2. Iodine is needed only in minute quantities, but it must be there. Take kelp (seaweed) to ensure an adequate supply.

3. Potassium should come from RAW fruit and vegetables, nuts and seeds, yeast and soya beans. In cooking most of it goes down the drain with the water. Health depends to a large degree on this mineral.

4. Sodium and chloride (sea salt or biochemic salt, never common salt). One bare level teaspoon (4 grams) is needed every day both in and out of cooking. Take between meals in a little water. If sweating a lot take a little more.

5. Trace elements such as magnesium, zinc, cobalt, manganese, aluminium, tin, arsenic, bromine, mercury, nickel, silica and silver are also needed. A mineral supplement is a useful way of ensuring they are adequately supplied.

N.B. Biochemic tissue salts (12 minerals) are best for illness, so keep them on hand and learn how to take them. They will improve your health tremendously and save innumerable chemist's bills and visits to the doctor. Everyone (particularly those alone) should use them.

ENZYMES

1. Are plentifully supplied in raw food, cooking kills them.
2. As you grow older you produce less in your own body and therefore need a proper supply as nature intended from raw food.
3. Everyone's digestion and assimilation can benefit from the enzymes in raw food.
4. Raw food should always be taken first at meals to stimulate the digestive process with enzymes (salads or fruit).
5. For the over-40's enzymes from raw food will revitalize in many different ways.

ANTI-STRESS FACTORS

1. Stress is defined as anything which harms the body or causes any cells to die (disease, overwork, anxiety, lack of sleep, no exercise or lack of food).
2. The anti-stress factors in certain foods can protect you from the effects of stress, so eat them regularly.
3. Liver is the best source of these, also wheat germ, some yeasts, kidneys and soya flour (full fat), green leafy vegetables.
4. In illness these foods are vital, but do not wait till you are ill before taking them.

THE DON'TS

1. It is as important to avoid certain foods as it is to take others. So remember these words and DO NOT EAT THEM.
2. White flour and white sugar or anything made from them come first on the list. Whole grain flour is all right, but even brown sugar is not particularly good or necessary. Have honey if you need something sweet, or molasses (if taken in very small quantities).
3. All processed animal fats or hydrogenated oils (solid ones)

should be avoided, and as little animal fat eaten as possible. It is so easy and much nicer to take your fat as oil or in nuts, seeds or pulses.

4. Processed cheese and meat have usually lost the natural elements they require for digestion and so clog up your blood vessels.

5. Fried food is hard to digest. Heated fats change their chemical composition and easily become rancid, then they destroy Vitamins A and E in the body and do untold harm.

6. Excessive coffee, tea, alcohol and cigarettes all cause toxins which need eliminating otherwise they poison you.

FOOD VALUES

CEREALS

1. Never eat cereals by themselves as they usually lack one or more amino acid, so always take them with other proteins. They combine best with green vegetables and badly with fruit.

2. Cereal digestion creates acids (poisons) particularly if taken separately.

3. Cereals take a long time to digest and while they do so they grow unfriendly bacteria which create toxins.

4. So never eat too many cereals; they certainly should not be the centre-piece of your diet. One dessertspoon of wheat germ is enough, or a couple of slices of bread, a handful of grain or sprouted seeds.

It may be helpful for you to know the following values:

Water percentage to know how highly concentrated it is.

Protein to plan your diet and ensure you do not take an excess which has to be eliminated by the kidneys.

Fat to ensure you get enough of the right sort, and not too much of either saturated or unsaturated.

Carbohydrate tells you how much natural sugar you are eating, which must be enough but not excessive.

Ash tells you the content of minerals which are vital to your health. A high intake will probably mean enough of all minerals.

Vitamins are too numerous to specify but if you eat lots of RAW food you will probably get enough.

100 grams of:	Water (per cent)	Protein (grams)	Fat (grams)	Carbohydrate (grams)	Ash (grams)
Whole wheat (grains)	12·5	12–14	2	70	1·7
Whole wheat (flour)	12	13	2	70	1·7
Wheat germ	11·5	26	10·9	47	4·3
Sprouted wheat	*	15	*	*	*
Bread (whole wheat	36·4	9	2·6	49	2·6
Bread (white)	31	9	3	55	1·9
Gofio (p. 180, No. 6)	*	16–18	*	*	*
Chapattis (wheat)	*	12	*	*	*
Spaghetti (dry)	10·4	12·5	1·2	75	0·7
Rye (whole grain)	11	12·1	1·7	73	1·8
Barley (whole grain)	11	13	1	73	1·3
Millet (whole grain)	11·8	9·9	2·9	73	2·5
Oats (whole grain)	9	12	1·9	73	1·9
Maize (corn) (whole grain)	72	3·5	1·0	22	0·7
Rice (unpolished) (raw)	12	7·5	1·9	77	1·2

* Values not known.

EGGS

1. Eggs are a complete food lacking only Vitamin C.
2. One or possibly two a day is enough. For the not-so-young 3 or 4 a week only, because of high cholesterol and fat.
3. If taken raw, eat only the yolk as the white destroys biotin (a B vitamin) in the intestines.
4. One average egg contains 6 grams of protein (12%), the yolk only 3 grams and the white is incomplete protein so needs combining with other protein.

5. One egg also contains 73·7% water, 11·5 grams of fat, 0·9 grams of carbohydrate and 1 gram of ash.

6. Eggs combine best with green vegetables, but not so well with fruit, although they do not clash seriously with anything.

DAIRY PRODUCE

1. Milk is better absorbed and utilized by the body if taken as a meal by itself. Otherwise it combines reasonably well with fruits but not so well with green vegetables. Cheese, on the other hand, combines well with green vegetables but not with other fatty foods or sweets.

2. Milk is even better digested if taken soured or as yogurt because the protein is then partly predigested. Also the bacteria in the culture creates a beneficial flora in the intestines which make Vitamin B.

3. Next best is soft white cheese (very little fat but all the goodness). Buttermilk is also good as it contains most of the lecithin from the butter.

4. Hard, natural, unprocessed cheeses are also all right if eaten in small quantities.

100 grams of:	Water (per cent)	Protein (grams)	Fat (grams)	Carbohydrate (grams)	Ash (grams)
Milk (cows')	87·4	3·5	3·5	4·9	0·7
Milk (goats')	87·5	3·2	4·0	4·6	0·7
Sour milk	As for milk				
Buttermilk	90·5	3·6	0·1	5·1	0·7
Evaporated milk (unsweetened)	73·8	7·0	7·9	9·7	1·6
Powdered milk (whole)	2·0	26·4	27·5	38·2	5·9
Yogurt (skim milk)	89	3·4	1·7	5·2	0·7
Cream (full)	56·6	2·2	37·6	3·1	0·4
Cheese (hard)	37	25	32·2	2·1	3·7
Cheese (soft white) (skim milk)	79	17	0·3	2·7	1·0

5. All pasteurized, homogenized or processed dairy products have partly changed their chemical composition, the antibacterial factors have been destroyed, the calcium and protein have become less easily obtainable and the vital lecithin lost.
6. Evaporated milk (if produced in a vacuum as in Switzerland) is least bad of the tinned milks. Powdered milk is useful to boost protein values of other foods, but only small quantities.
7. Providing you are not a Vegan, a small basic quantity of dairy products is a good addition to your diet. If the diet becomes inadequate for some reason, you can add extra amounts of this cheap whole food.

Quantities

The amount of dairy produce to be eaten entirely depends upon the rest of the diet. Outside a basic minimum it can be used to bring the diet up to standard as it is relatively cheap.

Milk (cow or goat). One pint ($\frac{1}{2}$ litre) is enough but no harm in more if unpasteurized. Milk is alkaline and useful as such.

Yogurt or *Sour Milk*. A little each day is a good insurance ($\frac{1}{4}$ pint).

Buttermilk. A good habit to acquire.

Soft White Cheese. Should be low fat. Amount depends on other protein intake.

Hard cheeses. As for soft white cheese but a little less.

Note. Too much dairy produce can overload the diet with fat which is not good when pasteurized, homogenized or processed: nature's balancing factors have been removed, so it is bad for heart, liver, kidneys and many other things too.

PULSES

Soya Beans are the most important and the most valuable. They are a concentrated food so never eat too many. About 14 grams of protein from this source is enough, which is about 35–40 grams of uncooked beans or soya flour.

Sprouted Soya and Mung Beans. Should be eaten daily for their vital qualities. A handful is enough at any meal.

Legumes are not complete protein on their own, so must *always* be combined with other protein food. This is particularly important for people with gout, rheumatism, arthritis, etc.

All Pulses combine well with green vegetables and badly with fruit, milk, sweets and fat. Soya flour can be mixed with yeast or flour from wheat or other grain to increase its nutritive value.

100 grams of:	Water (per cent)	Protein (grams)	Fat (grams)	Carbohydrate (grams)	Ash (grams)
Soya beans	10	34·1	17·7	33·5	4·7
Soya flour	8	36·7	20·3	30·4	4·6
Soya sprouts	86·3	6·2	1·4	5·3	0·8
Mung beans (dry)	10·7	24·2	1·3	60·3	3·5
Mung beans (sprouted)	88·8	3·8	0·2	6·6	0·6
Lentils (dry)	11·1	24·7	1·1	60·1	3·0
Peas (green)	78	6·3	0·4	14·4	0·9
Broad beans (green)	72	8·4	0·4	17·8	1·1
Beans (common, white)	10·9	22·3	1·6	61·3	3·9
Beans (kidney, lima)	10·3	20·4	1·6	64	3·7

NUTS AND SEEDS

Are a must for everyone *daily* due to:
1. Their unsaturated fatty acids (Vitamin F) for glandular secretions, proper metabolism, skin health and blood vessels.
2. Their Vitamin E, so vital for the sex organs, the heart, liver, muscles and conserving oxygen.
3. Their lecithin without which fat sticks to the blood vessels and degenerates the liver and kidneys, eyesight, hearing and heart.
4. Their minerals which turn food into flesh. They are a rich source. Lack of minerals can cause disease.

5. Their protein which, if correctly combined, is of the highest biological value (some are complete protein).

100 grams of:	Water (per cent)	Protein (grams)	Fat (grams)	Carbohydrate (grams)	Ash (grams)
Almonds	4·7	18·6	54	19·5	3·0
	Up to 50 grams a day if you can afford it.				
Brazil nuts	4·6	14·3	66·9	10·9	3·3
	Very oily, so only a few occasionally (20 grams).				
Cashew nuts	5·2	17·2	45·7	29·3	2·6
	Never salted. Quantity as for almonds.				
Hazel nuts (Filberts)	5·8	12·5	62·4	16·7	2·5
	As for almonds.				
Pecans	3·4	9·2	71·2	14·6	1·6
	Contain 71% fat. Only 3 or 4 occasionally.				
Pine kernels	3·1	13	60·5	20·5	2·9
	As for almonds.				
Pistachio nuts	5·3	19·3	53·7	19	2·7
	As for almonds.				
Pumpkin seeds	4·4	29	46·7	15	4·9
	A handful occasionally for the zinc (for prostate).				
Sesame seeds	5·4	18·6	50	21·6	5·3
	Not more than 3 teaspoons (20 grams) daily.				
Sunflower seeds	4·8	24	47·3	19·9	4·0
	A handful occasionally for Vitamins E and F.				
Walnuts (English)	3·5	14·8	64	15·8	1·9
	As for almonds (contain an acid, beware).				

N.B. Nuts and seeds combine well with green vegetables and fruit; not so well with other things.

FRUIT AND VEGETABLES

All fruit and vegetables contain some protein, often in worthwhile quantities of good biological value, but since it is not complete protein it needs combining with other protein at the same meal. The importance of fruit and vegetables in the diet is:

1. Firstly for their invaluable enzymes which perform much of the task of changing food into flesh, blood, muscles, nerves, teeth and bones.

2. Next for their vitamins without which health is not possible.
3. For their minerals which work with enzymes in performing all their tasks, preserve the alkalinity of the body and help balance the metabolic and other acid wastes.
4. For their roughage which helps to maintain proper elimination of wastes from the body.
5. For their pure water which is the best the body can have.
6. For their sugar which is properly balanced for digestion, absorption and therefore utilization to give maximum energy.
7. For their 'stored sunshine' (either as chlorophyll or otherwise) which performs unbelievable wonders for health.

100 grams of:	Water (per cent)	Protein (grams)	Fat (grams)	Carbohydrate (grams)	Ash (grams)
Apples (raw)	84·4	0·2	0·6	14·5	0·3

Apples (raw): Good all-round food to be taken daily. Perhaps 2 at night.

Apricots (dried)	25	5	0·5	66·5	3·0

Valuable for iron and copper, also Vitamin A and potassium.

Asparagus (cooked)	93·6	2·2	0·2	3·6	0·4

Lots of potassium and good for kidneys.

Avocado pears (raw)	74	2·1	16·4	6·3	1·2

Valuable protein, Vitamin E, unsaturated fatty acids, potassium and other vitamins and minerals.

Bananas (raw)	75·7	1·1	0·2	22·2	0·8

Starch becomes sugar when ripe (black spots), lots of potassium and a good source of energy.

Beetroot (boiled)	90·9	1·1	0·1	7·2	0·7

Best baked. Good for kidneys.

Blackberries (raw)	84·5	1·2	0·9	12·9	0·5

Valuable bioflavonoids and Vitamin C.

Blueberries (raw)	83·2	0·7	0·5	15·3	0·3

Same qualities as blackberries.

Brussels sprouts (boiled)	88·2	4·2	0·4	6·4	0·8

Good minerals and vitamins.

Cabbage (raw)	92·4	1·3	0·2	5·4	0·7

Good for ulcers. An excellent daily food.

Carrots (raw)	88·2	1·1	0·2	9·7	0·8

Best source of Vitamin A. Good minerals.

100 grams of:	Water (per cent)	Protein (grams)	Fat (grams)	Carbohydrate (grams)	Ash (grams)
Cauliflower (boiled)	82·8	2·3	0·2	4·1	0·6
	A good source of minerals.				
Celery (raw)	94·1	0·9	0·1	3·9	1·0
	Good minerals. Useful for salads.				
Cherries (raw)	80·4	1·3	0·3	17·4	0·6
	Good bioflavonoids, minerals and vitamins.				
Chicory (raw)	95·1	1·0	0·1	3·2	0·6
	Excellent source of Vitamin A.				
Cucumber (raw)	95·1	0·9	0·1	3·4	0·5
	Excellent calcium and other minerals.				
Currants (black) (raw)	84·2	1·7	0·1	13·1	0·9
	Best source of Vitamin C and bioflavonoids, also minerals.				
Custard Apples (raw)	71·5	1·7	0·6	25·2	1·0
	Excellent sugar, therefore energy.				
Dates (raw)	22·5	2·2	0·5	72·9	1·9
	Good iron and potassium. Contain 73% sugar.				
Endive (curly) (raw)	93·1	1·7	0·1	4·1	1·0
	Excellent Vitamin A and useful minerals.				
Figs (dried)	23	4·3	1·3	69·1	2·3
	Good against poisons or toxins. Good iron and copper.				
Figs (raw)	77·5	1·2	0·3	20·3	0·7
	All figs are a laxative and contain lots of potassium.				
Garlic (raw)	61·3	6·3	0·2	30·8	1·5
	Nature's best antibiotic. Should be eaten regularly.				
Gooseberries (raw)	88·9	0·8	0·2	9·7	0·4
	Good bioflavonoids and Vitamin C.				
Grapefruit (raw)	88·4	0·5	0·1	10·6	0·4
	Excellent Vitamin C and bioflavonoids.				
Grapes (raw)	81·4	0·6	0·3	17·3	0·4
	Excellent bioflavonoids and natural sugar (97% sugar and water).				
Guavas (raw)	83	0·8	0·6	15	0·6
	Super-Vitamin C content, good other vitamins and minerals.				
Leeks (raw)	85·4	2·2	0·3	11·2	0·9
	Same antibiotic as garlic but less strong.				
Lemons (raw)	90·1	1·1	0·3	8·2	0·3
	A good antiseptic and excellent Vitamin C and bioflavonoids.				

100 grams of:	Water (per cent)	Protein (grams)	Fat (grams)	Carbohydrate (grams)	Ash (grams)
Lettuce (raw)	95	1·3	0·2	2·5	1·0
		Should be eaten daily for Vitamins E and A, minerals and vital chlorophyll (stored sunshine)
Limes (raw)	89·3	0·7	0·2	9·5	0·3
		Same as for lemons only more so.
Mangoes (raw)	81·7	0·7	0·4	16·8	0·4
		Lots of Vitamin A and C. A healthy food.
Mushrooms (raw)	90·4	2·7	0·3	4·4	0·9
		A valuable food of the mould family.
Muskmelons (raw) (cantaloups/honeydew)	91·2	0·7	0·1	7·5	0·5
		Best eaten as a separate meal.
Nectarines (raw)	81·8	0·6	0	17·1	0·5
		Excellent Vitamin A and copper. Good dried.
Olives (cooked and canned)	80	1·1	13·8	2·6	2·5
		A good food but very salty.
Onions (raw)	89·1	1·5	0·1	8·7	0·6
		Same as garlic only less so. Should be eaten regularly.
Oranges (raw)	86	1·0	0·2	12·2	0·6
		Same as lemons plus good sugar. Take daily.
Papayas (raw)	88·7	0·6	0·1	10·0	0·6
		Excellent source of enzymes and Vitamin A.
Parsley (raw)	85·1	3·6	0·6	8·5	2·2
		Full of Vitamin A, iron, calcium, potassium Vitamin C and other minerals.
Parsnips (cooked)	82·2	1·5	0·5	14·9	0·9
		A useful root vegetable. Best baked.
Peaches (raw)	89·1	0·6	0·1	9·7	0·5
		Good iron and copper, also Vitamin A.
Pears (raw)	83·2	0·7	0·4	15·3	0·4
		A good daily food of all-round value.
Peppers (raw) (sweet)	90·7	1·4	0·3	7·1	0·5
		Lots of Vitamins A and C.
Pineapples (raw)	85·3	0·4	0·2	13·7	0·4
		An excellent source of enzymes. A healthy, acid fruit
Plums (raw)	86·6	0·5	0·2	12·3	0·4
		A bit too acid for many people. Take just a few.
Potatoes (cooked)	79·8	2·1	0·1	17·1	0·9
		Strongly alkaline with good minerals, but starchy.

100 grams of:	Water (per cent)	Protein (grams)	Fat (grams)	Carbohydrate (grams)	Ash (grams)
Potatoes (sweet) (cooked)	63·7	2·1	0·5	32·5	1·2
	Lots of Vitamin A, iron and other minerals. Best baked.				
Prunes (dried)	28·0	2·1	0·6	67·4	1·9
	Good Vitamin A, iron, copper and laxative. 67% sugar.				
Radishes (raw)	94·5	1	0·1	3·6	0·8
	An excellent root vegetable for salads.				
Raisins (dried)	18	2·5	0·2	77·4	1·9
	Good minerals. 77% sugar.				
Raspberries (raw)	84·2	1·2	0·5	13·6	0·5
	Good Vitamin C and bioflavonoids.				
Rhubarb (cooked)	62·8	0·5	0·1	added sugar	0·6
	Eat sparingly, contains an acid.				
Marrows (squash) (cooked)	95·5	0·9	0·1	3·1	0·4
	Useful potassium and Vitamin A.				
Strawberries (raw)	89·9	0·7	0·5	8·4	0·5
	Lots of Vitamin C but acid.				
Tangerines (raw)	87	0·8	0·2	11·6	0·4
	Same as oranges.				
Tomatoes (raw)	93·5	1·1	0·2	4·7	0·5
	Excellent Vitamin A, potassium Vitamins C, B and other minerals. Good daily food.				
Watermelons (raw)	92·6	0·5	0·2	6·4	0·3
	Good Vitamin A. Best taken as separate meal.				

Note: Dried fruit is concentrated food and very high in sugar. Soaking overnight helps restore better proportions, but it is only ever a second-best to raw fruit.

BREWERS' YEAST

1. Is a high-protein food (39%) so two tablespoons (50 grams) daily is more than enough.
2. Is one of the best sources of Vitamin B Complex (like liver).
3. Is an excellent source of iron, calcium, phosphorus, potassium and 14 other minerals.
4. Has no Vitamin C and only 1% fat.

5. Has given innumerable people a new lease of life and cured untold illnesses.
6. Is one of the foods everyone should eat daily for optimum health. It supplies so much for such a reasonable cost.

100 grams of:	Water (per cent)	Protein (grams)	Fat (grams)	Carbohydrate (grams)	Ash (grams)
Brewers' Yeast	5·0	38·8	1·0	38·4	7·1

ORGAN MEATS (offal)

1. If you are not a vegetarian and therefore eat meat, organ meats are where you will find all the goodness.
2. When animals kill for food, they drink the blood first, then eat the internal organs and leave the muscle meat for the vultures.
3. Liver is the best source of Vitamin B_{12} (vital for pernicious anaemia), also the other B Vitamins, and Vitamin A, and contains 26–30% protein.
4. Although it contains a lot of cholesterol, it has lecithin to metabolize it.
5. Kidneys, brains, heart are all good food and cheap, so have them regularly like liver.

100 grams of:	Water (per cent)	Protein (grams)	Fat (grams)	Carbohydrate (grams)	Ash (grams)
Liver (raw)	70	19	3·7	2·6	1·5
Kidneys (raw)	77	17	3·6	0·9	1·3
Heart (raw)	77	16.5	4–6	0·7	1·1
Brains (raw)	78·9	10·4	8·6	0·6	1·4

MEAT AND FISH

1. Meat and fish starts to putrefy the day it is killed and in warm weather this fact becomes obvious all too soon. Fruit and

vegetables on the other hand ultimately ferment. That by itself should be enough to make one leave well alone.

2. If you must have meat, twice a week is enough and then only in small amounts.

3. Meat contains 16–22% protein depending on the cut, but it also contains a lot of fat and cholesterol without the necessary lecithin to metabolize it.

4. Fish contains 21–26% protein depending on the sort. Some fish are much more fatty than others.

5. The biological value of meat and fish protein is not as high as vegetable protein, therefore it is not so well absorbed or utilized, even though it contains all the amino acids.

100 grams of:	Water (per cent)	Protein (grams)	Fat (grams)	Carbohydrate (grams)	Ash (grams)
Beef raw)	60–80	16–22	4–30	0	0·7–1·0
Lamb (raw)	61	16.5	21.3	0	1·2
Chicken (roast)	53·5	25·2	20·2	0	1·1
Veal (raw)	68	19	12	0	1·0
Cod (raw)	81	17·6	0·3	0	1·2
Flat fish (raw)	58	30	8·2	0	2·2
Sardines (canned)	62	24	11·1	0	3·1

HONEY

1. Is our best source of natural sugar, but it is a concentrated food (82% sugar) so 1 dessertspoon daily is enough.

2. Is good for the kidneys, heart, liver, lungs and skin, partly because it goes straight into the blood and needs no converting in the body. Therefore it is a useful source of quick energy.

3. Is said to be non-fattening as it increases the combustion rate of the body. Taken with lemon juice is a good nightcap.

100 grams of:	Water (per cent)	Protein (grams)	Fat (grams)	Carbohydrate (grams)	Ash (grams)
Honey	17·2	0·3	0	82·3	0·2

These are also all foods for the body because without them we should die and only with them are we able to maintain optimum health.

Sunshine makes Vitamin D in the skin, which for Vegans is important because they do not get it from any other source, since they do not eat dairy produce or eggs. No living thing could survive for long without sunshine (including us). Thus sunshine qualifies as a food and must be included in the diet as such.

Fresh Air is also a food because the oxygen in it is vital to all our functions and without it we die. This is important to people living in towns.

Exercise is also a daily must, otherwise the blood does not circulate properly to regenerate our internal organs or keep our blood vessels healthy. It need not be excessive but it must be enough.

WATER

1. Without it we die in 70 to 80 hours.
2. Three-quarters of our body consists of water.
3. The best we can get is from fruit and vegetables.
4. Spring water also gives minerals, particularly calcium.
5. If you are properly fed and nourished there should be no need to drink additional water, as all food is mostly water and the process of metabolism in the body creates more.
6. If you must drink water, have it between meals, otherwise it dilutes your gastric juices.
7. Always drink when you feel thirsty and completely quench your thirst then.

PREPARING FOOD

Now at last comes the question of preparing food. It is an essential part of nutrition because it is here that the vital elements in food are retained or lost, increased and utilized or wasted. To know how to prepare food simply and quickly is of value because people will usually do whatever is easiest, particularly if they live alone.

RAW FOOD

The first and most important point to make about preparing food is that there is no need to cook it, in fact most of it is best eaten raw in its natural state. It will nourish you better this way because the enzymes are not destroyed which helps with digestion, the heat-affected vitamins are retained, the minerals do not change their chemical composition nor does the fat, so both are better utilized.

Anyone suffering from digestive trouble can cure themselves with raw food, as can almost anyone who is ill. That may sound a sweeping statement to make but it is based on fact and borne out by the world's leading nutritionists. Meat and fish are excluded from this as they putrefy so quickly.

For many years the only cooked food I ever ate was one boiled egg for breakfast and some meat or fish at lunch, then I became a vegetarian and substituted nuts, seeds, brewers' yeast and soya flour for those foods. The difference in my health was quite exceptional and I only wish I had become a Vegan (raw food vegetarian, no eggs or dairy produce either) much earlier. Principally it is the meat which creates the acids and affects the capillaries but eggs are best reduced and dairy produce cut to just yogurt, raw milk or soft white cheese.

All pulses and rice must be cooked but grains can also be chewed or sprouted. The plant of yeast needs to be killed by drying to give the greatest benefit (this is done before you buy it as powdered yeast). Personally I could never eat raw liver, but many do to the greater betterment of their health. Meat should be cooked. Raw fish is delicious in places like Japan where they know what they are doing, but otherwise it is safer cooked.

All raw food needs to be cleaned before eating and preferably cut up. Several foods are best combined at the same meal, and if presented nicely help to create the right mental attitude towards eating. Harmony and tranquillity add a lot to the nutritional value of food. Eat the meal immediately it has been prepared, do not keep it waiting.

The first test of your eating habits is to look in your rubbish bin to see whether there are any tins, packets or plastic containers. If you pass that test, the next is to search for cooked food. After that one must inspect the fridge and larder for left-overs or partly eaten foods, which should never be present (within reason) as once a food has been opened it should all be eaten. Opened food (i.e. not as sealed in by nature) grows microbes, attracts undesirable smells and oxydizes.

COOKED FOOD

1. If you must cook food use as little heat as possible for the shortest time.
2. Use the least amount of water and never throw away that water. Use it in soup or drink it.
3. Never fry food, any other way of cooking is better. If you must fry, use only vegetable oil and never use it a second time. Animal fat goes rancid quickly and then does you a lot of harm.
4. Salt in cooking is quite unnecessary. Take salt between meals in water (one bare level teaspoon (4 grams) no more.
5. Never heat up left-overs, it is a bad habit.

SPROUTED SEEDS

1. All whole seeds can be sprouted, like soya or mung beans, peas, sesame seeds, wheat, oats, barley, rye, etc.
2. Their nutritional value is greatly increased during the process. The vitamins, minerals and enzymes multiply out of all proportion, so does the protein, and the starch becomes digestible. Their anti-ascorbic factor sky-rockets and sometimes exceeds that of lemons.
3. To sprout: wash and clean, then soak overnight in ample water. Next morning drain, rinse and put in a flower pot or collander with a damp rag over the top. Rinse under running water three times a day. Once they have sprouted, no matter to what length, you can eat them.

CEREALS

Whole Grains
1. Can be chewed if held in the mouth a short time so your saliva softens them.
2. Can be ground in a coffee mill and used to make bread or chapattis (very thin flour and water pancakes).

3. Can be crushed and mixed with other grains, milk, dried fruit and nuts as in muesli or turned into porridge.

4. Can be sprouted and then mixed with salads or put through a mincer and made into bread.

5. Can be mixed with soya flour to increase their value, either as flour or when sprouted.

6. Can be toasted for a few minutes and then ground in a coffee mill and turned into what the Canary Islanders call 'gofio' (usually maize or wheat). Add to milk powder and sprinkle it on vegetables, soups or anything else, including coffee, and you have greatly enhanced your diet.

7. Can be turned into spaghetti or any other pasta, but if not made from whole grains it does you little good and makes you fat.

8. Can be milled to separate the wheat germ which has a much higher nutritional value than the whole grain. A little of this each day would work wonders with your health.

Brown Rice (unpolished) is also good food (although some have to make it the basis of their diet). To cook it, use 2 parts water to 1 of rice. Cook in boiling water for 10 minutes, then turn off the flame and leave the lid on till eaten. The water will all have disappeared by then.

EGGS

1. Only the yolks should be eaten raw as the whites are said to destroy biotin (a B vitamin) in the intestines. There is disagreement about this, but it is better to be on the safe side. Whites are incomplete protein, so need combining with other protein food or with the yolks.

2. If cooked, eggs are best boiled or perhaps poached or baked. Omelettes are just permissible but fried eggs are not advisable.

3. Keep eggshells, crush them to small pieces and cover with lemon juice. This dissolves the shells and gives you a high-calcium health drink.

DAIRY PRODUCE

1. Fresh, raw, unpasteurized, unhomogenized cows' or goats' milk is best. Skim off the cream and drink the milk as a meal in

itself (slowly with a spoon). Milk is extremely alkaline which is most beneficial to the body.

2. Many races will not drink milk until it has soured, but yogurt, which partly pre-digests the protein, creates some good acid for protein and calcium digestion, increases the friendly bacteria and decreases the unfriendly ones. In the intestines it helps to create B vitamins and keep them healthy. For souring, keep in an open vessel in a warm place and whisk with a fork or whisk regularly every few hours until a solid curd forms. Then put in fridge.

3. Yogurt is made by adding a few teaspoons of another yogurt to any sort of milk: Fresh, pasteurized, homogenized, powdered, condensed, plant, soya or other vegetable kinds. Simply stir the yogurt into the milk and keep in a warm place until the curd forms (about 3 hours). A proper electric yogurt-maker is obviously best, otherwise put the mixture in the airing cupboard or oven.

4. Cheese made from raw milk is best, whether it be hard or soft white cottage cheese. The lower the fat content the better it is for you, but never eat more than two ounces.

5. Powdered, evaporated or condensed milk, although devalued by processing, is useful to mix with other foods to increase the protein and mineral content. During processing the milk becomes more concentrated, so a little goes a long way. Keep supplies handy in the kitchen or ruck-sack and get into the habit of using them.

6. Raw natural cream, as it comes from the cow, is said to be good food, but it contains a lot of fat and it is difficult to ensure it has not been processed or added to.

7. Buttermilk, on the other hand, is positively health-giving, mostly because of its lecithin content. Take between meals like milk.

8. Too much fat and cholesterol from dairy products which have been pasteurized, homogenized or otherwise processed is definitely bad for you, as nature's compensating factors have been removed so the body cannot cope with them.

PULSES

Can mostly be sprouted (as already described), otherwise they *must* be cooked.

Soya bean flour (already cooked) is an extremely nourishing food and can be taken daily with benefit. It combines well with most foods (wheat or other flour, brewers' yeast, soup, vegetables or other protein) and does not dominate the taste.

NUTS AND SEEDS

Seeds can all be sprouted if you wish, but nuts are best eaten whole.

Seeds can also be sprinkled on salads or other mixtures, eaten raw or worked into a paste with honey (sesame seeds).

FRUIT

1. Is best eaten raw in its entirety, pips, core and skin, with the obvious exception of bananas, melons, oranges, etc.
2. Most fruit is best rubbed clean on a cloth or in the hands, except grapes, cherries, currants, etc.
3. Immediately it has been cut, eat it and do not leave any over to oxidize in the fridge or larder. If you must make fruit salad, eat it immediately it is ready.
4. Never add sugar to fruit, it is not necessary and spoils the goodness of the fruit.
5. Fruit juices are good for you but should not be kept once they are made.
6. Fruit retains its goodness better if kept in the fridge, at second best in a cool place out of the sun. The worst place for it is in a warm airless corner in the sun.
7. Fruit combines well with milk, yogurt and most dairy produce, nuts, seeds. Best eaten last at a meal or first if you do not have raw vegetables instead. It helps to balance the acidity of high protein foods.

VEGETABLES

1. Are the most important part of the diet (assuming the protein part is adequate) and the most trouble.
2. The first golden rule is to have green leaves *daily* (lettuce, spinach, cabbage, endive, sprouts, watercress, parsley, etc.).
3. It is best to eat all vegetables raw. You will find they taste

better that way, once your taste buds have been re-educated.
4. If that is not possible, one salad each day will help. Have it first at meals for the enzymes.
5. If you must cook vegetables, use minimum heat, minimum water and minimum time.

Preparation
1. NEVER soak vegetables as their vitamins, minerals and protein seep away in the water.
2. Wash and dry quickly.
3. Chop hard vegetables finely, soft ones large enough to mix and leaves to a convenient size for eating.
4. Use only vegetable oil to dress (lemon or vinegar are quite unnecessary) and mix three or four different sorts together for best results. Everyone needs two dessertspoons of vegetable oil daily from all sources (nuts, seeds, beans and oil). Mashed pulp of avocado pears is also delicious for dressings and nutritious (oils, proteins, vitamins and minerals).
5. If vegetables are cooked in water, drink the water afterwards or use as stock for soup and gravy

BREWERS' YEAST

1. Since this wonder food does not taste very good it is best to buy Torula Yeast which is grown on molasses and with other special ingredients.
2. It should never be eaten when there is carbohydrate in the stomach as it will ferment this and cause gas.
3. Therefore it should only be eaten before going to bed or first thing in the morning or possibly one hour before the evening meal.
4. It should only ever be mixed with water or milk or with the saliva from the mouth.
5. Sometimes it causes gas for the first two or three weeks but this soon disappears.

ORGAN MEATS

1. Are best grilled (rubbed with vegetable oil) or put in a stew, otherwise gently fried (if no other alternative).

2. Include them in your diet several times a week, they are your best medicinal food outside vegetables. Some people eat them daily.

3. Lives have been saved with raw liver and uncurable diseases cured, but the liver must be fresh and the person capable of eating it (not me).

MEAT (for non-vegetarians)

1. Two-thirds of the world either cannot afford it or do not eat it for religious reasons and they are healthier for it.
2. Cut off the fat and only eat the lean meat.
3. Grilling is best, baking in aluminium foil next, stewing with organ meats is also good, frying is worst.
4. If it smells the slightest bit off, throw it away.
5. Never eat raw meat, it is dangerous (worms, bacteria, toxins).

FISH (for non-vegetarians)

1. Is usually less fatty than meat and contains better protein and minerals. Have at least once a week.
2. Grilled is best, also baked in aluminium foil. Otherwise boil in a very little water.

HONEY

1. Taken with lemon juice, some water and Vitamin C (1 gram) is a wonderful nightcap. Use as much honey as you want and drink it with a teaspoon for best assimilation.
2. If you are addicted to sugar, try to use honey instead on all occasions.
3. Don't forget it is a concentrated food, so always dilute in some way for the best effect and do not eat too much.
4. Books have been written about honey and legends told. There is no doubt it is a good food, but in moderation.

MENUS

Since this section is principally for people without much money, I will now show you how to organize a cheap, easy and quick diet.

MY OWN DIET

Breakfast
Vitamin and mineral supplements (particularly Vitamin B_{12}).
Some fruit (oranges).
A handful of almonds, $2\frac{1}{2}$ teaspoons sesame seeds.
More fruit (acid or sub-acid).

Lunch
An enormous salad with lettuce, cabbage, parsley, tomatoes, cucumber, carrots, radishes, garlic, onions, avocado pear, etc. No salt, but 1 tablespoon vegetable oil (if no avocado).
Some bananas or other sweet fruit.

Dinner
2 apples and a pear or other fruit. One pint of milk.

At Bedtime 2 dessertspoons Torula Yeast mixed with milk.

Between meals
1 bare level teaspoon of biochemic or sea salt in $\frac{1}{4}$ glass of water (half each time).

Nutritional Value
This diet gives you 60 to 70 grams of protein, up to 2,600 calories (depending on the fruit and vegetables), more than enough fat, abundant vitamins, minerals, trace elements and enzymes, any amount of 'stored sunshine' and cell regenerators. All the food is taken raw.

Fasting
Once a week I fast, eating only 3 oranges three times a day or having the juice of 1 orange with water every 2 hours (8 a.m.–8 p.m.)

Health Building
This is the way to build up your health gradually. You can change to this diet immediately providing you follow the instructions exactly. It is not particularly cheap, but worth the extra money if you can afford it.

If you do not want to follow my diet, set about organizing your own as follows:

1. Consider protein first. Work out how you can get 50 to 70 grams (1 gram per kilogram of body weight) of protein most economically. If you use soya flour and brewers' yeast as I do, one pound (453 grams) of each should last you 9 days at a cost of about 6p a day, giving you 37·6 grams of protein daily. Where else can you get it so cheaply or of such a high biological value?

Fruit and vegetables should add another 10 to 20 grams of protein each day, or maybe more, which gives you about 47 to 57 grams in all.

That allows you leeway to choose additional protein from whatever else you like to eat:

½ pint yogurt (4½ grams of protein), a handful of nuts (4 grams) or seeds, a glass of milk (8 grams), two slices of whole wheat bread (5 grams), an occasional egg (6 grams) or one ounce of cheese (7 grams), but not in excess of 70 grams of protein.

2. Do not be put off by a diet which follows a regular pattern, even to the point of repetition. All the longest living and healthiest races do the same, usually because they cannot afford to vary their diet much or because alternative food is not available. Therefore it is better to find a suitable pattern and stick to it rather than try to be clever and fail.

3. For breakfast you need protein, carbohydrate and fat to start your metabolic process working (like starting an engine or lighting a boiler) for the whole day.

Lunch is best as the main meal, vegetables should predominate with a large protein course plus fruit (and maybe cheese).

Dinner should be light, mostly fruit and milk. If you have been properly nourished by the other two meals you will not need more.

4. You may now be wondering if there is anything wrong with the conventional diet of an egg or two, a piece of toast, fruit and yogurt for breakfast. Dinner and lunch, meat and 2 vegetables, some fruit, possibly some cheese. These meals contain about 74 grams of protein. If the food is all whole and unprocessed

there is no great objection (except possibly not enough raw food), but not everyone can afford this diet and those who live alone will almost certainly not be prepared to do that much cooking. Consider therefore the following foods:

SPROUTED SEEDS

Always keep some growing in your kitchen and make them part of your daily diet, because they contribute so much to your well-being.

CEREALS

1. Find out if you can buy whole grains cheaply from your local corn merchant or elsewhere. Some you can sprout and mix with salads or mince and use to make bread.
2. Some grains you can chew. If they are too hard even with your saliva, let them soak in fruit juice overnight which makes a nourishing brew next day.
3. Try making flour from whole grain in a coffee grinder and then bake your own bread. If that is too much trouble, make chapattis with flour and water, thinly rolled out and quickly heated on either side (this is what the Hunzas do, the healthiest people in the world).
4. All grains can be crushed either with pestle and mortar or even a hammer, then mixed with other grains, milk, some fruit and dried fruit and turned into a muesli. Dr Bircher-Benner (the inventor of it) recommends it for breakfast and dinner daily.
5. Soya flour can be added to whole grain flour to make a very nourishing mixture.
6. Wheat, maize, rye, barley or oats can all be toasted for a few minutes, then ground in a coffee grinder and mixed with anything from milk or milk powder to soya flour, vegetables, soups, etc. This is gofio as eaten in the Canary Islands.
7. Wheat germ can be bought separately and contains most of the nourishment of the grain, so should be used regularly mixed with milk, fruit or sprinkled over vegetables, etc.
8. Brown rice (unpolished) is good occasionally. Eat it when it is ready, do not let it stand around and do not eat left-overs.

EGGS

Are usually cheap and a very valuable source of complete food. Poached eggs served on green vegetables is a cheap and easy meal, and good nutrition. An occasional raw yolk is good. If you are poor, include eggs regularly in your diet. The old should not eat too many.

DAIRY PRODUCE

A small carton of yogurt or a glass of unpasteurized milk in the afternoon is really enough. Both of these are cheap and complete food.

If your diet is inadequate you can add sour milk, buttermilk, cheese or more milk. The danger is taking too much animal fat, so be careful.

Do not forget powdered milk as a useful source of protein, minerals and milk sugar. It can be added to almost anything with benefit and it is cheap.

Too much dairy produce can give you too much calcium and thus create a magnesium imbalance. This can be detected by a craving for carbohydrate (including alcohol).

PULSES

1. Soya flour I have already mentioned but I will refer to it again here because it is so important. It is cheap, pre-cooked, easy to use, of high protein value, contains abundant vitamins, minerals and unsaturated fats. Mix it with brewers' yeast as I have suggested, with milk, flour or vegetables. Experiment with it but have it daily.
2. Soya beans themselves are also wonderful food but need boiling for 2 hours. However you can cook enough for 5 days at a time and keep in the fridge. Otherwise pressure-cook them.
3. Other beans, peas, lentils, etc, are also good food but contain starch, so eat sparingly. They must *always* be combined with other proteins as they are incomplete themselves.
4. Sprouted pulses are even better food as the starch is converted during sprouting, so no cooking is necessary.

NUTS AND SEEDS

Within reason eat as many as your pocket permits. Keep a selection on hand and have some daily. They are particularly useful for travellers and a great rejuvenator for the old.

If your teeth can manage it, they are best chewed whole, otherwise mince or grind them or make into nut milk, cream or whip. Keep an eye on their fat content and do not overdo it. Eating excessive unsaturated fat still puts on weight, although less water is retained than with carbohydrate.

FRUIT AND VEGETABLES

Here lies the secret to good health, so work as many into your diet as possible. I know someone who has raw vegetables for breakfast and says it makes all the difference to his whole day. If you or someone else have the time to prepare them, I should follow that example.

Otherwise make lunch your big vegetable meal unless circumstances force you to have them in the evening. The important thing is to have them, it doesn't really matter when, except that they should balance your main protein intake.

Raw fruit should come at every meal and even between meals if you cannot wait. When the grape season begins and all the other sugar-laden fruits appear, it is an idea to check your carbohydrate intake and see it is somewhere within bounds, although your waistline is the best guide and anyway winter is ahead!

Never cook your fruit and never add sugar to it.

The more vegetables you have raw, the better will be your health.

Fruit and vegetables are the panacea for illness and all the great cures have been based on them, so start the habit now.

BREWERS' YEAST

Is a must for its Vitamin B content, iron and other minerals, and since two dessertspoons are recommended as the daily intake, why not use it as a protein food as well (40%)?

Do not worry about the gas it creates when you first start taking it as this soon disappears.

Have brewers' yeast in some form each day and you will not regret it.

ORGAN MEATS (offal) (for non-vegetarians)

Liver and/or kidneys should appear on your menu at least twice a week. They are usually cheap and not difficult to grill lightly (rubbed with oil). If you have to fry kidneys, cover the pan with a lid to avoid dehydrating them.

Brains can be baked in bacon rings, then liquidized with milk and added to scrambled egg or soup, otherwise steam and cream them with tuna fish or ham.

Never forget the nutritional value of organ meat if you are a non-vegetarian, and learn to cook them so everyone enjoys eating them.

MEAT AND FISH

Two or three times a week is enough for these if you have organ meat as well.

Both are best grilled, otherwise baked in aluminium foil. Stews are also good nutrition but inclined to hang around too long. Only fry if there is no other way and then use vegetable oil, not animal fat.

Put animal bones into a pot au fêu to extract their calcium and other goodness, then add vegetables when you want to eat it. This is strongly recommended for everyone but particularly for the old.

Too much meat or fish can cause an excess of uric acid and be the beginning of rheumatic and arthritic complaints, heart and kidney troubles and many degenerative diseases.

HONEY

Always keep some in the house and eat it dissolved with lemon juice, water and Vitamin C by the teaspoon. It acts as a mild laxative and a wonderful nightcap.

Honey is a great help to the old who make energy less easily than the young.

Don't forget you need these every day, they are as important as food and lack of them will equally make you ill. To these I might also add relaxation, but with the other three this will come.

WATER

Can be a tonic if it contains minerals or a poison if it contains filth. Be sure of your supply because even if you do not drink it as such, you will need it for mixing and washing your food. The spa water at health resorts is no fantasy, the minerals and other factors help a lot.

SUMMARY

That is about all I have to say with regard to food. It is really very simple:

NON-VEGETARIANS

Can have as their main meal once a week, fish, liver and kidneys once each, nuts, cheese and vegetables together twice, and fast on fruit for one day. Breakfast will probably follow the same pattern every day, perhaps fruit, eggs, bread and possibly muesli. The evening meal can be mostly fruit and milk.

VEGETARIANS

Must concentrate on finding the best protein combination, then fill in the rest of the diet with fruit and vegetables. My diet is reasonably cheap if you cut down on the almonds and sesame seeds, but there are lots of alternatives which you can select for yourselves. If you do not eat eggs or dairy produce Vitamin B_{12} and D are a must.

VITAMINS AND MINERALS

If you are eating along the lines I have suggested you have no need to worry unless you are ill, although if you are over 40 it is wise to take additional supplements of all the vitamins and minerals daily. Additional calcium foods are also advisable for the old and a set of 12 biochemic tissue salts (minerals) to replenish daily deficiencies.

DON'TS

No white sugar or white flour or anything made from them.
No common salt, only biochemic or sea salt.
No *processed* fats or cheeses and the least possible amount of animal fat. Cook with vegetable oils.
No *frying*, or excessive *coffee* (even *tea*), alcohol, cigarettes.

NATURE'S MEDICINES

1. Garlic, onions and leeks are nature's antibiotics and good for high blood pressure and as a prophylactic.
2. Lemons are an antiseptic, a de-fatter of the liver and good for colds.
3. Charcoal attracts poisons in the stomach. Good for diarrhoea.
4. Vitamin C saturation is first aid for most diseases. To do this take 3 grams every three hours (add calcium, bioflavonoids and honey for extra effect) until better.
5. Biochemic tissue salts supply missing minerals direct to the cells in a size they can utilize immediately.
6. Wheat germ oil works wonders for hearts, sex organs, diabetes and any muscular or nervous troubles.
7. In most illnesses, fasting for one day on fruit will usually bring the patient to the turning-point.
8. Raw food is the best medicine of all because it goes straight to the cells and regenerates them.
9. Your mind can also talk you out of most illnesses and it is incredible how quickly you can get well if you really want to or have to. Do not give in, fight it all the way.
10. Other vitamins in drug doses (very strong) can produce quick results.

LIVING IN THE MIND

That's where it's all done, in the mind. All our reactions take place there, our sense of enjoyment and pain, of love and hate, of appreciation. So the actual art of living is more an attitude of mind than anything else, for it colours our thinking and really creates the world in which we live. It can destroy us as easily as it can make us sublimely happy. The key is positive thinking not negative, self-respect not self-pity, an outward-looking, giving attitude not a resentful, bitter one. This may be easier to say than put into practice, nonetheless it is the mental starting-point for living alone because all else depends on it.

Before anything else, I must make it quite clear that circumstances are the one great limiting factor to all I said in *About Happiness* and all I shall say here. Of course one can learn to be happy within the circumstances in which one lives and one can prevent oneself being destroyed by those circumstances, but their presence will always mark your boundaries and restrict your view. So don't forget that point if there is someone else dependent on you, don't pretend it doesn't matter because it does, most profoundly. If you are clever enough to change your circumstances and better them, then you have contributed considerably towards opening up a better life for yourself, although ultimately it depends whether you have the mental ability to appreciate those new opportunities.

To live alone, indeed to live at all, one must organize one's life, one's eating habits as well as one's way of living, that is the first essential, otherwise nothing gets accomplished. Men seem to be better at this than women: they usually seem to know exactly what they want to eat and when they take it home, find the easiest way of making it eatable, after which they are probably cunning enough to leave the washing-up for some passing girl friend. So concentrate on organization, make a permanent shopping list with all the items you like to eat on it, putting lots of columns to note how many you have in the larder.

Discover how you can eat almost entirely raw food (see My Diet on page 185) because it is much better for you and saves a lot of time. Of course if you lived in the country I would suggest you get a goat and some chickens, then you would be more than halfway to being properly nourished without having to worry to go much beyond your back door. They would eat up your scraps and you could ensure they were always healthy, so their produce would be too.

Another part of organization is always doing jobs as they appear and not leaving a clutter to weigh on your subconscious. You will be surprised how grateful your subconscious is if you try just that. Make your bed when you get out of it in the morning, wash up as you work in the kitchen (it's one less eyesore and ensures food does not harden on the plates) and put your laundry in a bucket of detergent at the end of the week so it virtually washes itself (keep a broomstick with it and prod every time you pass). It is all part of self-esteem as well, part of self-respect without which you cannot possibly live alone. Unshaven and unwashed you do not last long.

The undisciplined sink into a well of despair and despondency from which they can never escape unless they have the character to become masters of themselves. So remember that and start giving yourself orders, then seeing they are carried out. Try taking a cold shower occasionally, wash in cold water, say no to your carnal lusts once in a while, deny yourself a drink, make yourself do some little routine task each day, learn some poetry or another language. This is all part of moving forward, of progress and therefore keeping alive. Do not forget that 'When it is no longer possible to progress it is necessary to take the last step forward, otherwise you live a living death and the smell of rotting humanity in the end suffocates you,' that is suicide and is the first line of a book I wrote in the form of a suicide letter.

Now a word about your problems. When you have done all you can to solve them, that is an end of it, there is nothing more you can do. So do not continue to worry about them or talk about them, even think about them or refer to them again in any way until a new development arises. That is part of positive thinking. Work out quite cold-bloodedly what your course of action must be, then start the ball rolling, after which you can move on to the next problem and treat it in exactly the same way. When you have cleared your mind of them all, you have gone a long way to relieving yourself of the worry they caused you. But do not doubt your actions and do not interminably refer to them, either in conversation or thought.

Next comes the fear of living which affects so many people who were once part of a family, partner in a marriage or member of a community, and are then thrust upon their own resources. That fear comes partly from lack of confidence which is mostly lack of knowledge and practice at living alone. Gradually that confidence must be acquired by learning to do things on your own. There is no need to be self-conscious if you are alone, people really wish you well and would like to help you if they could, so you are amongst friends. Also do not forget that you can never get anywhere if you do not take your car out of the garage, both metaphorically and literally, even if you do run the risk of having an accident or being fined. That is part of life, the risk you take in living.

If you have always been cared for, it may be hard to find you are no longer, but there is little point in being sentimental about it, so try to rise above it. Learn to do without that luxury and harden yourself to real life. With the exception of one's own family, there are few people who would cross the street to help you if you needed it. If you come in for a little kindness be grateful for it but do not expect any more. This may sound hard but you are not going to survive alone if you are soft or sentimental.

Of course there are other aspects too, for you may have the courage to live on your own but be too lazy to do so. Naturally this does not apply to you, but there are people to whom it does. Laziness is also linked with enthusiasm and enthusiasm largely comes from ideas. Ideas can dominate a person's mind, rule their lives and destroy their character. Some ideas are simply inhibitions, others are wrong thinking or ignorance, but they are all ideas and somewhere along the line they burrow their way into the subconscious and there remain, dominating your will by their all-pervasive force.

Ideas are made of powerful stuff, they cause revolutions, give birth to religions and alter the course of the world. People will die for ideas, slave for them and wage wars on their behalf. This germ which so insidiously attacks one's mind can also be made to work for one's advantage, if one is clever enough to pick the right one.

But in spite of all this talk about the mind, there comes a time when one's feet must touch the earth, and one's stomach must be filled. It cannot be denied that there is a difference between living in a palace or a shack, between eating fillet steak or bread and dripping. Of course one's mind helps one to accept what one has and be grateful for it, and you yourself can help your mind by insisting it obeys your orders. To look around your living room and see some flowers can help a lot, so can pictures, cushions, cosiness. A tidy, clean and homely room with lots of light and sunshine will give you more than millions spent on grand effects.

However one cannot live by just having a house or an apartment; action must take place in the mind and movement in the body before one can qualify to be alive and living. One must amuse oneself and not expect to be amused, create and not always receive, make an effort and not remain dormant. Friends are also a help to do things with, some outside interests and perhaps some hobbies. You should never have time to do all you want to do, yet always be in command of time, which is asking a lot these days.

For a change of scene you can go to any occasion which presents itself, a fête or show or any public gathering. Weekends away are also a good diversion. Even going away for one night makes a welcome change in routine. Then there is window-shopping which for much of the world has to take the place of more expensive pursuits, but that too can be diverting and a change of scene. All this is part of being alive.

Doubtless some comradeship would be nice if you could have it, but you can live without it just as well, it is not a vital need. But everyone needs to communicate, and by that I mean taking from your mind some thoughts and either speaking them or putting them on paper. For that reason people who cannot read, talk and are gregarious, while studious types are usually the opposite. It isn't enough that people have something to think about, they need an end-product for those thoughts, they need to be creative and achieve something.

So also you cannot divorce the body from the mind, they go together, they live and die together, they share the same bloodstream and therefore the same nourishment, so we are back to food again. To eat properly you must plan how you are going to do it, as you must also plan your daily living, otherwise nothing will happen. It is not enough to trust to luck, you must know what you are doing.

That probably means acquiring some new habits and dispensing with others, both of which are extremely difficult to do. For living is largely a habit, like cleaning one's teeth, smoking, having coffee for breakfast or anything else one does every day of one's life. Our daily life becomes ingrained in our subconscious unless we are versatile enough to take each day as it comes.

Lastly don't forget that it must also sometimes rain, that too is part of life, otherwise we could never appreciate the blue sky and sunshine when it comes. Without a sense of appreciation life has no meaning, the beautiful and the ugly become the same. So be like the Chinese who say that before you can begin to enjoy life you must be able to enjoy the simple pleasure of sitting under a tree drinking tea. If you cannot appreciate that then you will never learn to live or understand the meaning of life.

Try to eat properly and make your old age profitable, fun and useful, otherwise you are better dead. All you need do is learn how to be properly nourished and if you are a woman do not skip meals to become slim, that is not the right way of going about it. When you know how to eat you can have as much as you like without putting on weight, then you will be healthy and enjoy living, as well as living alone.

Don't forget that the final test of it all is whether you are happy or not. If you are unhappy something is wrong and that cause of unhappiness must be eliminated from your life, unless of course you can come to terms with it. This may sound very elementary, but it is very basic because your subconscious sets the whole tone of your life and festering thoughts can make you as ill as festering sores, even more so.

If necessary, clean out your mind by telling your closest friend the worst pains you have to bear, or put them down on paper even if you don't intend anyone else to read what you have written. After that your subconscious will be relieved and you will feel much better, for it is more active if you live alone and has more time to make itself felt, so it is doubly important it should not be offended.

I hope this advice will help to make you happier, because if you are not happy there is no point in staying alive. Don't live isolated in the country, a village or town is much better, even a city, although I have sometimes found London (my own home town) the most lonely place in the world. If you are alone you need human contact, and that you cannot find in the fields. Try to be part of a community, if only by living amongst other people.

May I leave you with one last thought. Bernard Shaw, when he was trying to define happiness, concluded that those who gave themselves to one of the world's great causes and were consumed by it and for it were perhaps some of the most fortunate people. He may have been right, for surely the most glorious way of dying is in battle, not in the lingering agony of disease as is mostly the case today. So die fighting and keep on living until that day arrives, then you will not only not be lonely, but you will have a happy ending too.

6. About Health Foods

ABOUT HEALTH FOODS

Health Foods Generally	203
Health Foods Specifically	205
Health Foods	205
Food Supplements	207
Herbal Remedies	208
Homeopathy	209
Cosmetics	209
Books	210
Mechanical Aids	211
Health Foods Individually	211
Fruit and Vegetables	212
Dairy Produce	212
Eggs	214
Cereals	214
Pulses	215
Nuts and Seeds	216
Honey	216
Molasses	217
Raw Sugar	218
Vegetable Oils	218
Yeasts	219
Salt	220
Dried Fruit	220
Coffee	221
Tea	222
Jams	222
Diabetic Foods	223
Vegetarian Foods	223
Cider Vinegar	224
Canned Fruits and Juices	224
Sweets (Candy)	225
Low Salt Products	226

- Soups and Gravies — 226
- Baby Foods — 226
- Soy Sauce — 226
- Food Supplements — 227
  - Multi-Vitamins — 228
  - Vitamin A — 229
  - Vitamin B Complex — 229
  - Vitamin C — 231
  - Vitamin D — 232
  - Vitamin E — 233
  - Vitamin F — 235
  - Vitamin K — 235
  - Minerals — 236
  - Kelp — 237
  - Bone Meal — 238
  - Salt — 239
  - Biochemic Tissue Salts — 239
  - Other Mineral Supplements — 241
- Special Food Supplements — 241
  - Garlic Oil Capsules — 242
  - Wheat Germ Oil — 243
  - Charcoal — 243
  - Lecithin — 244
  - Bioflavonoids — 245
  - Desiccated Liver — 247
  - Royal Jelly — 247
  - Pollens — 247
  - Digestive Aids — 248
  - High Protein — 248
  - Concentrated Vegetables — 248
  - Herbal Remedies — 248

HEALTH FOODS GENERALLY

I OFTEN see people dithering about in health food shops not really knowing what they want to buy, yet clearly in pain or looking so ill that my heart goes out to them. The sight of so many products seems to overwhelm them, yet they know that on the shelves before them lies the answer to their ills, and they are right. It is not just that they have been told by friends how wonderful these natural cures are or that they have read some advertisement, it is also their native instinct to survive which makes them so sure. But how to find the right product for their complaint? That is the big question and I hope this section will produce the answer.

Since time immemorial people have known that what they eat affects their health, so they have experimented and refined that knowledge until they were able to pin-point specific foods and herbs to treat their symptoms. Unfortunately in the very early days insanitary and filthy conditions outweighed that knowledge, and 99% of the world suffered from near starvation, so deficiency diseases were rampant and resistance to infection so low as to make the chances of survival very slim.

Then suddenly one day vitamins were discovered, not because people were looking for them but because researchers knew there was some element in food which made the difference between health and a state of disease. That element was labelled 'vitamin' before it had even been isolated. Now, after nearly a hundred years of experimenting, we are still discovering more vitamins, although the basic five or six are time-tested and well established.

Vitamins have proved to be what they were thought to be, namely that element in food a deficiency of which makes the difference between health and disease, but mineral imbalance has been found to be equally vital and just as frequently the underlying cause of disease. Gradually also foods have been analysed and their contents disclosed, to show the individual amino acids which make up protein, the intrinsic and anti-stress factors, trace elements and enzymes.

Out of all this knowledge has grown the health food trade

which more and more people are suddenly discovering is the only way to cure their ills, as drugs simply relieve the symptoms but leave the body to cure itself. Nutritionists, nature cure and biochemic practitioners, homeopaths and herbalists are at last laying before the world the store of their knowledge and many people are suddenly realizing they are right, that what was learnt thousands of years ago is as right today as it was then.

There is little doubt that correct nutrition and health foods will win in the end, although the issue is not as simple or as straightforward as that, because correct eating amounts mostly to eating only whole food and some people are unwilling to do that. Nonetheless the cure to disease itself is fairly straightforward, although no one way is necessarily the only right one. There are many combinations or individual cures from different branches of nature cure: herbs, minerals or vitamins, homeopathy, enzymes, pollens or intrinsic factors, chlorophyll, anti-stress agents or fasting.

When I started to write about nutrition, I realized that people do not have the time nor sometimes the intellect and will to study the subject for six or seven years just to discover how to eat correctly to cure their ills. I also realized that some people know that nutrition is the right remedy but do not know how to go about putting it into practice. I therefore wrote *About Nutrition*, which was a simplification of the whole subject, both vegetarian and non-vegetarian. Having done that I saw that even though I had told people how to eat, I had not cured their ills, so I wrote *About Diseases*, explaining simply and briefly how to go about it.

When I had completed that I knew I still had not finished with the subject, because one's mind rules one's body and is blindly obeyed, so I wrote *About Happiness*, to probe this aspect. That seemed to cover it all except to tell people specifically what to eat and why, which I have just done in *About Living Alone*. Now I am writing *About Health Foods*, which is equally necessary if you are to be really healthy. Just one item from a health food shop can make the difference between health and disease, so it is important to know which one. Study this section carefully and make particular use of the index at the back which should guide you to what you want.

HEALTH FOODS SPECIFICALLY

Now let's go inside the health food shops themselves and find out what is what.

Basically there are:

1. Health Foods (nutritious foods)
2. Health Food Supplements (vitamins and minerals, etc)
3. Herbal Remedies (specially prepared for specific complaints)
4. Cosmetics (soaps, toothpaste and make-up from nature)
5. Books (the most confusing of all because there are so many)
6. Kitchen Appliances (mixers, juicers, etc).

These six groups contain the essentials for you to cure your ills and keep yourself healthy and beautiful. Something from each is probably necessary, and of course the more you are able to afford the better is your chance of complete recovery and remaining well.

You may well ask, 'Why can't I do it all with natural food?' The answer is, 'You are.' Let me explain.

HEALTH FOODS

These are no more nor less than foods which, for the most part, have been organically grown on compost-manured ground without any insecticides, fungicides or poisonous sprays. They therefore contain all the elements which nature intended for them and since they have not been forced by chemical fertilizers, but allowed to ripen in situ, they are rich in stored sunshine with all its healing balm. This goes for most of the fruit and vegetables sold in health food shops, as well as the packaged cereals, pulses, nuts, seeds, molasses and oils.

The dairy produce comes from healthy cows which have been properly fed on clean pastures. Likewise with the eggs, the hens are allowed free range and are healthy as well as being fertilized naturally. The sugars are as natural as possible, the salt is from the sea or biochemically balanced so as to be harmless, the dried fruit is mostly sun-dried or otherwise specially treated without harmful chemicals, the coffee contains no caffein, the tea is the best quality or made of herbs, the jams are prepared from natural products, the honeys genuine and centrifugally extracted, the yeasts specially fed while growing.

Also there are special foods for diabetics, meatless dishes for vegetarians, low-salt products for kidney and heart complaints, baby foods from untreated, natural foods without additives, also vinegars, canned fruit, vegetables and juices, soups and gravies, all as natural as they can be. Add to that sweets from real honey, molasses and butter, marmite, soy sauce, charcoal biscuits, slippery elm, rose hips drinks, plus some others I have forgotten and you have about the lot.

Amongst the cereal products are all sorts of breads: black, whole wheat, rye or four corns, starch-reduced or with added sultanas, honey, milk powder, soya flour or other delicious ingredients. There are rolls and biscuits, scones and cakes made likewise. Breakfast foods cover a wide range of whole grains, crushed, toasted, flaked or mixed with dried fruit as in muesli.

From this selection of food you can make up all your daily menus without any need to go elsewhere, in fact the diet I live on is all obtainable from such sources.

You may now ask, 'Why is it necessary to live on such food?' The answer is, 'Because food manufacturers have traded on the fact that everyone is lazy and will do whatever is easiest: they follow the course of least resistance. So manufacturers have packaged food specially for them, all ready prepared in cans and plastic containers, frozen or otherwise processed to give it a long shelf-life.'

But I can hear you say, 'What is wrong with processed food?' The answer is, 'Raw, natural, unprocessed food is a harmony of perfectly balanced mineral and organic substances which, if eaten as such, will do you nothing but good. Immediately you destroy some elements, wash them away or otherwise lose them, your body must re-supply them from its reserves, otherwise digestion is adversely affected. This is alright in isolated instances, but once you make a habit of it, you develop deficiency diseases of those particular elements. That is how most diseases originate, by your body getting out of balance and your resistance becoming lowered. To cure yourself, the harmony must be regained by adjusting those food elements which are out of tune.'

'Can't I do that with ordinary food?' you may ask. 'If you are lucky, yes, but to be sure, get it at a health food shop.' However, if your deficiency is long-standing and your health anything other than perfect, you will need to take supplements of vitamins, minerals, enzymes and so on, which I will go into now in more detail.

FOOD SUPPLEMENTS

These are concentrated vitamins, minerals, protein, oils, enzymes or pollens from natural sources. They are in fact the medicines of nature cure, because it is usually a deficiency of one of these which causes illness.

All that these supplements contain are a part of normal, healthy food which we eat daily, but we have learnt to isolate these special substances from them and use them in case of disease. There is nothing extraordinary about them, they are food, but since they contain only that particular section of it after which they are named, they are called food supplements.

It is in this particular part of the health food shop that you must know what you are doing so as to select the right supplement for your particular complaint, although you will do yourself no harm by selecting the wrong one, as all these supplements do nothing but good. However your object is to cure one special complaint, so you may as well try to do so.

Food supplements break themselves down into the following groups:

Vitamins. The oldest established are: A, B complex, C, D, E, F (vegetable oils) and K (made in the body). New ones have been named, but the first five are the ones used in everyday nutrition, with the addition of F which is really a food (vegetable oils) and K which is manufactured in the body and practically never deficient. Vitamin deficiency can cause disease.

Minerals. Are as vital as vitamins because they help food to play its part in nourishing and repairing the body and retaining its alkalinity. In 1873 Dr Scheussler discovered he could cure most curable diseases by administering these inorganic minerals in highly triturated potencies (i.e. by subdividing the particles to ultra-microscopic sizes); a process he called biochemistry. Those mineral cures are available in all health food shops.

There is also a general working need for the body to be supplied with minerals from food or food supplements, but in the case of disease the Scheussler cell salts act more efficiently. Just exactly where you draw the line is hard to say, so it is best to know that both are available to you at any time.

In the Scheussler method there are 3 calcium, 3 potassium, 3 sodium, iron, magnesium and silica cell salts. In nutrition generally there are other minerals also, with additional trace elements like zinc, cobalt, manganese, bromine, nickel, arsenic, mercury, silver and gold etc, which are needed in minute quantities.

Digestive Aids. Come in the form of enzymes, yogurt culture and liquid vegetable preparations.

High Protein. Is offered in tablets, beverages and desiccated liver. It is all simply concentrated natural protein.

Pollen. From plants cures many complaints, mostly nervous.

Concentrated Vegetables. Are no more nor less than what all these food supplements consist of, however these contain one specific vegetable with many vitamins and minerals.

Garlic Oil and Wheat Germ Oil. Are two of the most remarkable natural vegetable cures, which I will deal with at length later.

Royal Jelly. That is food for the queen bee which has been found to have such extraordinary qualities.

Charcoal. Something which dogs always take when they feel sick. We produce biscuits and tablets for convenience, instead of burning toast or eating charred wood from the fire.

HERBAL REMEDIES

These are rather a specialized subject, but health food shops are able to advise about which preparation is needed for what disease. The study of herbs goes back into past ages and has been handed down from generation to generation. All this information has now been correlated and studied intensively so as to present a comprehensive subject.

Herbal remedies come in dry powders, liquids and tonics. All have been tried and proved over hundreds of years, but many of them are without a scientific formula to qualify them. However the fact that science does not necessarily acknowledge them means nothing. It is in the cure that the proof lies, and only a sad reflection on science that it has not progressed far enough to be able to understand and endorse them.

HOMEOPATHY

This is the art of curing like with like in highly subdivided potencies as in the Scheussler biochemistry. This all makes sense when you think we use oil (soap) to remove oil from our skins and inoculate ourselves with disease germs to prevent ourselves getting that disease.

There is much more to homeopathy than this, but it is a specialized subject which requires a book, even a dictionary and a practitioner to put into practice.

COSMETICS

Man cannot improve on nature and I doubt whether he ever will. We have still only scraped the surface of what the laws of nature have to tell us, and we only know about the obvious substances in natural food. How therefore can the chemist hope to nourish the human skin which is one of the outward signs of inner health? The most he can do is to paint over the ugly signs of bad health to improve the visual effect. However it is the visual effect that women seek, but nature cure encourages you to go deeper than that and produce more lasting results.

Vegetable sources offer you all you could ever need to treat the human skin, hair, nails, teeth, eyes and lips. Nature cure also offers you powders and foundations, lipsticks, cleansers, soaps, shampoos, toothpaste, eye lotion, sun oil, bath salts, scents and many other equally natural aids to beauty and seduction.

All of these will have a lasting effect and can do you no harm whatever, so they are a good investment if you want to be attractive. Make a lasting contribution to your looks instead of spreading some synthetic salve over yourself in the hopes that it will produce the right effect. Use preparations made from almonds, lemons, wheat germ oil, Vitamin E, yeast, marsh mallow, sunflower oil, avocado, cucumber, and honey. Protein skin cream, seaweed bath essence, lanolin soaps, and many other natural aids can all become part of your beauty routine.

BOOKS

Books about health are vital if you really want to be healthy, because no person or health food shop can instruct you in all you need to know. It is necessary for you to read about it and to some degree study the subject.

If you are interested in going further into the subject, you should buy one of Adelle Davis's books: *Let's Eat Right To Keep Fit* or *Let's Get Well* because she has the gift of being able to get nutrition across to people. This may be because she herself wholeheartedly believes in it and is dedicated to her task.

Should your interest in nutrition be to lose weight, then Dr Carlton Frederick's *Low Carbohydrate Diet* will achieve this for you. He was once like a baby elephant and numerous doctors were unable to help him. Finally he discovered how to do it for himself, wrote this book and became head of the American Nutrition Society.

There is another book everyone should have and that is one about biochemistry, because this will save you innumerable chemists' bills and visits to the doctor. Such a book needs studying, and you must persevere at trying out various cell salts on every conceivable occasion, but your reward will be glowing health and an immediate antidote to the slightest upset. In England the best books are put out by the New Era Laboratories. They go into such detail that you cannot go wrong. Should you become absorbed in the subject, read *The Earth Heals Everything* by Justine Glass, which tells you the whole story of biochemistry. *Good Health and Happiness* by J. Ellis Barker explains the cause of disease.

I recommend these particular books because they carry you with them. The standard works are a little dry and more for the student of nutrition than the enthusiastic amateur. However don't be put off by me, delve as deep as you can, because it is an absorbing subject and one which is concerned with your own well-being. The Swiss nutritionist Dr Bircher Benner is a useful authority, so are: Harry Benjamin for nature cure, Dr Herbert Shelton for the Hygienic Movement (raw food only), Sir Robert MacCarrison, the British doctor who was one of the first in the field and did some outstanding experiments in India, Dr Kirstine Nolfi who cured herself of cancer with raw food. From there on it should be your choice.

MECHANICAL AIDS

The mechanical side of the health food shop offers you electric liquidizers, mixers, juice extractors, graters and choppers, but there are also hand-operated machines, particularly a vegetable chopper, which I find invaluable for raw vegetables. Other than that, electric yogurt makers are also available.

If you take to nutrition in earnest, these are all useful additions to your kitchen because they save time and give you a better finished product. With gadgets like these there is no end to the experimenting you can do and it is all great fun, as well as being healthy.

With liquidizers, for example, you are able to disguise the contents of your dish, which is helpful with children and also older people who are set in their ways. If it tastes delicious, that is all they care about, and it is not difficult to add some mouth-watering taste to the nastiest of foods and so make the result appetizing.

HEALTH FOODS INDIVIDUALLY

Now for the detailed information you need about all the items in health food shops. The greater part comes under the heading of health foods, so it is probably best to begin there.

FRUIT AND VEGETABLES

These are your best medicines, particularly raw. Never forget that cattle are vegetarians and produce all the beef you eat and the milk you drink from eating grass. How much more should we be able to benefit from all the exotic vegetables and fruit available to us. There is no substitute for vital, living food.

Reasons for eating:

Abundant enzymes, if eaten raw (mostly destroyed by cooking) for good digestion and absorption, for turning food into flesh, etc.

Vitamins and minerals are both abundantly supplied which help ensure good health.

Protein in small amounts but of high biological value.

Sugar for energy comes from fructose in fruit and starch in vegetables.

Roughage for bowel movements.

Stored sunshine (that vital element) in green leaves and fruit.

Are medicines for:

Nearly every disease. All the great cures in nutrition have been achieved by raw fruit and vegetables only, with the possible addition of milk. The best protein to go with them is nuts, seeds, pulses and yeast.

With the addition of short fasts, raw fruit and vegetables will bring new life to nearly every ailing patient.

Quantity:

Your body will guide you, so eat as many as you can afford and want.

N.B. With the exception of dairy produce, eggs, marmite, desiccated liver and possibly some other minor items, everything in health food shops is derived from fruit and vegetable sources. That should indicate their value to health.

DAIRY PRODUCE

Health food milk and dairy produce comes from properly fed,

disease-free cows, so the milk is safe, nourishing and healthy to drink.

Milk (cows' and goats') is a complete food in itself, providing it is not heated, pasteurized, homogenized or otherwise processed, and is best taken as a meal by itself.

The danger of dairy produce lies in taking too much animal fat from processed products. Natural, raw, untreated milk and its products should not be harmful, in moderation.

Reasons for eating:

Because it is extremely alkaline.

For its good quantities of calcium, protein, milk sugar, vitamins (particularly B_{12}) and anti-stress factors.

Yogurt and sour milk make intestinal flora which create B vitamins in the body, also friendly bacteria to destroy unfriendly ones. The protein is pre-digested, the calcium easily accessible and the acid helpful for absorption.

Cottage cheese (white soft) is a source of fat-free protein and calcium.

Other cheeses give concentrated protein and calcium (but very fatty).

Powdered and condensed milks have high protein and calcium values (a good cheap supply).

Buttermilk contains lecithin which helps break down fats and make them useful to the body, instead of harmful.

Raw cream is said to be good food (essential unsaturated fatty acids) but still it is a lot of concentrated fat.

Are medicines for:

The old because of their calcium, protein, vitamins and anti-stress factors (particularly yogurt).

The after-effects of antibiotics which kill your intestinal supply of B vitamins. This is a must for everyone.

Poor digestion, absorption and all sorts of intestinal ills.

All troubles due to lack of calcium and protein, also the B vitamins.

All malnourished states and convalescence.

Everyone daily to ensure something of all the nutrients.

Quantity:

A carton of yogurt, a glass of milk and under 2 ounces of cheese is enough. But increase if diet is inadequate in protein or calcium. Too much fatty cheese causes a calcium deficiency by the fat combining with the calcium in the intestines and forming a hard soap. Milk sugar is needed daily to feed the friendly intestinal bacteria.

EGGS

Are a complete food like milk, but are very acid-forming, therefore bad for rheumatism, kidneys, hearts, etc.

Reasons for eating:

Health food shop eggs come from healthy hens, fed on properly balanced rations, kept under free-range conditions and fertilized by a cock. Therefore they are good food, in moderation.

They are high in Vitamin A, contain Vitamin B_{12} (and other B vitamins), lots of iron, protein, minerals and lecithin.

Quantity:

When you are young it does not matter, but later in life 3 or 4 a week is enough, or even fewer.

Eat them boiled or poached, as cooking in animal fat or hydrogenated oils makes them more acid than they already are.

CEREALS

Barley and oatmeal are acid-forming, bread less so.

The available range is wide: whole grains (for sprouting, grinding or chewing), whole grain pasta, crushed or flaked breakfast foods, porridge and muesli, whole grain flour of various extractions, bread, rolls, cakes, scones, biscuits (all whole grain), starch-reduced rolls and bread, wheat germ, unpolished rice (various types).

Reasons for eating:

Refined white flour has lost most of its vitamins, minerals, enzymes and intrinsic factors which are needed for digestion, therefore the body must re-supply them. In the end this causes deficiency diseases. Whole grain products contain all the goodness, particularly Vitamin E.

All cereals take time to digest but white flour products sit in a lump in your stomach growing putrefactive bacteria.

Wheat germ contains high protein, Vitamins E and B, lecithin and minerals. A valuable food for the sick.

Are medicines for:

Cereals are only medicinal if taken in small amounts and if eaten as whole grain products. Then they improve health for their Vitamin E content, the life-factor from the germ and their valuable oils and minerals. Since they are digested slowly they offer a long-lasting energy supply and help to satisfy hunger. Too much cereal, eaten without other food, forms too much acid.

Wheat germ on the other hand is medicinal for its concentrated Vitamin E and other factors. Again only small amounts are needed. Hearts and debility respond well.

Quantity:

A few teaspoons of cereal go a long way and should always be combined (green vegetables are best or sweet or sub-acid fruit).

PULSES

These consist of soya beans, soya flour, Mung beans, lentils, peas, broad beans, common white and lima beans, canned soya beans in sauce or otherwise, other canned beans.

Reasons for eating:

Vegetarians obtain quite a lot of their protein from this source, particularly soya bean products.

Correctly combined pulses make protein of high biological value (soya beans are complete in themselves).

Soya beans are a wonder food, not only because of their 35% protein, but also Vitamin E, lecithin, Vitamin B complex and minerals. There is no better addition to the diet (in moderation).

Are medicines for:
  Nothing in particular but a useful food.
  Soya beans are good for all complaints which Vitamin E and lecithin cure.

Quantity:
  Soya products are concentrated food so two tablespoons a day is more than ample (30-35 grams).
  Eat other pulses sparingly too (they contain a lot of starch).

NUTS AND SEEDS

Almonds, Brazils, cashew, hazel, pecans, pistachio, walnuts, coconuts. Pine kernels. Sesame, pumpkin and sunflower seeds. Nut: milks, creams, meats and coffees.

Reasons for eating:
  They are a daily must because they contain the 'life' factor for new birth.
  The best source of Vitamin F (unsaturated fatty acids), high in Vitamin E, lecithin and minerals.
  Good protein too, but some need combining with other protein as they are not complete.

Are medicines for:
  Everyone for their valuable contents.
  The old who need rejuvenating.
  Degenerative diseases to stimulate new life.
  Most deficiency diseases to supply valuable minerals and vitamins.

Quantity:
  Not too many, a handful of almonds or 2-3 teaspoons of sesame seeds. Likewise with the others, a little goes a long way.

HONEY

Comes to health food stores from every corner of the earth as clear, clotted, dark, light, centrifugally extracted, in combs, from orange blossom, heather, acacia, clover, etc.

Reasons for eating:
Honey sugar enters the blood directly (it needs no breaking down) and is therefore an immediate source of energy. For the old this is useful as they do not make energy so easily.

This type of sugar is food for the heart, fuel for the brain, muscles and nerves.

It strengthens the heart, is good for the liver, kidneys, lungs and skin.

It increases the body's combustion rate and attracts water, so is not fattening (in moderation).

Is medicine for:
All convalescents and surgical patients.
With lemon juice and Vitamin C for colds, flu, fevers, liver troubles, fatigue, asthma, ulcers and sores.
Poor digestion or absorption, for young and old.

Quantity:
Honey is concentrated food (82% sugar) so needs diluting or spreading thinly. It mixes well with water or fruit juice.

If you take a lot of exercise, eat as much as you like, otherwise use in moderation. Carbohydrate is carbohydrate and neither necessary nor desirable in excess of body needs.

MOLASSES

The darker and thicker the better.
It is the residue left behind when sugar cane is refined.

Reasons for eating:
It is a concentrated vegetable juice and therefore its vitamins and minerals are also concentrated.

Its particular value is for iron, calcium, potassium and the B vitamins.

Its sugar however needs converting, like table sugar, so an excess is unwise.

Is medicine for:
Constipation (a mild laxative).
Anaemia (its iron, copper, calcium and B vitamins).
Arthritis and allied complaints.

Quantity:
Such concentrated carbohydrate (50% refined sugar) should be taken sparingly and well diluted (possibly in warm water or milk).

One or possibly two teaspoons is enough.

Never take straight from the bottle as it sticks to the teeth and causes decay.

RAW SUGAR

This includes everything from soft, dark, brown to lighter brown crystals, from fudges to toffees made from it.

Reasons for eating:
This sort of sugar still has some of the vitamins, minerals and other factors necessary for digestion.

Strictly speaking additional sugar should not be necessary, but if you cannot do without it, this is the sort to have.

Is medicine for:
Nothing and your teeth, digestion and metabolism are better without it.

Quantity:
As little as possible.

VEGETABLE OILS

These include corn, sunflower seed, safflower, olive, soya, peanut, linseed, sesame and cotton seed oils. All cold pressed and first extraction (no sediment or noxious acids).

Reasons for eating:
For their essential unsaturated fatty acids (sometimes called Vitamin F).

All body processes need these oils.

Are medicines for:
Prostate gland in particular.
All the other glands.
Healthy and clear skin.
Energy production.

Quantity:
Everyone needs 1½ tablespoons daily (in and out of cooking).
An excess will produce no extra benefit and may make you fat.
The right amount will help keep you healthy.

YEASTS

These include debittered brewers' yeast, Torula yeast and bakers' yeast. The latter is not for eating, but for making bread. The other two are excellent food, having been dried to kill the plant and sold over the counter as powdered yeast. The wet live yeast as used by brewers is not recommended.

Reasons for eating:
Contains 39% protein of high biological value.
One of the best Vitamin B sources.
Contains calcium, iron, phosphorus, 14 other minerals.
Is only 1% fat.
Best value-for-weight food there is.

Is medicine for:
All sorts of fatigue as it is a great energy producer.
Nerves, nails, blood purifying, liver health, anaemia, constipation, digestion, heart and insomnia (all Vitamin B complaints).
Resistance to disease and to combat infection. Used in treatment of oedema.
Eaten daily it helps to ensure health.

Quantity:
Two dessertspoons a day. More is too much. It creates gas at first but this soon disappears (it is a good sign).
N.B. It should only ever be eaten last thing at night, first thing in the morning or one hour before the evening meal, because if there is any sugar in the stomach it will ferment. Yeast can be mixed with water, milk or your own saliva but never anything else.

SALT

Common table salt is never found in health food shops, only sea salt or biochemically balanced salt.

Reasons for eating:

Common table salt has none of the additional minerals necessary for proper utilization, therefore if thrown off into the tissues (from excess or incorrect use) can cause water retention and other troubles.

Is medicine for:

Biochemic or sea salt is necessary for cell division, water distribution, glandular activity, combating low spirits, some types of constipation, thin and watery blood, watery colds, dry mucous membranes and sneezing, slow digestion (water brash), great thirst, flow of tears from wind, excessive saliva, hay fever, muscular weakness with drowsiness, very dry skin with itching, hang-nails, unrefreshing sleep (tired in morning), loss of taste and smell, troublesome insect bites. Excessive moisture or dryness anywhere in the body is a salt imbalance, which is often manifest by a watery or bloated appearance.

Quantity:

No more than 4 grams (one bare level teaspoon) in and out of cooking daily, unless sweating a lot or urinating excessively. Take between meals in $\frac{1}{4}$ tumbler of water, never with food. In very hot weather, if sweating a lot or urinating excessively due to kidney troubles or incontinence, it may be necessary to take a little additional salt (the symptoms will all too soon become apparent).

N.B. Those with high blood pressure should never take additional salt and should consult their doctor about it.

DRIED FRUIT

Figs, prunes, dates, sultanas, raisins, currants, apricots, peaches, nectarines, bananas and others. Many of them are sun-dried or specially treated to avoid chemicals.

Reasons for eating:
Figs and prunes are full of Vitamin A, iron and other minerals.

Apricots, nectarines and peaches are rich in Vitamin A, also copper and iron.

Dates are 73% sugar, raisins 77% but with the necessary minerals and vitamins for digestion.

Most dried fruit is a good source of minerals and some vitamins. All contains concentrated sugar.

Is medicine for:
Figs and prunes are laxative and effective against poisons.

Apricots, nectarines and peaches supply Vitamin A for skin, antibodies and mucous linings. They also have copper for iron utilization, so are good for anaemia.

Dates, raisins, sultanas, currants and bananas offer 73–80% sugar for energy, also bioflavonoids and minerals.

These are best for hungry children or for winter lack of fruit.

Quantity:
Dried fruit is concentrated food so it is best soaked in water to regain better proportions and balance.

If eaten unsoaked it is too easy to have a carbohydrate binge, sometimes causing great thirst, possible magnesium or vitamin B_6 imbalance, excessive sugar in blood and urine (the cure for which is to take $\frac{1}{2}$ teaspoon magnesium oxide and Vitamin B_6 for a day or two).

Eat as you would ordinary fruit once it has been soaked.

COFFEE

Ordinary coffee, either instant or otherwise, is not sold in health food shops. Decaffeinated coffee is available or coffee made from dandelions, nuts and other plants.

Reasons for not drinking:
Coffee is a stimulant, in fact its caffeine is a habit-forming drug. Excessive users get drug withdrawal symptoms when they give it up (I did).

It is bad for the liver which has to detoxify it.

It is bad for the heart because it stimulates it beyond its strength, also other reasons.

It can cause ulcers, grey hair, even convulsions (through magnesium loss).

It elevates the blood sugar, then causes it to drop below normal, causing fatigue, even confusion.

Drinking coffee creates stress and therefore adversely affects the whole body.

If you must drink ordinary coffee take milk with it.

Decaffeinated coffee is much better.

Nut or plant coffee, on the other hand, will improve your health.

TEA

Contains 75% less caffeine than coffee and if made correctly the tannin need not be liberated. Never allow tea to stand more than 2 or 3 minutes after making without pouring into another pre-warmed pot. This way the harmful elements are not released.

Health food shops sell China, Ceylon, Indian and green tea. Also Matté and herb teas: camomile, lime blossom, peppermint, rose hip, hibiscus and many others.

Reasons for drinking:

Matté and herb teas are positively health-giving. They are soothing to the digestion, medicinal for the body and an addition to the diet.

For more information consult health food shops about the individual types.

Quantity:

Too much liquid is never advisable unless perspiration or incontinence account for excessive losses.

A few cups of any sort of tea is enough.

JAMS

Ordinary commercial jams are made with white sugar,

saccharine, other chemical sweeteners, artificial colouring and chemical preservatives, so are acid-forming.

Their white sugar content alone should be enough to make you avoid them, quite apart from all the chemicals which have to be eliminated from the body, unless they are absorbed and remain as potential trouble-causers.

Reasons for eating:
Trouble is taken to use tree-ripened fruit and as far as possible to see it is organically grown.

Jams are made with nothing but natural products, such as honey, molasses or raw sugar.

No colouring, flavouring, chemical preservatives or other chemicals are used.

Quantity:
Since they are made from natural products you can eat what you want within reason (but too much carbohydrate is always bad).

DIABETIC FOODS

These include jams, fruit and vegetable juices, chocolates, health drinks, tinned fruits and other food specially tinned free from sugar.

Reason for eating:
These are obvious to the diabetic and it must be a relief for him to have such a large choice now available.

Quantity:
He and his doctor will know the answer to that.

VEGETARIAN FOODS

These include meatless stews, goulash, steaks, cutlets, rissoles, all made from soya beans, pulses or other vegetables with only vegetable flavourings. These will fool your guests so they will not consider you eccentric, and enable other members of your family to accept vegetarian food with ease.

Reasons for eating:
The same as those of being a vegetarian, namely to avoid acid-forming foods like meat and fish, amongst other reasons.

Quantity:
As for ordinary food.

CIDER VINEGAR

Has very special qualities.

Reasons for eating:
Because it is considered a perfect cleanser of the body, acting on the liver and disposing of poisons.

It closely resembles the gastric juices and is therefore helpful in digestive disorders.

It contains many valuable vitamins and trace elements.

Is medicine for:
The overweight because it improves metabolism and so deals with excess fat.

Aids digestion and absorption.

Relieves laryngitis, coughs, asthma, sore throats (if used as a gargle).

Arthritis and rheumatic complaints have been helped.

Liver and kidney troubles also respond.

Quantity:
As a gargle: one teaspoon per glass of water.

Otherwise use as ordinary vinegar with vegetables and other food.

Alternatively drink the gargle instead of gargling, or as well.

CANNED FRUIT AND JUICES

These are available in every conceivable variety and are meant for use in the winter when fruit and vegetables are a scarce commodity, or for convenience otherwise.

The fruit is carefully selected and only natural, whole food is used in the process. No artificial flavourings, colours, sweeteners or preservatives are added, so they are as near to nature as possible. Raw sugar is used, or even honey.

Juices from fruit and vegetables have achieved incredible cures, quite on their own. Usually they have to be drunk in large quantities for this.

Reasons for eating:
All that I said about fruit and vegetables applies here. These are your life-lines to health.

Are medicine for:
Most of your ills.

Quantity:
Be guided by your body and your pocket.

SWEETS (Candy)

Nothing is more delicious than health food sweets, the real genuine honey, molasses, raw sugar, butter, seeds and nuts ensure that. Their natural contents make them nourishing and healthy as well.

Reasons for eating:
The refined sugar in other sweets causes tooth decay and creates deficiency diseases.

The chemicals used in the manufacture of most other sweets need to be eliminated by the body as they are toxic.

Health food sweets are healthy.

Are medicine for:
Find out what they are made of and then consult that specific item in this book.

Quantity:
An excess of any carbohydrate retains too much water in the body and makes you fat.

Too much carbohydrate can also cause magnesium and Vitamin B_6 deficiency.

LOW SALT PRODUCTS

Are specially prepared for those who must not eat too much salt, like heart patients, and those with kidney and other complaints.

It is comforting for such people to know for certain that what they are eating is guaranteed to contain only the small amount of salt stated on the packet.

SOUPS AND GRAVIES

These are offered in tins and packets from a large variety of vegetables with mixtures of herbs and spices.

They are intended for those who do not have time to make their own.

Great care is taken in their preparation to include only natural foods and no chemicals are used.

They are a useful insurance for your health and a delicious addition to any meal.

BABY FOODS

These are to ensure that your baby starts life on the right food to develop his bones, internal organs and a sound network of blood vessels and nerves.

Nothing is more important than a good grounding in life and proper nutrition is the way to achieve it.

These preparations are convenient and easy to use, as well as being perfectly balanced with all the right food elements needed for the very young. Some old people also use them.

If you are doubtful about how to feed your child, these foods will end those doubts and give you peace of mind too.

SOY SAUCE

This is a concentrated soya bean product and everything which applies to them (see Pulse section) also applies here.

Since it is concentrated, you do not need much of it, but it can be added to nearly every vegetable dish, including of course rice, with the greatest benefit nutritionally.

If you wish to add special flavour to some dish, this is one excellent way of doing it.

FOOD SUPPLEMENTS

They are called food supplements because they supplement your food with their own particular highly concentrated vitamin, mineral or whatever else it is. They are the natural way of taking these additional substances which have become deficient in the body and caused disease, or which you need to ensure an adequate supply. The only alternative is to take them synthetically, manufactured by a chemist, and this does not ensure that all the necessary balancing factors are present. Of course in certain cases these can be taken with benefit, if added to supplements, and they are just beginning to be sold in health food shops in England now for that specific purpose. This applies in particular to the individual B vitamins and ascorbic acid (Vitamin C) which have been found by nutritionists to be especially beneficial to health in certain circumstances. So do not be put off by old-fashioned prejudice here.

Food supplements are invaluable for those who do not want to take too much trouble over their diet or who are not in a position to choose what they eat. All people over the age of 40 should start this habit because it is then their bodies start degenerating, although they would be wise to acquire the habit earlier, because habits take some acquiring. For people who are ill, food supplements in the form of vitamins, minerals, enzymes and other specialities are a must.

Health food shops are full of people who have been given up by their doctors because there is nothing more, they say, they can do for them (I was one such case). In desperation they come for help as a last resort and frequently not only cure their ills, but discover better health than they have ever had before.

Out of sheer gratitude those are the people who often go off and start health food shops on their own, or, like me, write about it to tell the world that there is some hope and to go on trying. To have found relief from their agony so simply from the ever-abundant and available source of nature, is something they are hardly able to believe and naturally they wonder why no one ever told them about it before.

All I explained in the last section about health foods applies equally to food supplements because they are one and the same thing, although the latter are more concentrated and specific. The one is only supplementary to the other. If you are ill, you would be best to start with the supplements to fill your deficiencies and then move on to the health foods, unless you take them both at the same time, which of course is obviously preferable.

As I have already said, food is not one element but many, perfectly balanced to produce the right effect. Processed food often has an imbalance which can cause disease and the cure lies in correcting it.

Don't be afraid of taking too many supplements, providing they are from natural sources. Vitamins A, D and E are the only fat-soluble ones which have to be taken in enormous quantities to become toxic. The other water-soluble vitamins are excreted in the urine if taken in excess, as with minerals. Study these explanations carefully and select your own remedy or ask at your health food shop. If you are wrong, do not worry, none of them can do you any harm, so do not be afraid of trying.

VITAMINS

MULTI-VITAMINS

These capsules are exactly what they say they are, a combination of all the vitamins.

For those who find pill-taking difficult, this is a good way of getting a little of what you need of them all.

The sceptics are sceptical, but let them be, vitamins are only needed in large doses when you are ill. For a daily addition to your diet multi-vitamins are perfectly adequate.

Take them as directed, then they will work for you as they were intended.

VITAMIN A

It usually comes with Vitamin D in fish liver oil, but carotene and other preparations are specific.

Halibut liver oil is the strongest, then cod liver oil.

Carotene from vegetables needs converting into Vitamin A in the body.

Its function:

For good sight and bright eyes, sensitivity to bright lights and the ability to see better in the dark.

For skin beauty. It is a must.

For anti-ageing. This is the youth vitamin, internally as well as externally.

For resistance to disease. It helps to create white corpuscles to fight infection.

Deficiency symptoms:

Pimples on the upper arms and thighs, night blindness, rough and dry skin, constant infection (particularly of the eyes, ears, lungs and sinus).

Additional sources:

All orange and yellow fruit and vegetables, green leaves (spinach, broccoli, tomatoes, turnip greens, kale, watercress, parsley, carrots, apricots, peaches, prunes, papaya). Liver and kidneys, dairy produce (milk, butter, cheese) eggs.

Quantity:

It is possible to take too much of this vitamin as it is fat-soluble, but it is not likely. However best be guided by what it says on the bootle. It can be stored by the body.

VITAMIN B COMPLEX

This is a group of vitamins and it is always best to take them all together, otherwise you create a deficiency of the ones you have not taken. To achieve this you can take desiccated liver or brewers' yeast tablets. However there are now also available individual B vitamins which can be used in certain cases for a short period of time. They are best taken in conjunction with high potency Vitamin B foods such as: brewers' yeast, yogurt, milk, wheat germ, whole grains, liver, kidneys, eggs, molasses, green vegetables, citrus fruit, nuts and seeds.

Its function:
The group as a whole is generally helpful for:

> Nerves and preventing irritability.
> Purifying the blood (thus skin health).
> Most liver functions, therefore its health.
> Energy production and thus preventing fatigue.
> Relieving constipation, thus normal bowel movements.
> Cracked lips and sore mouth.
> Poor digestion and memory.
> Healthy arteries and heart function.
> Resupplying B vitamins destroyed by drugs (a must).

The individual B vitamins also have specific functions such as B_2 for eyesight, pantothenic acid for stress, para-aminobenzoic acid for sunburn and preventing grey hair, but it is best to consult an expert or a more detailed book than this before taking.

Deficiency symptoms:
There are many obvious signs to look for:

> Tongue very bright red or purplish, shiny and smooth, cracked appearance with abnormal taste buds, enlarged and beefy.
> Cracked lips, vertical lines, lines in the corner of the mouth or burning sensation in it.
> Lack of energy and depression, poor nerves.
> A craving for carbohydrate (including sweets and alcohol) (B_6).
> Eczema, skin eruptions and boils or whiteheads.
> Pernicious or ordinary anaemia (B_{12}).
> Pellagra, poor blood.

There are other symptoms as well and they are all interrelated, but these are the basic ones.

Quantity:

Within reason the more the better, as it is a water-soluble vitamin and therefore excess is excreted. Two tablespoons of brewers' yeast is a good daily intake.

VITAMIN C

Is also a group (complex) of vitamins like Vitamin B, although not spoken of as such. That is why health food shops sell rose hip and acerola supplements instead of straight ascorbic acid as sold by chemists. However it is now commonly accepted that when large doses of Vitamin C are needed, ascorbic acid is a perfectly satisfactory method, and in most diseased states this is probably the only way of getting enough. The bioflavonoids (rutin, citrin, etc) can be added for increased effect, as can any form of calcium.

Its function:

It acts directly on the blood-forming centres.

It neutralizes toxins and poisons in the body and rejuvenates the liver.

It increases resistance to disease and infection.

It maintains the integrity of the gums, joints and connective tissue.

It helps to fight stress and prolong endurance.

It strengthens the capillaries and helps the other blood vessels.

It assists the absorption of iron and therefore oxygen, thus increasing energy.

It stimulates the thyroid gland and aids sufferers from schizophrenia.

It helps the utilization of calcium and therefore the bones and teeth.

It assists in speeding convalescence and healing wounds.

These are just some of its many functions. It is a most useful and versatile vitamin and should be used as first aid in most diseases.

Deficiency symptoms:

All forms of weakened blood vessels: bruises, bleeding gums, piles, varicose veins, nose bleeds, loose teeth, pyorrhoea.

Premature ageing with flabby and wrinkled skin.

Malfunctioning adrenal glands, therefore fear, lack of fight, poor resistance to disease and stress, exhaustion.

Slow healing, brittle bones, scurvy.

Anaemia and unhealthy blood.

All forms of intoxication (including alcohol).

Additional sources:

Almost all fruit and vegetables including:

All citrus fruit, blackcurrants, pineapple, raspberries, strawberries, tomatoes, sprouted mung and soya beans and other sprouted pulses and cereals, cabbage, lettuce, watercress, etc.

Quantity:

Vitamin C is water-soluble and cannot be stored in the body, so must be taken daily. Any excess is excreted in the urine.

In illness vast doses must be taken: 1 gram every hour (or 3 grams every 3 hours), maybe more. Otherwise 1 or 2 grams a day. Less for acerola and rose hips.

VITAMIN D

Is manufactured in the skin from the sun's rays. Otherwise it is only available in animal foods. Vegetarians therefore have no source of supply except the sun.

The richest source is fish liver oil (halibut or cod liver oil) which is sold in health food shops. Minute amounts are also available in some milk and butter, eggs, fish and mushrooms.

Its function:

Without it calcium and phosphorus cannot be absorbed from the intestines.

From this comes good teeth and bones, strong nerves and sound sleep.

For the proper functioning of the thyroid and parathyroid glands, therefore proper metabolism.

Deficiency symptoms:

Nervousness, muscular fatigue, tooth decay, brittle bones, insomnia, constipation, possibly osteoarthritis, rickets.

Additional sources:

Minute amounts are also available from milk and butter, eggs, fish, mushrooms, liver, salmon, tuna fish and herrings, but it is unwise to rely upon these as your sole source of supply.

Quantity:

Vitamin D is fat-soluble so can be stored by the body, but in winter when there is little or no sun and its rays are weak, everyone should take an additional supply. Large amounts cannot be taken with safety, as an excess is toxic, so abide by the label on the bottle.

VITAMIN E

Is sold as d-Alpha Tocopherol (which is the active natural ingredient). Wheat germ oil capsules also contain a high concentration.

Its function:

It oxygenates the tissues and therefore reduces the need for oxygen.

It has an anti-blood clotting quality (and can even dissolve clots).

It prevents scar tissue formation and can even dissolve some scars, therefore vital for heart complaints, kidneys and ulcers.

It is especially involved in reproductive and sex functions, therefore fertility, miscarriage and normal childbirth.

It relieves the unpleasant symptoms of change-of-life (menopause), such as hot flushes and dizziness. Also menstrual disorders.

It dilates blood vessels and increases the circulation.

It tones up the muscles through its oxygen conservation.

It has a sparing effect on Vitamin A.

It softens and beautifies the skin, getting rid of wrinkles.

It has been used to cure diabetes.

It detoxifies the liver and is therefore useful in all liver complaints.

It acts upon the thyroid gland and therefore stimulates metabolism, so reducing weight (also by its diuretic effect).

It is vital for burns to prevent scar formation and reduce the pain involved (also externally).

It stimulates the activity of the brain and sometimes remedies mental retardation.

It is associated with Vitamin C in preventing cell permeability and therefore resistance to infection, also all diseases of the cells such as cancer and leukaemia.

It acts on the pituitary and adrenal glands and normalizes their functions.

It has helped varicose veins, haemorrhoids, varicose ulcers, purpura.

It helps to withstand the demands of stress, even multiple scelerosis.

Deficiency symptoms:

Most degenerative diseases are due to lack of this vitamin: sexual degeneration, diabetes, arteriosclerosis, heart disease, liver disorders, circulation, thyroid and other glandular degeneration, miscarriages.

Painful and irregular menstruation.

Poor muscle tone and diminished circulation (weak blood vessels).

Lack of sexual libido, impotence and infertility.

Paralysis has been induced by feeding a diet deficient in this vitamin.

Additional sources:

Cold pressed, natural wheat germ oil (sold at health food shops) has a very high concentration of Vitamin E as well as all the allied vitamins and minerals. This source alone works wonders for all the conditions which need Vitamin E.

Ordinary wheat germ is a less powerful supply. Most vegetable oils contain some: corn, soya, cottonseed, olive, sunflower, safflower, etc. Milk and dairy produce contain a very little. Whole grains are a useful daily supply (whole grain bread and cereals).

Quantity:

People are usually advised to start with 100 i.u.'s and build up to a dosage which is well tolerated by the body. You can usually be your own judge on this.

Vitamin E is fat-soluble and better absorbed by the body when taken with fat or lecithin. The body stores it together with its own fat.

N.B. Vitamin E is one of the great discoveries of the century, do not be put off taking it by people who know nothing about the research and cures which have been done with it. Dr Evan Shute of the Shute Foundation, London, Ontario, Canada, is the greatest living authority on the subject and has produced several books about it. Insist on the natural sort, labled d-alpha tocopherol.

VITAMIN F

Not officially a vitamin (although it is essential to health like the other vitamins) but many people (in particular Americans) talk about it as such.

Vitamin F is the essential unsaturated fatty acids so you should refer to vegetable oils which gives details.

Do not omit these from your diet and remember that many people are deficient in Vitamin F and this can cause a number of diseases. Simply by taking vegetable oil and so filling this deficiency you can cure them. In particular prostate disorders, skin and hair disorders, asthma, arthritis and blood vessels.

Fish liver oil and wheat germ oil are concentrated sources as well as providing many other nutrients. Nuts, seeds, avocado pears are excellent sources.

VITAMIN K

Vitamin K is synthesized in the intestines like the B vitamins and can be likewise killed by antibiotics. If this happens, the process can be restarted by taking yogurt. Being fat-soluble it can be stored in the liver.

Some preparations in health food stores contain this vitamin, should you need it specifically. Consult them.

Its function:
Is to maintain a certain level of prothrombin in the blood,

which is one of the essential factors needed to make blood clot.

Without Vitamin K prothrombin is not stored in the liver and therefore cannot prevent haemorrhaging.

It is obviously vital for childbirth, operations, tooth extractions, cut fingers or any wounds.

Deficiency symptoms:
Nosebleeds or any form of haemorrhage (the failure of blood to stop flowing). Best used in conjunction with Vitamin C.

Additional sources:
Green leafy vegetables, kelp (seaweed) and liver.

Quantity:
More than 10 mgs can be toxic to infants (2–3 mgs are enough).

Women in labour receive 10–20 mgs as newly-born infants are especially deficient.

MINERALS

Minerals are as vital as vitamins.

Some of the more important are: Calcium, magnesium, potassium, iron, sodium, phosphorus, iodine. Also oxygen, carbon, fluorine, hydrogen, sulphur, manganese, silicon and trace elements.

Their function is to:
Maintain the alkaline reactions of the fluids in the body.
Provide digestive and other secretions with the necessary elements.
Regulate the flow of fluids to and from the cells and tissues.
Help the formation of bones, teeth and cartilage.
Help blood clotting.
Keep nerves and muscles elastic and thus healthy.
Work with enzymes in turning food into flesh, etc.
Distribute oxygen.

Deficiency symptoms:
Calcium: Brittle bones, debility, poor circulation, slow convalescence, abscesses, anaemia, poor memory or nerves.

Sodium Chloride (salt): See details under sodium in nutrition section.

Potassium: For balancing sodium, constipation, acidity, nervous tension and sleeplessness, fatigue and irritability.

Iron: Anaemia, listlessness, lack of pep, sluggish thinking, tiredness.

Iodine: Malfunctioning of thyroid gland: therefore no zest for work or play, no energy, sensitivity to heat or cold, cold hands and feet, mental and physical sluggishness, weight easily gained, no sex urge, poor memory, early ageing, constant desire to sleep.

N.B. For more detailed information consult a larger work.

Sources of supply:

Biochemic tissue salts. If you learn about these, they will supply your needs and make more difference to your health than almost any other single health food supplement.

Bonemeal from veal bones for calcium and magnesium (also a vegetarian preparation specially made up).

Dolomite tablets: from the rocks of the Dolomites which are very rich in minerals, particularly magnesium.

Calcium and iron preparations are also available.

Kelp or seaweed for iodine.

Quantity:

Most of the minerals sold in health food stores are from natural sources and therefore properly balanced to ensure good health, so the quantities are not of great importance.

The biochemic mineral salts are in such minute potencies that there is no risk of taking too many.

KELP

This is the richest natural source of iodine and also abundant in other minerals (22 known ones) and trace elements. The iodine occurs in the same form as in the thyroid gland, where it is principally used, but all the endocrinal glands need some. Everyone over 40 should take it daily.

Its function:

Is principally to supply iodine for the normal working of

the thyroid gland and other endocrine glands. This ensures an adequate supply of energy and a freedom from all the other deficiency symptoms listed under iodine.

Is also to supply minerals and trace elements, of which it has an abundant supply.

Deficiency symptoms:
As listed under iodine.

Quantity:
On account of its salt content, take as instructed on the container, as too much salt is not advisable.

BONE MEAL

This is your best source of natural calcium because it comes balanced by phosphorus and magnesium in proper proportions. Other minerals and trace elements are also present.

It is literally the pulverized bones of calves or other cattle. It is cheap and easy to take. For the young it is vital for the development of their bones and teeth, for the old for their nerves and assimilation, to prevent anaemia and numerous other causes (see under Calcium).

Vegetarian bone meal is also available made from entirely vegetable sources.

Its function:
Is principally to supply calcium which the body needs daily (about 2 grams).

The young have sufficiently active thyroid glands, run about in the sun to get enough Vitamin D and naturally supply the necessary acid medium in their stomachs, all of which are needed for calcium absorption. But the old may have none of these requirements, so suffer from a calcium deficiency, even though they may eat enough of it.

The other minerals and trace elements which bone meal also supplies are not to be ignored.

Deficiency symptoms:
In young people: their teeth develop badly and their bones do not form properly.

For the old, it may mean poor assimilation of food, anaemia, sensitivity to pain, bad nerves, impaired memory, slow convalescence, brittle bones or poor circulation, amongst other things.

Quantity:
Although high in phosphorus there is little danger of taking too much, providing moderation is used.

SALT

See under nutrition section.

BIOCHEMIC TISSUE SALTS

Between 1873 and his death in 1898 Dr Scheussler established the vital role of highly subdivided mineral salts in the cure and prevention of disease and the maintenance of health. He named 12 vital cell salts (3 calcium, 3 potassium, 3 sodium, iron, magnesium and silica).

Since then all branches of natural therapy have acknowledged his genius and most now use his remedies, although some people will only use minerals obtained through inorganic sources. However the rocks, sand and other basic ingredients of the biochemic tissue salts seem natural enough to me.

These tissue salts are triturated (subdivided and spread) to the minutest homeopathic potencies so as to make them instantly acceptable by the cells and directly absorbed by the blood. Therefore their action is immediate, and relief from the symptoms of disease begins directly they are taken. For easy assimilation they are mixed with milk sugar which dissolves quickly on the tongue.

Their function is:
Basically concerned with cell metabolism, which is the changing of inert materials into living cells, the maintenance of their life and the elimination of the waste products. These changes are maintained by biochemic cell salts (the minerals).

To maintain the health of the cells and therefore the body

by supplying the blood, which in turn supplies the cells with these elements. This applies to the tissues, nerves or bony structures of the body.

To be available to the cells in any part of the body to correct an imbalance, which is claimed to be the cause of nearly every disease. Biochemistry explains clearly and logically the cause of diseases and its rational method of combating them. This is an exact science and has been proved by modern research.

To form the basis of bones, the chief solid constituent of muscles, blood cells, nerves etc, and to maintain the acid alkaline balance of the digestive juices and other secretions. Also to distribute oxygen and water throughout the body.

Deficiency symptoms:

These consist of any and every disease, so are obviously too numerous to mention here. However those who are seeking health should buy a biochemic handbook from a health food shop and study it. The larger versions give the correct cell salt for symptoms in every part of the body, including those affecting sleep and mental health.

The study of these tissue salts requires some effort but once you have mastered them, you will never be without them. When you understand them and use them regularly you will find how simple they really are.

Do not be put off by the extravagant extent of their claims. because they are all true, although if you have been long deficient it may take time to put you right.

Don't just buy the one cell salt which you think answers your particular complaint, because you will almost certainly find you need all twelve, and it is fun to experiment and find out how accurate they are in their definitions. Only by trial and error can you learn anything.

Quantity:

These are specifically stated on the bottles and depend on the seriousness of your ailment.

OTHER MINERAL SUPPLEMENTS

There are other mineral supplements available too. Some are made from the mineral-rich rock of the Dolomites, then there are calcium preparations and iron in an easily assimilable form. But the range of individual minerals is not wide, as it is considered better to obtain them from food. There are always the biochemic tissue salts which are the ideal answer to mineral nutrition of the cells, fluids and bones of the body. However if you know you are in need of a certain mineral, ask for it specifically.

SPECIAL SUPPLEMENTS

There are certain special food supplements which have come down through the centuries and which are invaluable to health unless your nutrition is extraordinarily adequate, and even if it is, they improve your well-being. Garlic oil, charcoal, royal jelly and pollen preparations come into this category.

Then there are improved techniques for extracting special elements from food, which include wheat germ oil, desiccated liver, high protein supplements, lecithin, bioflavonoids, concentrated vegetables, enzymes and elixirs. These all use a special part of various foods, or concentrate them, to give you a high potency, special purpose supplement.

This is the treasure house of the health food store, because here you have some of the most powerful health-giving food substances in their natural but concentrated form. There are vitamins, minerals, unsaturated fats and if you can afford to, you would be well advised to take some of all of them every day of your life. There is no better guarantee of good health and the happiness which can come from it.

I take all the vitamins: halibut liver oil (A and D), brewers' yeast (B), additional B Complex ascorbic acid (C), Vitamin E, vegetable oils (F). Added to these I have lecithin, the bioflavonoids and wheat germ oil which are also part of the vitamin group. Minerals I get from kelp and a special calcium-magnesium biochemic preparation, plus biochemically balanced salt (or sea salt) and the 12 biochemic tissue salts (when needed).

That list I consider to be my insurance card for daily health, so that I have to spend no money on doctor's bills or extras from the chemist. If you eat properly and add these to your daily diet, you should have glowing health and save yourself a great deal of money, as well as the misery of being ill. All you need to do is to study this book carefully.

Now let me explain these special supplements in more detail.

GARLIC OIL CAPSULES

These are what they say, the concentrated oil of garlic. The capsules are specially made so that they do not dissolve until well down into your stomach to avoid any possibility of smell.

What it does:

Garlic is nature's antibiotic (together with onions and leeks which are much weaker). Being a natural product there is no limit to the dose and it assists friendly bacteria. Even more important, it has no after-effects like the other antibiotics.

What for:

The immediate effect of garlic oil is to give you a wonderful feeling of well-being.

It is effective against many stomach troubles, and if taken regularly helps to prevent them ever occurring.

It improves digestion and assimilation.

It reduces blood pressure.

It is effective against catarrh and other lung troubles.

It has been used to treat cancer and to try and prevent sea-sickness (by aiding the digestive process).

It was used in the Middle Ages against plague and the Pyramids were built on it (as a prophylactic measure).

It is said to prevent pneumonia, typhus, T.B. and diphtheria.

It has cured colds, bronchitis, asthma and influenza.

It is an intestinal antiseptic for: diarrhoea, colic, some dyspepsias, food poisoning.

As an external ointment for boils, bites and septic wounds.

Quantity:

Three capsules a day is recommended, but you can take as

many as you like quite safely. I usually take one before going to bed.

WHEAT GERM OIL

This is exactly what it says, the cold pressed oil from the germ of wheat, which is where all the goodness lies. Its principal quality is that it has the highest Vitamin E content of any supplement, also some B vitamins, lecithin, unsaturated fatty acids and the undefined germ factor for new life.

What it does:
Wheat germ oil is the great heart tonic by its actions on the heart muscle and blood vessels.

Its oxygen-conserving qualities help prevent fatigue and increases endurance, tone up the muscles (the heart too) and add to your energy.

It is a great rejuvenator and gives a new lease of life.

Diabetes has benefited from it, so has the change-of-life (menopause).

Since E is the sex vitamin, it is a cure for infertility, miscarriage and lack of sexual libido.

There are few states of disease which it will not help, unless fat cannot be tolerated.

Quantity:
One teaspoon a day is effective but three tablespoons are recommended. It rather depends on your pocket.

CHARCOAL

This supplement does not come from the drawing-room fire, but is specially prepared for medicinal purposes.

Man has sensibly learnt a lesson from dogs here, because when they are suffering from impurities, they too eat charcoal.

What it does:
Principally it is taken by people with dyspepsia, but it is also effective in a great many gastric troubles.

Diarrhoea, suspected infection of any part of the digestive

tract, and self-induced problems of digestion, all respond well to charcoal.

Charcoal is said to attract the poisons of digestion and otherwise, which includes purifying the system.

Quantity:

People usually take a tablet after each meal, but if the need is great take more. It can be bought with garlic oil added, which is even more effective, or as biscuits.

LECITHIN

Is a by-product of vegetable oil and is sometimes referred to as the beauty vitamin, although it is not strictly a vitamin. However, since it always occurs together with Vitamin F (the unsaturated fatty acids) and contains two B vitamins (inositol and cholin) from which it is manufactured in the body, it does seem to be essential to health and therefore qualify for the name of vitamin. When oils are processed (hydrogenated) lecithin is removed, as with cereals, where it is contained in the germ (wheat germ and its oil). Eggs, liver, brains, soya beans and sesame seeds are all abundant sources.

What it does:

Lecithin is removed from the oil used in paint-making, otherwise it smears. This same lecithin is then used to emulsify chocolate and sweets (candy) to keep their contents in suspension, and it is used in other industries where oil must be broken down into tiny particles. It does the same thing in the body, breaking down fats to make them useful to us instead of causing us harm. It acts on cholesterol likewise and so prevents heart attacks.

What for:

It is essential for preventing cholesterol or saturated fat from harming the blood vessels or heart. These two substances are not harmful when held in suspension by lecithin.

It serves in a structural capacity to the cells of the brain and nerves.

It forms 30% of the brain and 73% of the liver fat (which also manufactures it).

It is essential to the function of the endocrinal glands (particularly the pituitary, the master gland, and the pineal), also the gonads (sex organs).

It plays a vital role in sex, in all stages of the manufacture of spermatozoa.

Through its homogenizing qualities, it helps to put down a layer of fat under the skin, and therefore prevent eczema as well as enhancing skin beauty.

It has helped diabetes by reducing the amount of insulin needed.

It assists in the production of bile and therefore plays a part in digestion.

It aids liver health by supplying the two B vitamins, inositol and cholin.

For health, vitality and beauty take lecithin, either as a supplement to ensure an adequate supply, or together with another supplement or in food.

Quantity:

Great quantities are not necessary, but enough is vital. One teaspoon of the liquid or granules plus a food source is quite enough (the liquid is the cheapest).

BIOFLAVONOIDS

A symposium held in Russia recently decided that there is no diseased state which is not improved by bioflavonoids. This is because every such state causes weakened capillaries.

The principal source is the peel and pulp of citrus fruit, all brightly coloured fruit, grapes, rose hips, parsley, spinach, cabbage, lettuce, buckwheat. The Swiss have synthetically manufactured a super-strength bioflavonoid called Venoruton P_4 for those who are not averse to chemicals. Natural sources plus Vitamin C can be very effective very quickly.

What it does:

It increases the strength of the capillaries (and their permeability), thereby increasing the body defences at a basic level, for it is here that immunity to disease can be created. It also keeps the collagen (the cementlike substance between cells and tissues) healthy and so the state of the body. Healthy capillaries should prevent viruses from entering the cells and tissues, as well as ensuring waste products are eliminated and nourishing food supplied. The bioflavonoids (rutin, citrin, hesperidin and others) act with Vitamin C to increase its effect.

What for:

It is the most famous cure for varicose veins and haemorrhoids.

It assists all cases of haemorrhage from weakened capillaries, such as nose bleeds, blood spitting, anal bleeding.

It is useful in heart cases too, plus Vitamin C, to help dissolve clots, prevent haemorrhages and strengthen blood vessels.

It is invaluable in drug-taking, which can break down capillaries and therefore cause bleeding (bruises).

It has been given to animals to prevent cancer deliberately induced by bacteria, and to treat weakened capillaries in leukaemia.

Bruises, bleeding gums, poor healing, no resistance to disease are all signs of capillary fragility and need bioflavonoids.

Fevers respond well to bioflavonoids, even flu.

It has prevented miscarriages and bleeding from pernicious anaemia.

It has improved blood pressure from kidney weakness and assisted kidney complaints.

It has been used successfully in diseases ranging from colds to rheumatic fever, coronary thrombosis, arthritis, diabetes, polio, T.B. and respiratory infections.

Quantity:

Any excess is excreted in the urine, as with Vitamin C, so there is no danger in larger doses. It is destroyed by boiling or exposure to the air. Take at least 100–200 units daily, but a great deal more will only add to your health.

DESICCATED LIVER

Is liver dried under vacuum and sold as a powder or tablets.

Its object is to supply all the goodness of liver in concentrated form, therefore it is truly a food supplement.

Its chief elements are Vitamin B_{12}, the other B vitamins not destroyed by heat, Vitamin A, the anti-stress factors and of course protein and many minerals (particularly iron and copper).

Vegetarians sometimes cheat and use this as their source of B_{12} and for all its other exceptional qualities.

It is useful for anaemia, all Vitamin B deficiency diseases, as a source of protein and a boost to health.

If the powder doesn't taste good, mix it with tomato or other vegetable juice or take tablets. Once you have discovered its beneficial effect on your health you will always take it. Very young children can also profitably eat it.

ROYAL JELLY

This is a glandular secretion of the worker bees and meant as food for the queen bee. It makes her grow twice their size and weight, increases her egg-laying capacity and makes her live 5 to 8 years instead of 2 to 6 months like the workers!

This exotic food supplement is said to help cancer patients, normalize weight and reduce fat, regularize bowel movements, increase appetite, improve mental and physical power including sight, reduce nervous tension and bring sleep.

It is manufactured from pollen which is the bees' food.

POLLENS

You have just read about the magic of royal jelly and I see no reason why pollens should not be just as remarkable. Russian scientists discovered pollen to be the active substance in honey as a rejuvenator.

Pollens are a part of several food supplements, such as Biostrath, Elixir, Sleepwell and nerve tonics. All honey contains them.

They are taken for purposes of rejuvenation and sexual

stimulation, also as medicine for gastric disorders, asthma, hay fever and prostate troubles.

DIGESTIVE AIDS

These are all natural products which nature intended us to use for proper digestion. They include:

Enzyme tablets. Some made from papayas or pineapple (two of the highest sources), but there are other sources as well. Enzymes are supplied by all raw vegetables and fruit and are the secret of proper digestion and absorption.

Yogurt culture. This is the substance to make yogurt from. Yogurt will improve your digestion enormously.

Bioflora and others are also natural vegetable products.

HIGH PROTEIN

This is made from natural whole foods and intended for those who suffer from a prolonged deficiency or to ensure an adequate supply. Take as instructed, as too much protein causes acidity and all the complaints that brings.

CONCENTRATED VEGETABLES

It would be difficult to eat all the vegetables you need each day for glowing health, but this is one way of increasing your intake.

They have many uses not only for the health-conscious, but for babies, invalids, travellers, people living alone, the aged, office workers and many others.

HERBAL REMEDIES

These are a subject for a work on its own and they require specialized knowledge. However health food stores are able to advise you and carry stocks of the better-known and most commonly used ones.

There are liquid mixes of herbs as well as dry products and many of them are made up specially for such complaints as:

catarrh, asthma, indigestion, constipation, headaches, haemorrhoids, liver troubles, stomach and nervous ailments, kidney trouble, rheumatism, coughs. Name your complaint and they have the remedy.

The history of these cures goes back thousands of years and there is no doubt of their efficiency, so even if you only have a herbal brew of tea as a trial run, make that effort, because it is all part of building health as well as curing disease.

Cosmetics
Refer to page 209.

Homeopathy
Refer to page 209.

Books
Refer to page 210.

Mechanical Aids
Refer to page 211.

7. Stepping Stones to Health

STEPPING STONES TO HEALTH

Part 1 INDIVIDUAL STEPPING STONES

Why Stepping Stones At all?	255
My Own Steps	256
First Steps	260
The First Step	262
The Second Step	265
The Third Step	268
The Start of the Journey	271
The Rest of the Way	273

Part 2 COMMUNITY STEPPING STONES

The Family	279
The Community	282
The City	285
The Nation	290
The World	295
In Conclusion	298

PART 1

INDIVIDUAL STEPPING STONES

WHY STEPPING STONES AT ALL?

ALTHOUGH I have now written five sections on how to acquire health by natural methods, I have never divulged the stepping stones which are necessary to achieve that end. This I intend to do now.

Health and happiness are, I suppose, the two principal quests of the world at large, yet people mostly associate health with freedom from illness and doctors, in a negative sense, instead of with a progressive and positive way of life which builds health day by day. Happiness they link with eating ice creams, getting drunk or some other equally material pleasure, but seldom with their own peace of mind or the simple delights to be derived from nature. In the other sections I have written about the essential ingredients for health and happiness and explained them; now I must tell you how to approach the problem because people naturally have misgivings when asked to start a new regime, and have no idea where to begin.

Trades and skills we learn from each other and from handbooks written by those who have acquired them. So with the art of being healthy, because it is a skill and must be learnt, it is not enough to know what symptoms are caused by which vitamin or mineral deficiency, one must also know what food to eat to ensure an adequate supply of all the necessary elements of proper nutrition. Then there is the problem of breaking with past habits and maintaining a new-found way of life in face of less enlightened or malicious people. That is the first part of what I have to tell you.

The second is to show you as a householder what you can do for your own household in your search for health and happiness, so that you can all live in an atmosphere which will promote those ends. From there comes the community effort, then that of the city, state or district, so to the nation, then the world. It is not easy to accomplish, any of it, but then one would not expect so great a prize to fall into one's lap for the asking, nor for it to be retained without an effort. However there are short cuts to be had from those who have trodden the path before you and who have blundered on the way, so take this opportunity of discovering those pitfalls, as well as the stepping-stones which were used to make their journey easier.

MY OWN STEPS

Let me begin by telling you my own experience, for I am a rugged individualist who has always had to learn the hard way. But painful though that process has been, it has at least ensured the lessons were properly learnt and understood.

After a third attack of jaundice I realized I might never again feel well enough to enjoy life as I had, and under those circumstances I was not prepared to go on living. Therefore I had to find out how to regain my health, because the doctors had said there was nothing more they could do for me. This is a very common story, in fact it is the one which has been mainly responsible for the emergence of the health food trade. Every day sick people come into health food shops desperately imploring the proprietor to help them as they have been given up by their doctors, or should I say more accurately, the doctors have not known how to make them well again. Taught as they are to treat disease at germ level instead of to build health as a cure and prophylactic measure, when their latest drugs do not produce the right results most doctors either resort to the knife or tell their patients there is no longer anything wrong with them.

Those with the will to live and the character to ensure they do, realize that these drug-dispensing practitioners have been misled and that with all the goodwill in the world they simply do not possess the knowledge to put them right, so they look round for a different approach. Quite naturally they end up by taking the advice and the remedies of those who treat the cause of disease and not its manifestations, because those are the people who can make them permanently healthy again.

However the unfortunate part about the new advice is that it means eliminating from their diet and their life certain harmful foods and habits which people find extremely hard to do. Consequently they follow the next best course which is to take vitamin, mineral and other food supplements to replace those elements which have been processed out of food. Usually it works, if they are persistent enough, but it means taking all the vitamins, not just one, and ensuring their intake of minerals covers the complete spread. Then they must also eat a minimum amount of raw food, if only for the enzymes, and eliminate all drugs from their medicine chest.

You may think all this sounds very easy, but it is not. If you live alone, as I have for a number of years, your problems will be fewer, but still you will need fortitude to persist with a regime which entails going against the fashions rather than with them. That is why I have subdivided this section into different parts, because it is not just an individual problem nor even one for the household, it belongs to the district where you live and to the country of which you are a citizen, indeed to the world as a whole. Of course as a start we must believe that our rulers have the improved health of the world at heart and that their intention is not to drug us through our ills, but effect a cure. Given this premise, let me tell you more about how I tackled this problem.

'There's nothing more I can do for you,' said my doctor. 'You no longer have jaundice, because if you did you would be dead, and I can find nothing seriously wrong with your liver. If you want some good advice, go away and eat lots of first-class protein to regenerate your liver.'

I thanked him and wondered whether to say I still did not feel very well or very strong, but there seemed little point and anyway he must have seen my eyes were still slightly yellow. What I did ask him was, 'What exactly is first-class protein?'

'Duck and grouse, salmon, fillet steak and all that sort of thing,' he replied.

My face sagged, for I was poor, as indeed I still am. When I returned to where I was staying I was delighted to find some copies of the *Encyclopaedia Britannica*, so I set about investigating first-class protein. That night I went to bed much relieved to know that milk (even dried milk), cheese, soya beans, almonds and other nuts, eggs, fish, organ meats (liver, kidneys, etc), yogurt, certain seeds and vegetables also qualify as first-class protein, although it had taken me most of the night to extract this information.

In those days health food shops had hardly come into their own and there had not been much publicity about their value to health, so my next step did not lead me immediately there. Instead I told my friends about my ignorance over protein and found that they too did not know such a simple basic fact of life. This made me wonder: why did people in England who were supposed to have had a good education not know these things? Obviously because they were not taught them.

I reached for the *Encyclopaedia Britannica* again and tried to find out why first-class protein was supposed to be so good for my liver. After a week of study I was not much nearer the answer, although I had learnt something about amino acids (of which protein is composed) and their individual role in nutrition. I was angry to be so frustrated in my quest for knowledge about what to eat for health, even from such sources as public libraries and medical books. So, for the first few months after being told I was alright but knowing perfectly well I was not, I followed the advice I had been given and ate my fill of first-class protein. I gorged myself on meat and eggs, cheese, milk and fish, little knowing that the nitrogen and other waste products from excess protein have to be eliminated by means of the liver and kidneys, otherwise they can contribute towards rheumatism and many other diseases.

So my first piece of nutritional advice was of doubtful value, in fact it was useless because I did not know how to turn it to my advantage. Proper nutrition is not just a question of eating sufficient protein, even though protein is the only food element which can sustain life on its own. However I was now aware that my salvation lay through what I ate, even if I did not have the least idea where to turn next.

Fortunately I have many good friends and equally fortunately I discuss my troubles with them. Their first response was to suggest I read a health magazine called *Prevention* which is put out by an American organization under the auspices of J. I. Rodale. From this journal I gleaned my first piece of vital information: that white sugar and white flour are the cause of most illness today because of what has been extracted from them to make them white. Natural cane sugar and other sugar sources, whole wheat and other whole grains contain all the necessary food elements to make digestion possible, but when refined and concentrated create most frightening and accumulative deficiency diseases. Armed with this piece of information and many other copies of *Prevention* I went abroad for a winter's writing.

But how to give up white flour and white sugar? That was quite another question, because I used to half-fill my cup of tea or coffee with sugar and practically everything I ate contained white flour, often combined with white sugar: cakes, biscuits, bread, rolls, etc. I considered my meals and found them all to be offending and everything I ate between them even worse. If I was going to dispense with white sugar and white flour it meant completely reorganizing my meals, and then adhering to a new plan. Firstly I had to know with what to replace the offending items, and secondly I had to have the strength of mind to put the plan into practice.

Nonetheless it was from these beginnings that I cured myself, not only of a seriously impaired liver but of all the other ailments I suffered from as well. I did not do so in the first winter nor in the first year, in fact it took five years or more to reach a high degree of health, and even now I find that by taking new natural health remedies I can still improve what seems to be otherwise perfect health.

This winter for example, I have set out to recolour my hair by biochemic methods and to rejuvenate my glands and other internal organs in the same way. The improvement is clearly visible and as a by-product I have achieved other things as well. That is the way to build health through nature cure, it is not done in a day or even a week; it may take many months to get results but once they begin the process is continuous. Now let me describe the steps I took to achieve this end.

FIRST STEPS

Fortunately my choice of winter quarters was not only one of the most beautiful islands, but also somewhere I could buy the fresh fruit and vegetables I so badly needed, a place where nature has not quite yet been perverted. That first winter in Madeira proved the turning-point in my life, and it was accomplished with little more than the raw materials which this charming island has to offer, plus the knowledge that it was necessary to eliminate processed foods from my diet.

The result of the winter's programme were spectacular. From a certain part of my body a group of warts suddenly disappeared, plaques of cholesterol vanished from my face and elsewhere, my weight decreased by more than twenty pounds and my ribs and neck became visible, as did the contours of my face. These were immediate results, more appeared as I progressed: cuts healed quickly and provided they were kept clean never went septic, scars began to soften and after I had learnt to rub them with Vitamin E some completely disappeared, blackheads ceased to exist and the enlarged pores reverted to normal smooth skin, the rest of my skin became soft and very slightly moist instead of hard, thick and dry, the sparkle returned to my eyes as did their whiteness, joints no longer creaked, digestion and absorption became superb and I had more energy than I knew what to do with.

I will not go into the exact remedies I took this first winter in Madeira because at this stage it is not necessary; it is enough to know that by eliminating white flour and white sugar from my diet and by taking vitamin and mineral supplements I had wrought these changes. This is the starting-point for anyone who is ill or suffering from degenerative diseases, for no real or lasting improvement can be achieved without the elimination of the causes of vitamin and mineral deficiencies, nor can it take place unless these deficiencies are filled.

It is perhaps worth adding here that in disease, whether degenerative or otherwise, vitamin and mineral supplements must be taken in drug doses (i.e. large quantities) to fill the deficiencies before a complete cure can be effected. Whole, unprocessed, natural food, preferably eaten raw, will help the return to normal health, but long-standing deficiencies take time to fill. European nutrition still has not entirely accepted this fact, although the Americans have been working miracles by these methods for years.

I myself have proved this point over and over again particularly with Vitamin B Complex. If the person's inherent need for a particular vitamin is exceptionally high or their condition exceptionally low, the deficiency cannot be said to have been filled until the whole body and mind are working in harmony, as nature intended, which may take years.

So the first step to health is to educate yourself about what to eat and what to eliminate from your diet, and to discover exactly which vitamin and mineral supplements you must take to fill your deficiencies. That must always be the first step if you have been living on the normal Western diet of processed food, which has been devitalized and robbed of its vital balancing factors in the factories.

The Hunzas in the Himalayas, the Georgians in Russia, a large number of Chinese and certain other people who live close to nature have no need for this first step because they do not impoverish their food or their bodies by trying to outdo nature. By instinct, by trial and error and by sensitivity, they know what is good for them and those around them. You too must acquire that knowledge before you can begin to be healthy or happy. By taking just an occasional vitamin or mineral supplement you will not get far. You cannot wet a sponge with a drip of water, it needs a bucketful, nor can you rejuvenate by half-measures a body which has gradually degenerated throughout its life.

Although food is only one aspect of health, or happiness for that matter, it is the essential one because the workings of the body depend on the blood supply which consists of what you eat and what you absorb from that food. There is no other alternative, no substitution, that is where your health begins or ends; it can make you or break you, give you glorious, glowing well-being or reduce you to a frightened, schizophrenic, sour, neurotic mess. It is as important as that, so heed these words now and learn the steps which only you can take.

THE FIRST STEP

The first step is always the most difficult because you have to make a decision to undertake the journey at all, quite apart from preparing yourself to take it or finally setting out. This usually means breaking with a life-time habit of eating, learning from a nutritionist or some health books exactly what your diet should be and then having the courage and strength of character actually to put it all into practice. Many people dream about such a step and have visions of the prize at the end, but not so many actually do anything about it. That is why I am writing this section, to help you take those first few difficult steps and then lead you on to the open road to health. I have done it myself, and I have watched numerous other people also do it with varying degrees of success, so I know how difficult it can be.

The decision to tackle one's health through nature cure is usually forced upon one by the inability of the medical profession to help one throw off some fairly serious disease. It is nearly always in desperation that people turn to the health food shops for a cure. Now that is all very well, but it is not the job of health food shops to take over from there. How could they possibly treat all their customers as individual patients and guide them on their way to health? They do give a lot of advice and they are tremendously helpful, but their advice is uncoordinated and they are not always qualified to hand out the information people require.

So the first step to take, when you find you are committed to the natural road to health, is to educate yourself in the requirements of this new life. To do so you must read some books, buy some of the health journals and if possible consult a reliable authority on the subject. All this is a major undertaking and cannot be accomplished in a few days, or even a few weeks. It is the complete study of a subject which will probably take you years to understand fully. Therefore to help you overcome what must seem a nearly insurmountable barrier between you and nature's road to health, I have these proposals to make.

Since the first step is such a big one, a short cut must be

found to enable you to participate immediately in a regime which is really very simple, but which requires such a major change in your routine. As there is no difference of opinion on the basic principles of nutrition nor upon the dangers of eating processed food, this is the place you must begin and I will now set out very simply what it is you have to do.

The Don'ts
White flour and white sugar or anything made from them must never under any circumstances be eaten. This is the first golden rule. Both these foods have been so impoverished during the process of refinement that it is impossible for your body to digest them without robbing it of all the nutriments which were refined out of them in the factory. The result is that you suffer permanently from deficiency diseases through a lack of these elements. Some people are worse than others because they eat more white flour and white sugar and less of the foods which help to compensate by supplying these deficient elements, such as liver, kidneys, eggs, unpasteurized milk, yogurt, nuts and seeds, fresh, raw fruit and vegetables.

But even if you do eat large quantities of these compensating foods you will never be completely healthy, and most likely frequently ill, if you continue to eat white flour or white sugar in any form. The white sugar will almost certainly give you heart disease and rotten teeth, also diabetes, skin troubles, bad nerves, constipation, lack of energy and a serious deficiency of all the B vitamins. You will therefore be prone to every disease and a candidate for an early grave. The white flour will play havoc with your digestion and all diseases eminating from the digestive tract, quite apart from making you fat and waterlogged.

This is just a beginning of your troubles, because your body finds it impossible to work even remotely efficiently if it has to compete with these two unnatural, devitalized, semi-foods which are as dangerous as many poisons, drugs or putrefactive foods. No lasting degree of health can ever be maintained while these foods are eaten, nor can any disease be permanently cured.

So whatever else you do or do not do, white flour and white

sugar must immediately be struck from your shopping list. That equally applies to anything made from them. This is your first step and by far the most important, because just by giving up these two you really can regain your health – or at least a greater part of it – over a period of time.

The Do's
Having eliminated the two most lethal foods from your diet you must now take some positive steps. Start by only buying fresh food for your larder, never have anything that has been processed or interfered with in any way (no tinned, dehydrated or packaged food). If you can also go one stage further and eat at least 2/3 of your diet raw (fruit and vegetables, nuts and seeds, unpasteurized milk and yogurt, cheese, etc) so much the better.

By following these instructions you will be helping your body to fill its deficiencies and so regain your normal state of health. You will not be doing all that is necessary to follow the paths of nature cure nor to eliminate the cause of disease, but as a first step you will be making it possible over a period of time. You will also be doing something that is agreed upon by all the various branches of nature cure whether it be herbalism, homeopathy, biochemistry, osteopathy or general nutrition. All of them sound a warning against denatured foods, in particular against the two most pernicious and widely eaten, white flour and white sugar.

These two instructions should be quite simple and straightforward. I am not going to suggest that either of them are easy to put into practice, but then the first step is only to discover what you have to do. All you have done so far is to save yourself making a study of nutrition and then having to work out your own course of action from that. However you are being asked to consider doing something with which everyone in the field of nature cure agrees, although most of them would go a great deal further.

So read and re-read these Do's and Don'ts, learn them by heart and think about what it means to eliminate these foods from your diet and to add others to it. Learn to recognize processed food and shun it automatically. Know that any food which has been added to or taken away from by the hand of man is called processed, and therefore deficient in some of its vital elements which it must steal from your body to enable digestion to take place.

Also never forget that it is the enzymes in raw food which do a lot of the digesting for you and therefore make it valuable to you by absorption, quite apart from the vitamins and minerals which are retained in their entirety because they have not been heat-treated or thrown away with the cooking water. However even if you do cook some food, if you eat only what is whole in itself you will absorb most of the elements which are necessary for health.

THE SECOND STEP

When people are called upon to make decisions they tend to put them off until they are forced to do so. In this particular case I am asking you to read what I have had to say first, in other words to educate yourself, at least partially, in the demands of proper nutrition and healthy living before doing anything else. After that will obviously come a period of thought while you deliberate on what I have said and see how you can apply these words to your own daily life. This will be the crucial time because it is when you will be making up your mind about whether it is possible for you to do as I have suggested or not, also whether my ideas seem to answer your own problem.

You will be faced with deciding whether you can suddenly throw out of your life bread, cakes, biscuits, pastry, spaghetti and all forms of pasta, pizza and other flour-containing foods, as well as sugar and all the dishes to which it is added, such as ice-cream, jam, sweets, biscuits, cakes and practically every sort of pudding which comes out of the kitchen. You may be wondering what else there is left to eat if you do dispense with these foods, and I fully appreciate how you feel. I too was faced with exactly the same problem. How, if you dispense with these items, are you going to get enough to eat?

The short answer is that practically everything you eat turns to sugar, by one method or another, so there is no need to worry about ditching white sugar or its products from your diet.

White flour contains hardly anything worth eating anyway by the time it has been refined, bleached and robbed of most of its vitamins, minerals and special factors, so what little nourishment you might have been getting from this source can be obtained ten times over from natural, whole foods. Of course you can eat whole wheat flour, in any form you like, that is good for you. The dangerous stuff is white flour. Whole grain flour does little harm to those who take enough exercise to work it off, and anyway for many it has to be the staff of life. So it can be, if all the goodness is not taken out of it in the refining process.

Now I realize I still have not answered your question: you are worried by the fact that if you take white sugar, white flour and their products out of your diet you will not have enough to eat. What is even worse is that if you dispense with sugar and flour you will find yourself extremely hungry and you will blame it on me and accuse me of telling lies. The truth is that sugar and flour both take away your appetite, the latter because it digests so slowly, the former because it deluges your internal organs with its unnatural source of food, but an excess of any carbohydrate does the same thing. For this reason sugar and flour are useful to those who cannot afford to eat properly, although after the effects have worn off they feel just as hungry as they did before. However they can afford to satiate themselves again with these cheap foods and assuage their hunger once more. So it goes on.

For you the problem is presumably different, because you know that all fruit and vegetables contain sugar in its natural and most beneficial state. You also know that other carbohydrate which comes from nuts and seeds, legumes and other fruit and vegetable sources also turns to sugar and can do you nothing but good. These are the foods you must eat to become healthy, all of which you can find in their natural state as live foods not dead ones, as food with the spark of life still left in it, its survival factors still intact.

Soya beans and soya flour, brewers' yeast, almonds, walnuts and other sorts of nuts, pumpkin seeds, sesame seeds and other sorts of seeds, these are foods of the highest quality, supplying protein, fat (vegetable) and carbohydrate. There is no need to eat meat if you have these, but if you do, have lots of liver and kidneys, four or five eggs a week only, milk (unpasteurized), yogurt, a small amount of cheese, meat and fish in moderation, also fowl and game.

There is heaps left to eat, as you see. 'But,' you may say, 'these are all too expensive.' Not if you buy them in season and fill in during the winter with dried fruit such as dates, raisins, figs, prunes and apricots, also honey. If that is still not enough, then you must resort to small amounts of brown rice and whole wheat flour and its products, but see they are not overdone. Substitute vegetable oil for animal fat, have olive, corn, sunflower, soya, safflower oils instead of lard, margarine, butter or dripping. Try never to fry food, it makes it difficult to digest and the heated fat can become harmful.

As well as disposing of white flour and white sugar, try also to resist the temptation of falling back on any other processed food, its incompleteness makes you, too, incomplete and thus causes disease. What has been added to it in the way of preservatives, colourings, artificial flavourings and sweeteners are chemically detrimental to your health and sometimes even directly poisonous. But it is what has been taken away from them to make them keep which really signs your death warrant, because that spark of life which has been extracted from them must be found from inside you.

Don't be under any illusion, incomplete food is incomplete, what the manufacturers take away when they process it is the very substance which will keep it alive (that is why they take it out or else it would not keep), and a lack of it will also kill you. Only buy food that will go bad after a short time, food that still has the spark of life left in it, and eat it before that dies. Vital, living foods, full of the sun's rays and the earth's minerals and vitamins are the only ones which can keep you, too, vital and alive.

Now I hope I have done your thinking for you. I have tried to answer your questions as you went along and I hope I have satisfied any misgivings you may have had. So now, if you are ready to take the decision, do so while you understand how much good can come from it and do not wait till you are ill in bed and then wish you had done so before. To decide, you simply have to say to yourself: 'There is no other way of permanently curing my ills and ensuring good health for the rest of my life. I have tried the other methods and they have failed me. Now I am left with no other choice than to live as nature intended me to live, and so regain the health I was born with.' That is all you need to do, now it is just a question of putting it into practice.

THE THIRD STEP

You have been given the facts about nutrition, if only the barest outline, and I have answered your queries as you went along. You should therefore have no more doubts and you should know exactly what to do to turn your decision into action, so what is the force that will finally make you act?

What usually makes people want to live and take the necessary action is the sight of death. When they see their own grave they begin to appreciate life, because life and death go together, the one has no meaning without the other, and to meet death is one of the qualifications of learning to live. Should the clammy hand of the grave not have beckoned to you so far, you may have noticed some other ugly sign to warn you that you are going the wrong way: some incurable disease or a degenerative one increasing as the days go by.

Could you be so unwise as not to heed the first warning of disaster or so insensitive as not to feel the impending doom? Is it not enough that I have told you in simple language what you can do to alter your course from dying to living, from degeneration to building positive health, from sickness to the prevention of disease, from the miseries of being ill to the joy of living? If you have the will to live and to get well, surely you will take this chance of doing so.

Tonight perhaps, before you go to bed, you will put out what you are going to have for breakfast and you may have made a plan for what you will be eating at lunch. You may decide to go on having an egg for breakfast, but instead of bread, butter and marmalade to have some fruit and to begin with some muesli and milk. That is a start. Of course you could eat some oranges or other fruit first, then have liver or kidneys, even some cold chicken or salmon or grilled fish;

perhaps some dates or prunes, raisins or figs would end off the meal well.

But none of this really matters, all that is important is that you should not eat anything to do with white flour or white sugar, nor any processed food out of a tin or packet, which is dead. You can eat any other food you like; there is no food you cannot eat providing it comes to you as it was grown, vital living food, not dead and embalmed.

At lunchtime, if you have it at work, ask if the vegetables are fresh and say you would prefer fresh fruit instead of pudding, you could even have a small piece of cheese with it. Then when you get home at night try making yourself a salad of raw vegetables dressed with three or four vegetable oils previously mixed together in a bottle. Don't take any salt with it, nor any lemon, and if you can afford to, mix the pulp of an avocado into the dressing. After that, you might like to try mashing up two large bananas (or several small ones) with a dessertspoon each of soya flour. That is a meal in itself but a vegetarian one. If you do not like that you can have anything else you wish, providing it is fresh, in fact you can eat as you ate before with the exception of processed food, white flour and white sugar; it is really quite easy.

Now I realize the breaking of habits is a hard process and the first is the hardest of the lot, but once you have broken one the next will be easier, and so on, till you are complete master of your own mind. Unfortunately the first habit I have asked you to break is an addiction also, that of white sugar. It is a drug in all senses of the word and almost as harmful, so you will need to have at hand some kind of sop for when the craving overtakes you: dates, prunes, figs, raisins or sultanas will supply the sweetness you crave and their sugar is natural, whole and unrefined. Honey mixed with fruit juice or even ordinary water would also answer the need. Molasses is not so good, as it contains so much refined sugar together with its goodness, but ordinary fresh fruit will fill a gap if you feel hungry.

To occupy the space left by the white flour which used to be churning round for so long in your stomach I suggest you take extra large helpings of vegetables, preferably raw. If that does not work ask your health food shop for the biochemic tissue salts Calc Phos and Mag Phos. These may stop your craving for sweetness and take the edge off your hunger by ensuring you are properly nourished (i.e. by seeing your food is all absorbed and digested). Both of these are perfectly natural minerals, they have been used with success in obesity and to cure that hungry feeling immediately after eating.

If you are successful in destroying these two habits of white flour and white sugar, and in overcoming your desire for unnaturally tasty processed foods, you will be on the road to health. All that remains now is that you should make a routine of your new style of eating. Unfortunately routine is necessary if one is to accomplish anything, it need not be rigid, but it must be routine. So work out how much of the various foods you are going to need for a week or half a week, then decide where you can buy them best and cheapest. Keep the more perishable fruit and vegetables in the fridge. See if you can obtain a supply of unpasteurized milk and learn to make your own yogurt, it is very easy to do. Find out which butcher supplies the freshest liver and kidneys and who sells free-range eggs, then you are nearly set to go.

In these days of mass-production it is best to buy your vegetable oils at a health food shop, as also your dried fruit (to ensure they are not sulphur-cured). From the same shop you may have to get eggs, also your yogurt and possibly unpasteurized milk. Your local health food shop will be invaluable to you in other ways as well, because they stock all the vitamins, minerals, herbs and biochemic cures you will need, but more about that later.

By now you should be doing what I have suggested because I have shown you how. It is not difficult to apply the decision to your daily life. Maybe you will need to be strong-minded if you meet some opposition, but if you are already acquainted with the sight of your grave you will be, for others the prize of glowing health is enough. So now you are on the road to health I must wish you luck and a happy journey.

THE START OF THE JOURNEY

Now that you have successfully used the stepping-stones to start on the road to health you should not go wrong, unless of course you come to the conclusion that having made a successful change in diet you will automatically become healthy and so revert to some of your old ways. The road to health is not a very broad one, and there are many tantalizing turnings off it for those without the strength or the will to go straight on. So beware, because the bare outlines which I have given you are literally the bare outlines; you cannot pick and choose among the suggestions. The fact is that processed food is all incomplete and natural food nearly all properly balanced, so this must be your guideline.

However, outside this, there are certain other suggestions I have to make which will help you go on to strength, for health is a continuous process, you do not achieve it and then stay there. From illness or even from indifferent health you progress to health, building it day by day until you have freed yourself from disease. After that you must continue to progress, otherwise you slip back and you can never achieve any real degree of health.

So do not stop trying to improve your health, always be experimenting and learning something new, because I have only put you on the road to health, you have not achieved it yet. Also do not forget there are many degrees of health, because people feel well when they no longer feel ill, but that does not mean they are either healthy or well. In the same way it is always difficult to convince people that they are suffering from the most appalling symptoms of degenerative diseases because they cannot actually see inside themselves.

Therefore, once you have taken these first three important steps, continue along the road to health because it offers such enormous rewards if you will only persevere. Always be improving on your methods as you go, for although health is achieved and maintained by eating only whole food as nature intended, there are other contributing factors as well. For example there is never any need to drink (either wine or water) if you are completely healthy and properly nourished and have a healthy mind (which means a satisfactory emotional life). But perhaps I ought to be more specific.

Whole food you already know about and processed food I have explained. If you eat the former and forego the latter you should be properly nourished and thus you will not need to drink water. A large percentage of food is water and the body is designed to retain a reserve for emergencies. However if you must drink do not do so at meals, it only dilutes your valuable digestive juices. The same with salt, if you find you cannot live without it, take a very little between meals mixed with some water, and be sure it is sea salt or biochemic.

However proper food does not by itself produce perfect health unless combined with enough fresh air, exercise, sunshine and a healthy mind. When I say fresh air I do not mean you have to spend your whole day in it, but that you should get enough to give you the oxygen without which your body cannot function for many minutes. Exercise is equally important, so if you sit all the time at work, walk at least part of the way to the office and play some outdoor games at the weekend. Sunshine too plays its part, not just for the Vitamin D but for its mental effect also, because the mind needs relaxation which in turn relaxes the body.

A healthy mind is not so easy to accomplish as a healthy body, but it can be done, given time and patience. The mind's effect upon the body is mostly through the emotions and emotions are an agitation of the mind or feelings, or an excited mental state (*Concise Oxford*), so your answer is to keep calm no matter what the circumstances. Never underestimate the power of the mind over the body, because the body is in fact no more than the slave of the mind, which it blindly obeys. At the slightest behest of the mind, the body sickens and will not recover until it is told to do so.

But that is not the end of the story, it is simply the beginning, because I have only so far given you the vehicle in which to make your journey, the rest you must do yourself. So do not imagine that what I have told you so far is more than that, you still have to make the journey and there are numerous ways of accomplishing it, depending exactly where it is you want to end up.

THE REST OF THE WAY

The rest of the journey is comparatively simple, providing you have taken the trouble to prepare yourself properly and you have a good car. Both of these I have attempted to arrange for you by giving you the outlines of a diet as well as a way of life. With these as a basis you will begin to improve in health daily and as soon as they become a habit you should try out some new ideas, because people will continually tell you of the wonderful things which they have done to themselves with this or that. Now I do not want to throw cold water on what they may recommend but let me get in first, so that you will be better able to judge if their ideas fit in with what is accepted practice.

The first suggestion may well be to become a Vegan and eat only raw food. There is no sounder piece of advice and no better way to improve your health as a lasting measure, but you must read something about vegetarianism before you do. There are certain facts you must know, otherwise you will ruin your health in a few years. Vitamin B_{12} is a must for Vegans so may be a small amount of sea salt, otherwise you develop anaemia.

Raw food provides you with nature's enzymes which are otherwise killed in the process of cooking; it also ensures an adequate intake of minerals and vitamins, some of which are likewise affected by heat or get thrown down the drain in the cooking water. Raw fruit and vegetables, nuts and seeds, unpasteurized milk and honey offer you an abundance of all the most valuable food elements and more than enough protein, fat and carbohydrate to live on. Meat, fish and eggs are not for Vegans and anyway are best not eaten raw unless you are an expert in such things and know the history of what you are about to eat. But do become a Vegan, there is no better way to health. I am one and can strongly recommend it.

Vitamin supplements are the next item sure to come your way, so learn the facts about them before you start to use them. If you are ill you will have to take certain vitamins and minerals in large doses to regain your health, as small amounts will not do any good. The more natural the vitamin the better it is likely to be, but some may have to be taken as synthetic preparations of which ascorbic acid (Vitamin C) and Vitamin B Complex (if enough individual B vitamins are included in the right proportions) are both alright. Vitamins A and D are combined well in halibut or cod liver oil and Vitamin E is contained in wheat germ oil and other vegetable sources. The bioflavonoids (part of the Vitamin C group) are excellent concentrated from natural sources.

Food supplements can be extremely useful, particularly in the case of illness when larger than usual amounts of certain foods are advisable. Garlic oil capsules are marvellous as an intestinal antiseptic, and act as nature's antibiotic. Wheat germ oil has cured many heart complaints, retarded diabetes, restored fertility, normalized metabolism, renewed sexual vigour, assisted piles and rejuvenated many old people. Kelp has prevented thyroid gland disaster and all the associated complaints. Charcoal tablets assist in digestive troubles and intestinal disorders.

Then there are enzymes, cultures for intestinal flora, desiccated liver, pollen, royal jelly, concentrated vegetables, plant milk, quite apart from all the organically grown foods which almost qualify as food supplements. There are many others as well, and usually they are to be highly recommended if the manufacturer is at all reputable. Read *About Health Foods* for further information.

Biochemic remedies are the best way of solving your mineral problems, either as tissue salts for instant action or as specially prepared mineral supplements for long-standing deficiencies. I cannot speak too highly of these products because I have tried nearly all of them and also observed their effects on other people. I am convinced beyond doubt that their unbelievably extravagant claims are completely accurate and true, and providing the body is not excessively acid will always work. Their application needs a lot of study and a great deal of trial and error, but the more you experiment with them the more amazing do you find the results.

Homeopathy never really crossed my path until a homeopathic friend found a cure for my cystitis. Inflamed urinary tract is no easy complaint to cure but this is what the essence of nasturtium flowers and another homeopathic remedy succeeded in doing for me. I have tried other preparations and found them to be equally effective, although it is possible that others less healthy than me may take longer to react; in fact some may be so clogged with toxins and wastes that nothing will work until these are at least partly cleaned out. Nonetheless it is always worth trying.

Herbal remedies are as old as man and not only include the lesser-known herbs but also common vegetables like beetroot, parsley and rose hips. There is no doubt that their claims are correct, but as time has passed so much more has been discovered about healing disease by other natural methods that herbs are best employed in conjunction with them. But do as the herbalists instruct you for the most satisfactory results.

You may also be recommended to fast, which is one of the first-aid treatments of nature cure. Many incredible cures have been effected at health farms and clinics by fasting, but people are rightly frightened of conducting a fast on their own, although a four or five day fast on water only is safe enough. Another idea to improve your health immeasurably is to fast once a week on fruit only; this is what I do myself and I cannot speak too highly of the results. Oranges probably clean the system best but any other fruit would do as well (except bananas) taken three times a day (as many as you wish).

Osteopathy I mention only in passing because it is not something I have tried myself, but there are some clever and talented people employing their skills in this remarkable science, and if you find the right person to minister to the right complaint you could do no better.

These are some of the suggestions which will pass your way during the remainder of your journey along the road to health, and as you can see, most of them are useful ones. Of them all I would put raw food nutrition first because this is the way to get the maximum goodness out of your food and nutrition is the permanent remedy for your health.

Next come the vitamin, mineral and food supplements because there is no doubt that after a certain age and even before, these can make the difference between health and disease as well as preventing it in the future. You need not take them in vast quantities when you are well, but always have them at hand and use them as soon as you need to. Also experiment with them to find out the extent of their powers and your failings.

The same applies to biochemic remedies as to supplements and if possible more so, because one's daily balance of minerals varies, and once you have learnt how to use them you will always be able to correct deficiencies. Since their action is practically instantaneous there is no reason why you should not always be in the prime of health. Homeopathy is mostly useful in case of sickness but herbal preparations can be taken daily as a prophylactic measure. Fasting is best employed as part of your daily life where it keeps the balance in your weekly routine, like the weekend's rest and relaxation: physiologicaally fasting performs that same task with your vital organs and to a degree your mind. Never underestimate a weekly fruit fast, it can make the difference between super-health or just health, even between the appreciation of living and just an insensitive monotony.

But in spite of all these super-remedies and their natural cures, one always comes back to food as the basic provider of health, although of course all these are in fact food by a different name. So your diet is what you must concentrate on and strive to improve. From the very early beginnings of meals without white sugar and white flour or their products you must progress.

Next maybe you will cull out some of the excess starch such as potatoes, or have them only once a week. Then perhaps you might decide to be a vegetarian for a while to see how it suits you. To begin with you might give up meat, fish and chicken but retain eggs and dairy produce, then after finding out how well that works dispense with even those.

You will obviously have to include nuts and seeds, brewers' yeast and soya bean products to make up your protein, as well as being careful to see that you get enough calories, and at this stage it would probably be wise to weigh out your protein foods and calculate the calories in your average daily diet. It is important to check that you are getting enough of both.

You may finally decide that cooking does nothing for your food except destroy some of its most important elements and so undertake raw food eating. It is best to learn from others how that is done, although it is not so difficult to discover for yourself if you are only eating fruit and vegetables, nuts and seeds, brewers' yeast and soya flour, vegetable oils and possibly yogurt. However a diet like this requires the inclusion of a reliable Vitamin B_{12} supplement, and also 4 grams of sea or biochemic salt daily (one bare level teaspoon). Having refined your diet to this degree you will possibly want to ensure you do not eat an excess of food which only creates toxic wastes and has to be eliminated, so try to streamline your meals to the exact requirements. This is easily done with a table of food values, weighing scales and a nutrition book.

But even when you have reached this stage you cannot stop, you must always be adding to or taking away from your diet and the supplements and biochemics which go with it. I am suggesting for example that you might want to try a year's course of Vitamin E therapy or then again a year without any supplements at all. There are other natural remedies which need a year or even more to prove their worth and by the time you have tried them all it might be time to think of retiring from this world and taking your place elsewhere. So the job of improving your health is never complete.

All through the journey you will have to fight against those who disapprove of what you are doing and who fear you because you want the world to be a better place. Idealists of whatever brand are a nuisance to those who want their own way, but it is essential they should be tolerated because they do no lasting harm and supply a safety valve.

So now I have told you all there is space to say in this short section about the road to health. It should be enough to make your journey possible and after all, this book is only the first of many you will read to improve your knowledge. Once you have taken the first few steps and gone a short way up the road the rest of the journey is no problem. The difficult part is the beginning, which is why I have offered you these stepping-stones to health.

PART 2

COMMUNITY STEPPING STONES

THE FAMILY

THE problems of health, or happiness for that matter, are not only an individual responsibility but ones which concern us all, for whilst only the individual can accomplish it, the community of which he is a member can help to make it possible or impossible. We are seeing this at the moment when the world has suddenly become aware of its environment and is trying to prevent the mass pollution of land, sea and air by industry and private citizens. This is the negative aspect of what I want to write about now, but there is also a positive side from which we can all draw happiness instead of distress, so let us pursue it further.

We must start where we all began, in the bosom of our families, because from the milk of our mothers' breasts came our first nourishment, without which we should not have made a start at all. The quality of that first mouthful of food and the ones which followed made a big difference to how we developed later on, both physically and mentally. No one would deny that. It is also clear that those who are breast-fed for the longest period in their infancy not only receive a better physical base but have an emotional stability which other children lack. From this security they have the basis for happiness and health. I am not suggesting it is the only criterion or that it will necessarily bring either of these rewards, but the odds are stacked in your favour. So this is the first contribution parents can make towards the health and happiness of their children.

The next is to realize that the cells of all animate objects have an inborn intelligence, just as the objects themselves, although sometimes I think parents do not realize this as I watch them forcing food down their children's throats and behaving as though they knew better than the child itself. The same goes for laughter and tears, love and rage and the whole way we develop our physical and emotional character. Of course those who are disciplined stand a better chance of being happy and those who are self-disciplined of being healthy as well. That, however, does not mean we have no right to say no when our instinct demands it or that we should not be granted that right. Denied it, we can never properly develop.

Next there is the ambiance into which we are born, something akin to the type of soil in which a grain of corn first finds itself embedded to grow its roots and draw its sustenance. For what you are, your children will become and the world you create for them within your home will be their standpoint and their grounding for life. If it is cheerful, gay and happy, they will be laughing, carefree children who are an asset to the community and a pleasure to meet. If not, they may be the delinquent, problem children whom the world is best without.

On the physical side obviously their food is of the first importance. This is something over which you have direct, if not ultimate control, because although you can bring what is good and nourishing to your table, you cannot guarantee its contents. Of course you could compost your garden and use dung, as well as grow most of your own vegetables and fruit, which would not only save money but ensure that they were properly grown. You might even keep your own chickens and allow them free range together with the natural complement of a cock. Then you could also have a goat or perhaps a cow if you lived in the country, so you would hardly need to go outside your garden for your food, as well as making certain of its nutritive value.

Outside these suggestions there are some don'ts which every family should enforce. First is the candy habit. It is as bad to addict your children to the unnatural taste of white sugar as it is to give them drugs, and as sure to do them lasting harm. Most candy is made of white sugar and artificial sweeteners, so are biscuits, cakes, ice-cream, soft drinks and cola. If your children are properly nourished they will neither want these nor enjoy them when given them, but if they do need something between meals have some dates or prunes, sultanas or dried figs on hand.

Tea, coffee, tobacco, alcohol or any other stimulants are next on the list of don'ts because all of them are acquired habits, none of them are naturally required. If you smoke and drink it is 90% sure your children will too and the same goes for the rest of your habits. Take care to set a good example, for if you give them the wrong stepping-stones they will not know better than to place their feet where you have walked. If you do not know or care where you are going, you cannot expect your children to avoid disaster.

In the same way that you give them most of their stepping-stones for life, so does the power of your will for them to do well also motivate their minds. Unconsciously you drive them to success or failure. But need it be either? Could it not just be to contentment, for as the Chinese say: 'The contented man though poor is happy. The discontented man though rich is sad.'

There is more to what a family can give to their children, much more, but short of writing a whole book on the subject I can only make you aware of the fact so you can think about it and take the necessary action. It may be limiting that children are thus educated at home, but it is better that they should grow up in an atmosphere of love and affection than that they should become impersonal objects in an equally impersonal state machine. There is more to life than doling out money for the bare necessities of existence, there is the actual act of living too, which when you are young or old means more than the material needs. The family unit is designed by nature for that purpose and cannot be replaced by any other synthetic means.

So understand your responsibility to your family and learn what it is right for you yourself to do, so you can pass it on to them. For your routine will become your family's, and if they learn to have only fresh fruit and vegetables and other whole food in their homes they will find it hard to eat anything else. If they learn to treat their lives as a journey, they should always be refreshed like all those with a positive reaction to their problems instead of a destructive and negative one.

Of course you will not agree with your children when they

grow up, if only because they will want to break away and start a family of their own to make their imprint in the pattern of their world. But providing you do not want to run each other's lives and can resist the temptation of interfering, the stepping stones of family will go on from one generation to the next. Try to see those stepping-stones are solid ones, because families are only part of communities and communities make up nations.

THE COMMUNITY

Your family is part of the community which lives around it, so your life has an effect upon it. For this reason, it makes sense that so many districts have now organized community associations to voice their objections to whatever offends local opinion, because what is objectionable to one will probably also be to the other. Out of modern living has come the realization of the power of the united voice. This voice is neither political nor partisan and speaks only for you as a group of people who wish to live peaceful, happy and healthy lives, so there can be no objection to it.

Your first concern as a community is presumably your environment because that is the most important common ground you have. It does not matter whether it is polluted air or sea, rivers, lakes, or soil, or whether it is noise from the land or sky, desecration of a local beauty spot, redevelopment of a part of your area, inadequate drains, dangerous roads, pedestrian crossings, the water supply, milk deliveries, the state of the local shops, a proposed new highway or any of a thousand other matters which affect you all, they are a common problem and call for a united voice.

People who are not a part of your community are not particularly concerned with what goes on there, except so far as it affects them. Outsiders can never really be on your side, neither motorists travelling through at high speed nor pilots overflying, a group of redevelopers from financial institutions nor people who pollute your land and water, even air from some distance outside your perimeter. None of them are directly affected by their actions, but you are, hence the need for your common voice to carry weight. This is the smallest naturally combined unit outside the family which has a right to be heard, because many of them joined together become a state or county and in the end a nation.

Once one fully realizes the implications of the community in one's private life and the influence it can have on one's health and happiness, it is not surprising to expect some stepping-stones to be laid down in this direction. After all why should someone else be allowed to poison your water which they themselves do not have to drink? It may be less obvious as far as the desecration of a local beauty spot is concerned, but equally you all derive pleasure from looking at it and when it is gone you will notice the gap.

So the first step for the community must be that it speaks with one voice, after that so many things are possible which were not before. Each person or family will bring to such an association their own problems which may also be everyone's concern, and out of their joint interest will come a plan for action. For example, you are all affected by the local milk supply and how the eggs are produced, who grows the local fruit and vegetables and how they are husbanded, the local water could be over-fluorinated or be lacking in other minerals, there might be violence in the streets and it could no longer be possible to walk in peace, one's house might no longer be secure as burglars prowl the district every night. These matters all extend beyond your gates to the next family down the road, and their interest in them is as great as yours.

The solution to them need not be so difficult, if only because many voices are much stronger than one. Such issues as pasteurized milk which should be prevented, or arranging for free-range eggs, compost-grown fruit and vegetables, a supply of health food articles at your local shop, are all matters of common interest. Pollution problems can be handed over to your local parliamentarian or council representative and continual pressure put on him until matters are attended to. Noise might also become his responsibility because this has now become a major national issue as the greatest disturber of the peace. Why should everyone's life be made a misery because one man is thoughtless or selfish? That is exactly what the laws are for, to protect people from just such eventualities.

There is also something else. the community can do to improve its health and increase its happiness. One of the great by-products of this present age of high-pressure living is stress and tension. It accounts for more deaths than almost anything else because the extent of its inroads into the workings of the body are practically unlimited. From the stress of modern living comes tension and from tension comes heart disease, arthritis and the rheumatic complaints, even cancer, the common cold and degenerative diseases. Proper nutrition can prevent many of the physical ravages of stress but tension is not so easily dealt with, because to counteract it you need to relax, which some people find hard. Yoga was designed to give that serenity which, by practice, you can learn to achieve at will. However there are other ways as well.

Two particular examples come to mind: one of a Scandinavian girl who was so exhausted after work that she used to go home and get drunk until she discovered the local rhythmic gymnastic group which did their exercises to music. The second case was a middle-aged spinster in London who used to do Scottish folk dancing two or three times a week and who would rather have sacrificed her pay cheque than give it up. Both of these people were achieving what the adherents of Yoga accomplish with their mental and physical exercises.

If Yoga is not taught in your district, perhaps the community could organize some sort of local dancing club to be an anti-stress factor, or gymnastics, even bowls, tennis, netball or a hiking group. Then there are more cultural activities like theatrical, musical, choral, chess, cards or poetry groups which produce very much the same effect, that of relaxing the mind. Perhaps you could combine the two and have a perfect balance, because brainwork really requires physical exercise as relaxation, and cultural activities fulfil another need.

A social life of some sort is also a need within a community. In the modern dehumanized world the old have no sympathizers and the lonely are preyed upon, for the place of the family has been taken by the state who hand out cash instead of love, compassion and understanding, the security that they will never be forgotten or neglected.

Although the cash is important, to be part of a family is even more so because it is the only real security the world can offer, although some other artificial methods have been invented for political purposes. Social life can easily be organized within a community, as well as succouring those without a family who must necessarily fall back on it.

These are some of the functions of the community which can be put into effect if it is organized but which are neglected if it is not. The actual art of living is not exclusively an individual affair, because we draw so much of our pleasure and our health from all that lies around us, our environment. In the same way as someone must be responsible for noticing that the lovely old oak tree on the village green is in need of attention, so also must someone take notice of the old widow in the derelict cottage who is desperately lonely since her husband died, and is suffering from malnutrition.

I may be accused of seeking the ideal society by suggesting all this, but is it really idealistic to ask such small requirements from a world which has reached the moon and conquered such enormous technological problems? Could not the same brains which have been able to organize our scientific advance be applied to the human problems of living, of health and happiness for us all?

If you see the community as only an extension of the family, then a great many things are possible. It is a place to air your grievances and have them heard, instead of boring your wife, as well as a place to create a happy ambiance in which to live; but to achieve it you will need to be organized as some form of association. If you discuss at the community councils what local causes are affecting the health and happiness of your family, then you are part way to effecting a cure, because most things that affect the community also affect your family and call for action. This is not a political suggestion, it is simply commonsense and made for the benefit of you all.

THE CITY

From the family and its immediate surroundings of the community one comes to the next largest division of people, which is the city. Included in that is the state or county of which it is the capital. The community can be a section of the city, but not vice versa, because the scope in each case is somewhat different. The family and the community are concerned with what lies outside their front door, and all which directly affects them in this manner is for those two divisions of society to deal with. The city or state have more general interests, yet they become most personal when applied to you as an individual.

For example, the standard and amenities of the local hospital are of no interest to you for 90% of your live but on that rare occasion when you have to make use of it, its efficiency becomes a matter of life and death. The same applies to many of the other services provided by the city, whether it be the regional price control of local food, public lighting, marketing or public entertainment. These do eventually affect you and make a great difference both to the enjoyment of your life and the whole ambiance in which you live.

I am always staggered when I look round a city I have not visited before to find they have recently erected a modern hospital three or four times the size of the old one, which is probably still in use. This is not an isolated happening, at least in Europe, and it can have only one meaning: that the number of sick people has vastly increased and that the local authority estimates that the rate will increase. Is this progress? Is this what we are paying vast sums in National Health Insurance to insure? Are our enormous income tax contributions not providing enough money for research into the cause and prevention of ill-health, or is there so much money in sickness that the fire must be kept burning in case it should die out?

The first stepping-stone I suggest for your city is that it should attend to the health of its people as well as their sickness. Then, as their investigation grows, I should hope to find that the seekers after health will outweigh and absorb those who dwell on illness, and that finally the only concern will be the prevention of disease and the building of health, both of which are positive undertakings.

To learn the art of cutting out cancer or transplanting hearts, of suppressing the symptoms of disease instead of finding out their cause and tackling the problem there, seems to be the act of any monopoly defending its product. The only alternative to conventional medicine is through nature cure and all its various branches, and once you have studied it, you will begin to understand how simple is the building of health, the prevention of disease and even its cure. It may take time and perseverance, but in the end will come not just momentary relief from the symptoms, but an elimination of the cause as well. Doesn't that sound more like a solution to sickness than to build more and more enormous hospitals and plan ever-increasing areas for graveyards?

So this is the first step your city can take towards improving the general health, and while it is doing so it will come across some other problems as well. The first of these is the marketing of fresh fruit and vegetables, even fresh meat, poultry, game, fish, eggs, milk, cheese and other perishable items. Over the years the market-places in villages, towns and cities have disappeared and been replaced by supermarkets which stock almost exclusively tinned, dried, deep-frozen or otherwise processed foods. In the first part of this book I explained the dangers of processed food so it does not take much imagination to see why our hospitals are full, but the problem is how to bring back the markets and ensure a continual supply of fresh food for everyone. However that is not within the scope of this book, but I do suggest it is the next step for your city.

Another subject needing attention is the fact that the local flour mills are marketing only the worthless part of the grain of corn as flour, the rest is being sold at an inflated profit to the farming community to fatten their beasts. The result is that the beasts become fatter and healthier but the humans become fatter and iller. Unfortunately we do not realize why we are becoming more and more sickly, otherwise the public outcry would remedy for ever this iniquitous practice and in so doing restore, in part, good health to everyone. This is no small matter when you consider the number of people who make flour such an important item in their diet, and who are virtually being sold down the river for the price of the nourishing part of the grain. Your city as the capital of your state or county could put this right.

A part of this same theme is the growing of our food, because if it is produced in poor soil it will only be of poor quality. The substance of the soil depends on what is put back into it in the way of manure and compost, just as much as its indigenous quality, and over this we have complete control. Artificial fertilizer contributes an imbalance of one or two necessary ingredients and overgrows the product to an unnatural size, so it obviously attracts a great following.

Compost and dung contribute all the necessary factors in organic form and increase the humus of the ground. After a few years of natural manure, plant diseases completely disappear and the yield improves out of all recognition. Isn't this a worthwhile bonus and something every farmer or producer of food is trying to accomplish? All this your city can help to promote by propagating the use of organic methods of cultivation. The proof of this system is in the eating and in the freedom from disease of those who eat it, so here is another step for your city, state or county.

There are also many other stepping-stones to health which become known once a committee start to work on positive methods of improving the public health, but it is not within the scope of this book to delve into them all. The present cause of ill-health will be obvious once the facts about vital living food are known, and from that will come an appreciation of the methods of production. Subsidiary factors such as cleanliness in both public and private places must also not be overlooked, as well as sports grounds and play places for the younger generations. Some conscientious work by an intelligent and industrious committee could soon turn the state of public ill-health into that of good health.

Then there are other steps which the city can take to make the life of its state or county happier. People's peace of mind and therefore happiness can be greatly affected by unnecessary noise and that is within the scope of the city to control. Why should young men be allowed to race about the public streets on motorcycles which sound like machine guns or in cars which have no exhausts? Why should those same people be allowed to take transistor radios to public places and equally destroy the peace that others find there? This is but a beginning of the problem of noise which, since the invention of the internal combustion engine, has been growing every day, as has the problem of pollution of the air from its filthy fumes.

I suppose the answer to all this lies on the national level, but a beginning can be made in the state or county and heavy fines imposed on those who do disturb the public peace. If violence was meted out for violence, death for murder and crippling prison terms for stealing, crime would come to an end as it always has in countries which have followed this policy. In this permissive age where violence, burglary and crime are used as weapons, the public seem too weak and downtrodden to stand up and defend themselves. If they are that gutless, then perhaps they deserve what is coming to them.

Before leaving the city (for lack of space) might I just put in a plea for public lighting, because bright streets produce a happy ambiance and dark ones a depressing feeling. Cities which rigidly control the public supply of electricity always seem to be the most miserable, whereas those with bright lights are the most gay and happy.

I suppose this all comes under the heading of 'Beauty and Ambiance' because that is what helps to make a town an attractive place in which to live or not. Why should what is ugly not be improved by public will, and what is beautiful enhanced? All the little corners with a bench, some trees, a pond or piece of sculpture are what help to make a town, as well as the people who live there and the architects who build their houses. So let public concern create a happy place for everyone to live, because the public and their representatives can help to make that possible.

Lastly may I mention public entertainment and by this I do not mean television. There is more to life than toil and tears, there is also a need to be distracted. Of course for men there are bars and pubs for some social life, and cinemas and tearooms for women, but cities could promote clubs and associations for all the other light and entertaining pastimes which contribute to the public good. Individuals and even families do not always have the time nor the opportunity to start such things themselves, so need a lead from their city authority to get them going.

The responsibilities of the city towards the health and happiness of the state or county are many and significant. They do not end in the council chamber, but begin there. Their deliberations depend upon a positive attitude, upon building health and promoting the ambiance of happiness.

But first the council must know what is needed before they can act, so I hope these few words have guided them on to the right lines.

THE NATION

Beyond the steps which I have already suggested, there are others which best apply to the parliament of a nation and need the force of law to make them public acts. What is good for everyone is a national concern, so the welfare and health of us all must be debated in Parliament, for no lesser body can take the necessary action. Who but Parliament, for example, could prevent our towns and countryside from being despoiled by brash and vulgar advertising signs? Those who have ever lived somewhere without them know how different life can be with no such eyesores. But perhaps I am using a bad example to start with, because advertising does not directly affect our health or happiness, although it does to some degree destroy our peace of mind and make us want what we do not have (in fact that is its purpose).

But suppressing advertising is not the first step a nation must take towards improving its health or happiness, rather it is for Parliament to educate itself in the facts of preventing and curing disease the natural way, and to give priority to the happiness of the country instead of the issues of power. So Parliament must behave as we ourselves did in the first part of this book and re-educate itself in its basic thinking on the facts of health and happiness, for then it can put into effect the results of those findings and make them law. Any government strong enough and capable of putting such measures into effect would be saving the country hundreds of millions of pounds a year and have a healthy nation at the end of it instead of, as now, having to spend even more millions next year and having even more sickness.

So I suppose the place to start is where the doctors themselves are trained, because there is no doubt that if one is brought up to the fact that silver is gold one is never likely to know the difference. So with the medical profession, they can only practice what they are taught, and if they do not learn any other methods of healing they are not to know which is right or wrong, or which will produce lasting results or only palliate the symptoms. So with the general public, unless they understand what is continually making them ill they can do nothing to put it right. Why should they ever suspect the incompleteness of the food they eat as the cause of most of their disease? Even when they do discover the truth they will need the assistance of a national parliament to put their new way of life into effect.

Of course the medical profession may still not accept this new premise, but there must by now be sufficient weight of public opinion in its favour to carry it through. The bare fact which Parliament need to accept and propagate is that the processing of food is the principal cause of disease by the imbalances it creates within the body. That is the whole story. In the old days diseases were caused because people did not get enough to eat and because of atrocious living conditions. Now they get enough, even too much of the wrong food and die even more harrowing deaths from cancer and all the other degenerative diseases. How can Parliament put this right?

I doubt whether processing of food can be prevented by Act of Parliament, anyway the answer seems to me to lie in a way of life and not in laws. If people know that ordinary, natural, live food is the basis of their health they will see they get it, so the processors will not be able to sell their products. Thus the first step is to inform the public of this fact. Next perhaps is to ensure they are able to obtain that sort of food, which is a question of marketing and distribution. Both could be tackled on a national level and put into effect locally, while Parliament oversees its successful introduction.

But although it is not within the scope of Parliament to dictate what people should eat, it is within their rights to protect the public from being harmed and this they should do by making illegal the production of foods which are bad for us. This law alone would go a long way to preventing any amount of disease and help to produce a healthy nation.

Next on the list is to educate farmers, horticulturists and all growers of food in the use of natural methods of husbandry: the simple fact is that compost and dung, with the assistance of mineral supplementation, can cure most plant diseases and increase yields. Again this is a local matter, but if incorporated in a national policy from the government it might stand some chance of being generally accepted. Of course most farmers know these facts but find it easier to use the artificial substitutes, and who can blame them, but still it is not the right answer to food production.

If all this action was taken, the need for a National Health Service would become less. What was left of it would require the addition of nature cure with all its subdivisions of biochemistry, homeopathy and conventional nature cure, for they all warrant a place in the prevention and cure of disease and should be granted that right. Otherwise, sick people are only being offered a portion of the valuable knowledge available for the maintenence of health and prevention and cure of disease.

I have often wondered whether the right way to achieve all this is not something like a Consumers' Council, because we are the dupes who buy the rotten goods put out by the manufacturers, swallow the drugs dished out by the doctors and harm ourselves by eating denatured food, yet our views about it all never become loud enough to be heard. On the other hand perhaps something like that is on too large a scale and too centralized, and therefore too much in danger of being manipulated. If communities were able effectively to communicate their views and express their wishes this might serve their purpose better. But it does need some sort of reflection of the public will.

One last thought on health is that a nation must to some degree be judged on what and how it eats, it is a test of its civilization and culture, as well as its goodwill. China, up to her fairly recent past, seems to have known all and more than we do at present about eating and health, although the word vitamin had not even been invented and minerals were used for industry, not nutrition. Italy at one time put into practice the principles of good nutrition and its way of life embraced them. Austria led the world a hundred years ago in the study of medicine by natural methods but opposition soon destroyed them, although their findings are still the basis of much of what is being accomplished in this field today. The Jews have had sound nutrition at the basis of their civilization for many thousands of years, and still heed those words of wisdom. All people who value their health, and they are fools if they do not, learn the relationship between it and food, because that is the starting-point of a successful and happy journey through life.

It is the details of life that matter, contrary to what most people think. What is important is to know from which cows your milk came and what those cows ate, how they were cared for and under what conditions they were milked. The fact that National Dairies is stamped on the bottle means absolutely nothing, nor do the words Pasteurized, Homogenized or any other patent phrase. Were your eggs gathered from forced-fed, battery-reared chickens or did they pick freely from the food in the fields? This is the sort of detail you need to know. Just to buy vegetable oil is not enough, you must know what sort and how it was extracted from the plant. Honey could come from pollen extracted from flowers (which is what should happen), or from bowls of white sugar deliberately fed to the bees.

Fruit and vegetables grown organically bear no relation to those which are forced artificially and kept a long time before being eaten. Some Vitamin B Complex pills contain a large number of individual B vitamins in high enough strengths to make them effective and safe, but others very definitely do not. Some people know they take pink, yellow or brown pills but do not know what they contain. So learn what your food and pills contain, that is vital and see that your government make manufacturers divulge that information on labels.

About happiness on the national level, I would only add these few words. F. T. Cheng in *The Musings of a Chinese Gourmet* said this: 'Thanks to the widsom of their sages, the Chinese as a people have been taught since ages past to find enjoyment of life and to be happy even in the meanest circumstances.' I believe that is true and I believe it is possible, with only a small amount of goodwill, to achieve this for any nation. It isn't that we do not have the sages or the wisdom to go with them, but we seem to lack the goodwill. As Han Suyin said in one of her books. 'One day a man of goodwill will come along . . .' She said it at the end of a diatribe on the misery in the world, as if that was the panacea for our troubles. If that man of goodwill had any power she is right, but power is not vested in individuals any more, if it ever was.

However, outside the philosophical aspect, there are things a nation can do about its environment and that is a direct contribution towards its happiness. Noise and pollution are the first step because they have both reached such enormous proportions. When the first cars and aeroplanes were introduced they did not affect us adversely, but now there are so many that the ground and the air shudder with their vibrations and the water and atmosphere have become filthy with their vile excreta. It is all a question of degree, for to smack a naughty child is permissible but to hit it harder might kill it. Yet we are being killed by poisonous wastes which are wantonly ejected all round us, and our peace of mind and ability to think are being disturbed by excessive noise. Both can be remedied by Acts of Parliament to the great relief of the whole nation.

All the other matters which affect our environment can also play their part in making life more agreeable for everyone, whether it be parks and gardens, public places or amusements, clean streets and lighting, sports and recreations; there are endless items with which it is concerned. But the basis of it all is in our head, how we think and what our values are. After that comes nutrition, because once our long-neglected deficiencies are filled our personality changes, and we become happy, positive people instead of negative obstructionists, calm and understanding instead of nervous and highly strung, law-abiding instead of criminals. These qualities are the natural accompaniment to proper nutrition. This could spell the end of jails, even lunatic asylums, and all the other corrective institutions, for a soured mind comes in part from a soured body and can be put right the same way.

What our country is we become, at least in part, regardless of our race, religion or upbringing. The climate and customs embrace us and our house becomes like all the other houses, if only in style. Our environment overwhelms us, and the most we can do is to make it as agreeable as possible for our benefit and that of our nation. People are basically weak and they remember very little of what they are told for long, so what is for our good must become a part of our way of life, or else it may never benefit us at all. I suppose that is the basis of religions because by practising them we are practising what is in our own interests, learning the ways of those wiser than ourselves who attracted a great following.

We are all creatures of habit, from getting up in the morning and what we eat for breakfast to how we part our hair and wear our clothes. New habits are hard to acquire and old ones even harder to dispense with, so a sound and solid way of life is worth acquiring because it plays such an important part in our well-being and happiness. That is the problem for the nation because a way of life can be given to a people, and there is no doubt that this is what will produce a happy and a healthy country.

THE WORLD

Since 75% of the world hardly get enough to eat it may seem far-fetched to talk about good or bad nutrition, but those are just the circumstances in which it is necessary. A handful of wholewheat flour can sustain a person, with the addition of a small amount of other food, but if that flour is refined and white it very definitely will not. So we are back to the same problem which has recurred throughout this book, that of educating the world in the basic facts of good nutrition, and as far as 75% of the world is concerned those facts make the difference between living or starving. That is the importance of passing on this knowledge.

The majority of the world only regard food as something to satisfy their hunger, not as nutrition to prevent disease and keep them healthy. Of course most of them are not in a position to choose what they eat anyway, they must take what their money will buy and what is available locally, so the responsibility for seeing they are properly fed lies with their government. Most governments do not know about the relationship between good health and proper nutrition, because like the medical profession itself they have not been taught the facts about it.

So the first step for the world is to be told the facts about nutrition, even one basic fact would do: that whole food is the basis of health and processed food the cause of most disease. That fact is enough to stamp out much of the disease in the world and make it a considerably healthier place in which to live, yet one does not hear of any international welfare organization having propagated this elementary knowledge. One reads of shiploads of corn being dumped into the sea because it cannot be sold, or of apples being left to rot because it was not economic to transport them to be auctioned at the current prices. One is always reading of food going to waste because of the poor prices, but never does one hear of any world organization doing anything to recover that wastage or take any action to ensure it does not happen again.

So we are back to that man of goodwill again. But he was not there before nor does he seem to be here now. Thus people are left to die of starvation and the world sighs with relief that there are a few million less to feed. What a thoroughly negative approach! People can always be put to constructive use if organized, as they can also be fed if the country grows the right kinds of food. There are many high protein crops such as soya beans which could wipe out starvation practically overnight, or it could be brewers' yeast which does not even require land for cultivation.

If, instead of grazing cattle on valuable grass and then eating the cattle when they have turned it into flesh, we grew nuts and seeds on the same ground, we should greatly contribute towards solving the protein problem of the world. I do not believe that the world food shortage is so much a matter of fact as it is of distribution, and with some goodwill that could easily be organized. So we are back to the politics of food, which like that of life and death are the trump cards. In some ways we have tried to solve the world food shortage by tinning, drying and freezing food, but in doing so we have wrought our own destruction because we have not taken into account the laws of nature, only the discoveries of science.

Unfortunately science still does not know very much about nature although it discovers hair-raising facts every now and again, only to be proved completely wrong 50 or 100 years later. Yet during those years we change our eating habits to fit in with the fashions of the scientists, and find we have completely crippled the population of the world because we thought we could improve upon nature.

Had we paid attention to the laws of nature we should have noticed that it is food like nuts and seeds which last the winter out, also beans and other legumes, that dry grain will keep indefinitely and retain its enzymes and its goodness. Fruit which is dried in the sun, cheese which is made from sour milk, onions, garlic, herbs, potatoes and a great many other foods all have excellent shelf life. Had we concentrated our efforts on growing and storing such items the world would be properly fed and healthy as well, instead nature has had the last word and we are still not conscious of what is happening. Can it be that a few are making a living out of suppressing the facts? Is the world being blindly led to its destruction? Are we so dumb that we cannot see the truth about such basic facts as food in relation to health?

The general standard of living throughout the world has at last been raised so it is not a large step to make it healthy as well. That step could be taken in the councils of the world with a small amount of goodwill, but in the same way as the United Nations has digressed from what it could once have become, so perhaps has the nutrition of the world as well. When the history of this era comes to be written it will be told how much white flour and white sugar, how many tins and packets of food were distributed to this or that starving nation which staved off famine – true enough – but it also addicted them to that type of food and so ruined their health.

Some people seem to think that by moving a few pieces of antique furniture or *objets d'art* into their house they can become civilized, whereas in fact they would really do better to remove all their possessions and educate their minds instead. So with food, people fill their larder with tins and packets and their deep freezes with frozen stuff, and think they can be well fed and properly nourished. But they know nothing about nutrition, and that is the whole point of food. If they sold their possessions and went out to the fields and learned about nature, they would discover its beauty and absorb its wisdom. This is your starting-point and that of the world. This fact of nutrition and health has been proved over and over again, yet the world takes no notice, it seems to think it knows better than nature. How unwise can one be?

IN CONCLUSION

I suppose Yoga was the first real key to the health and happiness of the world, as those who follow its various paths must have discovered, and its invention dates back thousands of years, even tens of thousands. Unfortunately others have come along since who thought they knew better, and great institutions which were once dedicated to truth have fallen into other hands and been corrupted. So the world is now left without a unified course of action to achieve what every person alive must dearly wish: to be healthy and happy.

My suggestion to you is that you return to nature, because according to those laws you will learn how to acquire enough of the right sort of nourishment, fresh air, sunshine, and exercise as well as leading a satisfying life. On top of this, there are few emotional problems which cannot be worked off by physical labour and there is no doubt that when you are tired you sleep. Also do not forget that a mind which works constructively helps to prevent illness instead of inducing it, that those who cannot afford to be ill usually are not and that those who really want to get well always do. The cheerful and the givers are happy, the mean and the miserly are miserable. It is all in the mind, for those who want to be sick can usually manage it and of course they do not get better, although sometimes this is a subconscious reaction, not deliberately invoked.

Do not forget that the human body and mind are evolutions of nature, that they have grown and developed according to the laws of nature from their earliest beginnings millions of years ago, so how can we expect to cure their faulty workings by methods which do not obey those laws? Of course if the heart was mechanical and worked by clockwork, the problem would be much simpler, likewise if the brain was an electrical instrument, but this is not the case. They are activated by blood and nerves which require food and nerve regeneration as their source of power. No amount of chemical compositions can ever assist the body in its daily fight for life or in its efforts to throw off disease. Of course the symptoms of disease can be suppressed by such methods, but this only forces the uneliminated poisons further into the body and makes certain that later on in life the person is afflicted with arthritis, rheumatism or some other progressively degenerative disease.

Why do we always think we can improve on nature? Everything in the world has some purpose or function, if we have the wits to discover what that is. So with disease of the body, it means we have been doing something wrong and caused an imbalance of some sort which needs to be corrected. But before we can do that the poisons from that disease have to be eliminated or the inflammation allowed to subside, then the imbalance corrected before we can get well again. It is really very simple. Yet people still continue to go against nature by taking drugs and other unnatural cures and wonder why they are always ill. Unless the cause of disease is eliminated you cannot say the disease is cured, and the cause lies in the normal workings of the body or mind which requires a natural cure.

The hope for you and the rest of the world is to discover exactly what the laws of nature demand in sickness and in health and then abide by them. Many books have been written on the subject and in essence they all agree that nature is the starting-point. Of course one will differ from the other in its individual approach, but that is the same with anyone practising the art of healing, he follows his own particular ideas which he has proved and believes in. But at the basis of health lies ordinary common natural food, eaten as it comes to one from the ground or from the animal. When we are sick we refrain from food like all animals, and when we are ready to eat again we become hungry. But in the first days we only eat very little because that is all we want and gradually we take more and so increase our health. That is how nature meant us to behave and if we do, we become and remain well.

Why otherwise do you think our bodies would feel so sick that we have to retire to bed? What other reason can there be, when we do not feel like eating, than that we are meant not to eat? If we therefore go to bed and abstain from food (but not drinking) we shall be doing what nature dictates and can therefore expect to be cured, providing we take the right sort of food when we are ready to eat again. That is the basis of nature cure and if followed with intelligence, some knowledge and guidance, it will not fail. What more to nature can there be than nature itself? There lies the answer to health as well as happiness.

8. About Sex

ABOUT SEX

Sex	309
Just Sex	309
The Idea of Sex	310
The Act of Sex	319
Food For Sex	325
General Nutrition	325
A Balanced Diet	328
Vegetarian or Meat-Eater	329
Specific Sex Foods	333
Wheat Germ Oil and Wheat Germ	333
Nuts and Seeds	335
Sesame Seeds	336
Kelp	337
Honey and Dried Fruit	338
Milk and Brewers' Yeast	340
Raw Fruit and Vegetables	342
Supplements for Sex	343
Vitamin E	344
Vegetable Oil	344
Zinc	345
Vitamin B Complex	345
Vitamin C	346
Vitamins A and D	346
Lecithin	347
Minerals	347
Ginsen	348
More About Sex	348
Stimulants	348
Inhibitions	350
Perversions	352
Change-of-life	354
The Prostate	356
Drinking and Smoking	358

FOREWORD

I WROTE these few words about sex on a ship going out to the East. When I arrived there I found that they treated it as a normal everyday function which men living in hot countries have a need for, and it was therefore available in agreeable circumstances and at reasonable prices. Of course sex for men and for women were two completely different things because one was supposed to be experienced and the other a virgin in the marriage bed. For that reason men did not spend their time trying to seduce their girl-friends or their friends' wives but went where there were women prepared to sell what was wanted. This way the integrity of the family was maintained, the messy and untidy business of social sex avoided, and the problems of homosexuality and lesbianism non-existent. Sex for men was not tied to some petty morality which creates a bad conscience by this very normal act, but equally not encouraged and considered bad for the mind and body.

Sex in the East is something which takes place between man and wife for the procreation of children and outside that is not much thought about. It is not an obsession as in the West where women without clothes – sometimes even the act of sex – appear on the stage and screen, in the press and television, even at social functions. Because sex is not brooded about and not forever pushed at people by the mass communication media, it presents no problem; if it worries some men before they are married, they know where to go as they do for other public conveniences. That is the end of the matter. Society is not disrupted by it nor is the integrity of the family. What a different picture from the one in the West.

I was therefore rather ashamed that I should have taken upon myself to put pen to paper about such a normal, natural subject which does not really need any explanation, except perhaps the few words I have just written. However I have decided to let them stand because for the young and inexperienced there may be something they can learn from them. Perhaps this will help to prevent them from turning sex into a vice and thus ruining their lives, because that is what can happen with sex, as also with drink, drugs or any other indulgence. We must all learn to control ourselves and to be moderate in our habits because an excess of anything is bad, no matter what it is.

THE ACT OF LOVE

Sex is a dirty word
For those with filthy minds,
Yet they are a part of it
Or they would not be alive.

Sex is also beautiful,
No greater love exists
For people who perform it
With their hearts and not their wits.

Sex can be exhausting,
Frustrating sometimes too,
But even so it is by far
The nicest game for two.

So if you've never played it,
Delay the magic hour,
Don't abuse this pleasure
With unsatisfying fun.

Go to every effort,
Learn the art of love,
For everything needs learning
To get the best results.

Then when you've perfected
This simplest act of all
Go to she who loves you
And make her yours.

Take a lot of trouble,
Activate the mind,
Time is all important,
Then she'll respond.

When it all is over,
Cherish whom you've loved,
She'll re-live those moments
Till next you come.

This is your expression,
The only one she knows,
Of if you really love her,
Naught else counts.

So love her very often
Or else she may go wild,
All animals need petting,
A wife needs love.

SEX

JUST SEX

I SUPPOSE I should really start this section by qualifying myself to write it and I have no doubt that if I did, it would be a best-seller. Instead I shall leave you to judge from reading it whether my past experience has justified these few words, and begin by describing what I see taking place outside the window in front of me, because although sex is ideally an expression of mutual love, it is also a simple physical orgasm.

In the garden on the opposite side of the road is a puppy, desperately trying to copulate with a hen and becoming extremely hot and frustrated in the process, even though the hen is tethered by one leg. I have watched the performance with fascination for quite some time and it is not at an end yet by any manner of means, and doubtless it will go on tomorrow as it went on yesterday. That is sex! You may call it disgusting and perhaps you are right, but equally that judgement is relative.

When the urge comes animals and humans are no great respecters of man-made morals or codes, they relieve themselves of their need in whatever manner is available to them at the time, if they cannot control themselves. In the Andes it is said to be llamas, in other places other methods, in the navies of the world sodomy, and for others masturbation. The need is compelling, as nature intends it to be, otherwise the species would die out, but that need can be turned into a vice if the glands become overdeveloped by childhood masturbation or youthful promiscuity.

I say all this to explain the normality of sex which in modern times has been exploited and perverted and from there used as a weapon, both political and otherwise. What is not normal is not to want sex in one's twenties and thirties, and those men are rightly described as effeminate because they sometimes do not develop the obvious male characteristics. However in many civilized countries where sex is not used as a weapon, these unfortunate youths are given injections of the missing hormone which often stimulates the development of their manhood. Perhaps the same can be done for frigid females, because it would be a mercy for those women if they could be helped to fulfil themselves as mothers, which is their principal function in life and an act which makes them complete.

When talking about sex one must remember that man's appetite for it is apparently insatiable, providing he does not become bored or in some other way put off by his companion, although even then his hunger is there for someone else. In his prime of life that urge knows no bounds and thus the world becomes populated and his own family propagated. Normal men cannot help this urge although most of them can control it, but there are some who cannot and when they are young this desire is frequent and dominant. When they are old, I am told they still want what they cannot fulfil.

So it is no use pretending that sex can be dispensed with, at least in youth, or even trying to forget about it because, as the hackneyed phrase goes, sex will rear its ugly head, although why ugly I fail to appreciate. Instead it would seem more sensible to come to terms with it and learn about its function and fulfilment in the same way as one should learn what to eat to be healthy. Both are a need, both must be catered for, and there are right and wrong ways of coping with sex as there are of eating. Simply to do what our parents did in either respect is not necessarily correct, at least as far as the West is concerned. It is therefore important to learn in the light of current events, or even age-old customs, how to be healthy in body and mind by eating correctly and conducting a balanced emotional life.

THE IDEA OF SEX

Sex is not entirely physical, as those who have been distracted in the act of performing it will readily agree. Women also understand this, otherwise they would never use so much scent and bare their most attractive samples of flesh, nor paint, polish and perfect their most seductive smiles. All this is aimed at the mind because that is usually where the first idea of sex takes hold, although there are even more sensitive places.

Once the seed has been sown, it grows, or more accurately once the pituitary gland has sent out its messenger, the sex glands are quick to respond.

Of course some women can paint themselves and smother themselves with scent, even take off all their clothes and still find no response. Then obviously what they have to offer is either unacceptable, or the object of their attention is particularly resistant to their type of charm, or maybe more interested in something else. Either way it is the mind which causes the barrier. Of course if they were able to make physical contact where they had failed to make it mentally, they might succeed, but that is another story. Alternatively they could solicit the aid of alcohol which does a lot to confuse the mind and make people do what they had no intention of doing.

All our voluntary actions start in the mind, for that is where the orders are given, the body simply carries them out. If the result of taking certain action is pain, one's body automatically shuns repeating it. In the same way, if the reward is pleasure, one wants to do it again. By that principle animals are trained to perform whatever tasks their masters require, whether it be walking a tight-rope in a circus or retrieving game out shooting. Human beings are no different from other animals in this respect except perhaps that they have a greater capacity for thought. Our basic instincts and reactions are no less animal than the beasts of the jungle or field, one would not expect them to be. However we have refined ourselves, or rather some of us have, and civilization, which is no more than man's behaviour to man, has paid a passing visit to most countries. Some have developed their civilizations to a very high degree of culture, but unfortunately the more civilized they have become the less strong and virile, and the more decadent and effete, for in the end civilization causes its own destruction.

Thus we are back to the animal again and the brute force which makes us man, for that is how we survive in the jungle of the world, without those instincts we would play the female game which never can command. Of course the fashion is to have women wearing trousers today and men are encouraged to have long hair, use make-up, scent and other female garb; but although women now wear trousers they do not yet have balls nor men an orifice in front, and that is where the difference in their behaviour lies. Most women still give in and go the way the victor says, whether they wear trousers or not, whereas men for the most part do not, they fight and die if needs must be.

From these basic instincts and differences the male and female approach to sex and all the other things in life derives. It is the reason we are so completely different physically as well as mentally. It is why women have soft skins and silky hair, wide hips and large breasts. Of course there are aggressively masculine women who are made worse if they have weak husbands or financial independence, but they basically think the same way as their more feminine counterparts and react in an identical fashion.

You cannot change the physiological make-up of women by putting them in trousers or even by making them the boss, they would still much rather it was the other way round and that man would come and dominate their female frame. Man however can be turned into something much less than man: he can be debauched and weakened, perverted and demoralized till he has no strength or courage left to save his life in face of death. Drink and drugs, perverted sex and physical degeneration all work together to reduce the powers of man to be a man, then what is left is something for the garbage heap, not life with woman, worries, children, work.

So it is with sex: women do not do the chasing, seeking, lusting after sex, that is left to brutish man. They lay out the meal as attractively as they can and wait for hungry man to come and dig his teeth into it. That is all they can do, they are not the dominant sex, they cannot drag their quarry back to their cave and there possess it. They can say no, deny their pleasures to the passing tramp, but not usually in any firmer, stronger union. Of course if they want attention of a sexual kind there are many subterfuges which they can employ to make man hungry and create an appetite for what may not be a particularly appetizing meal.

There are all sorts of garnish, curry, herbs and frills which they can use to turn an aged cut of meat into a tender fresh young chop and man is fool enough to eat, but that is their survival trick, so let him go on being fooled. If all else fails they can always numb the senses with whatever kind of liquor comes their way, and then when drugged man does not care so much what sort of meal he has. If you are hungry, food is food and anyway not all the world can live on dainty early shoots, the rest must take whatever comes their way.

In Eastern philosophy these two forces of male and female are known as Yin and Yang, and great importance is attached to their relationship. In life there are always opposing forces, light and darkness, warmth and cold, positive and negative, only in death do they cease to exist. It would therefore seem prudent to keep a happy balance between the two for fear that one should suddenly cease to exist and death ensue. In the West we appear to have overlooked this finer point in maintaining life, and that is perhaps why our physical and mental health is degenerating rather than progressing.

Everything depends on a happy balance, too much of one thing or another is never right. In the world of nutrition people talk about a properly balanced diet, and practically everyone knows that term even though they may not know how it is achieved. Science is well aware that any perfect union produces inaction and that what was animate then becomes inanimate, yet in the field of medicine they do not use those opposing forces, and the constant interaction between them to effect their cures. Nutritionists on the other hand often judge the degree of a person's health by the state of tension between sodium and potassium, outside and inside the cells of the body, because that is life at its most basic level. Everywhere in life you find these opposing forces and everywhere there is constant action and a happy balance which produces progress, thus life goes on. Anything else is death or dying.

I particularly draw your attention to this point because it is of such importance in marriage and any other form of male and female relationship, therefore in sex. It has been referred to as sex hostility which I think is an inappropriate term. It implies the idea of opposition rather than a healthy balance, of war rather than interaction, neither of which should be in fact the case. The weak and the strong, admittedly, are always opposed to each other to some degree, for the one must necessarily slightly resent the other. But these forces are always found together in nature: a positive lead would not produce an electric current without a negative one, there would be no children in the world without women, no warmth without cold, no light without darkness. The secret is to find the happy balance because they are complimentary, that also is the secret of life as well as sex.

This balance takes place in the mind, although there is also a physical one, and if you analyse it you will find it mostly amounts to an attitude of mind. That attitude may be an accumulation of many years, it may incorporate injustice and hardship, resentment and fear and it may have become ingrained, like the grooves on a gramophone record, and be equally difficult to erase. But the human mind is logical and can therefore nearly always be reasoned with, that is the best way of dealing with a normal mind. Whatever is upsetting it must be eliminated and replaced by healthy material. Drugs can never do this, as equally they can never cure the body. However they can alleviate the symptoms, which are often pain, and thus allow the body or the mind to effect its own cure.

The greatest danger of drugs is that they do nothing for the cause of the trouble, which still remains active but driven even deeper into the body. That is the illusion of modern medicine and its greatest menace to health. With the mind, drug therapy usually creates dependence on the drugs because that is the only way the person can find relief from whatever is troubling them. Then gradually the mind becomes weakened and the will to continue the battle of life ebbs away, until the person becomes a drug addict, forever dependent on the potion which creates oblivion and deadens the horrors of real life.

I am explaining all this in such detail because it is in the mind, to a very large extent, that sex takes place. The physical side is a mechanical one dependent on the correct functioning of the glands, but these have to be activated before they can perform their task and this is done by the mind. If the mind says no, they cannot function, thereby is the basis of all inhibitions. Now inhibitions have to be put there by someone, by parents, teachers, priests or books, they are not a part of the mind at birth. This is not necessarily a process of reason, it could have been straightforward indoctrination and repetition, but the only way inhibitions can be removed is by reason, although temporarily by drugs. Any form of drug completely demoralizes a person so he does not know what is right or wrong for himself or anyone else. Far from re-educating a person's mind, this is simply another method of destroying it.

If a person is inhibited it means that he subconsciously rejects certain courses of action, he does not have to think about them, he automatically knows not to do them and therefore does not. His resistance can be broken down by a persuasive person, by alcohol or drugs, sometimes by fear, greed or weakness. When he has overcome his inhibitions once, the second time is easier and so on till he does not care. That is one sort of inhibition, but there are others also and they play just as important a part in sex.

These are the inhibitions which you put there yourself and as such take considerably more overcoming. If a certain sort of smell revolts you, you will do all you can to avoid it, the same with taste and sight and all the other senses. These are the inhibitions which make sex impossible for a great many people and some are genuine dislikes, others simply an attitude of mind. Love and hate are two particularly good examples, because during married life love can turn to hate, then sex does not happen. This is an attitude of mind. Maybe after a joke, some relaxation or simply some rest that attitude can change again to love, then the reconciliation will almost certainly include some sex.

But most men do not think about sex all the time! I presume the same is true for women, although I sometimes wonder! Essentially therefore sex is suggested, unless of course the urge becomes too great, in which case there may be abnormal functioning of some gland or another form of stimulation. That suggestion is usually a mental one although a quicker response can be gained by physical contact. Now suggestions are easy to transmit, in fact any association of ideas becomes a suggestion, which is how the world is led along its precarious path towards one end or another.

Of course some people's inhibitions will prevent them agreeing with what you suggest, and some (but very few) have minds of their own which makes them even more difficult to deal with. But for the most part, man in his lusty prime of life does not refuse sex if it is nicely served up to him on a golden platter with some form of finesse, unless it does not fit in with his work schedule or he is committed somewhere else. So suggestion goes a long way where sex is concerned.

Suggestion can also come from boredom and very often does. Those who are gainfully employed do not have the time or the opportunity to think about sex but when they are on holiday or out of work, the sight of a pretty girl goes a long way. An empty mind is the most fertile soil for the seeds of sex because once sown they germinate forthwith, and then the process is almost irreversible. This is physical and due to the outpouring of the glands which stimulate us into action to relieve the pressure they create. But all this comes from the mind, and can only be activated by it and with its co-operation. No form of physical contact, no type of perversion, no sort of mechanical aid can overcome the resistance of the mind to sex: it must be willing first or else there is no flow.

The reverse is also true, as many women must be sadly able to recount of their old and debauched husbands or even lovers. What they want to do they simply cannot accomplish, and nothing that their women can do will make the slightest difference. Their will is strong enough but the chain of cause and effect inside their bodies is not functioning as it should, so there the matter ends. Very humiliating no doubt for those concerned, yet it must be the most common occurrence in sex, and nothing for anyone to be ashamed of. Perhaps it will happen to us all, but I hope not and I do not believe it is necessary. One hears of centenarians sireing families in places like Georgia and amongst the Hunzas in the Himalayas, but in the West this is not the case. This is mostly nutritional.

I remember once chatting up some gorgeous Nordic girl while doing some writing on one of those islands off Morocco, and we had gone a long way to getting to know each other. The moment seemed ripe for more intimate relations but the circumstances were not suitable so I had to resort to words as my first line of attack. This is always a satisfactory beginning anyway, because it breaks down so many barriers and creates that most precious of unions, a contact in the form of communication which is necessary before the act of sex, unless it is bought. After we had talked about sex for some time I had no doubt whatever that she had made up her mind about what she would do when the moment arrived. I had talked about the subject generally and she had replied from her own experiences, so gradually I had led her mentally into the bedroom and prepared her for what was to come. That is always necessary with women, they need time to adjust, they cannot cope with shocks!

Since women are more dependent on their emotions than men and since their bodies respond even more readily to their thoughts, it is not surprising that so many women are neurotic. Were they able to control their thoughts and discipline their minds, their neuroses might not have such ravaging effects on their bodies and behaviour, but few of them seem able to and so they suffer and sometimes even destroy themselves.

Next we come to the dreams of the young and sometimes not so young. Such dreams are a mental act even though they may have been stimulated by something physical, but perhaps there are two kinds. Could it be that all these naked ladies on the front of magazines today help to make them dream that way? Could it be they sow the seed and leave the young frustrated for the act of sex? It is surely unnecessary to arouse such feelings. For the young married it is more a question of restraint than creating the desire, at least in the early years, so there is small fear of a population decrease. With the unmarrieds, it is rather pointless, also harmful to work them up and then frustrate them. After all they will marry when the time arrives, because marriage is a part of life, not something which one undertakes to satisfy a need. Of course if the urge is great enough they can always buy it, but that also is rather unsatisfactory, although not nearly so unsatisfactory as masturbation which is positively harmful, both physically and mentally.

So the idea is the first food of sex and the nourishment most needed for a satisfactory sex life, and one which can cause impotence if not supplied in the right manner and of sufficient substance. Man, as a result of developing his mind, is now frighteningly dependent on it, particularly in modern times when machines do most of the work while we simply sit and use our brains. What goes into them, like what is fed into a computer, remains there; it becomes part of us so we must learn to discriminate before switching on to record. Even better, we could pick through all the rubbish which gains admission with the pitchfork of reason and discard what we do not like or need or use or want. That is a start to disciplining the mind which is the first step to making us happy, healthy and the enjoyers of a satisfactory sex life.

So, if you are a man, wanting to seduce your girl-friend, remember that a few ideas go a long way. Women are romancers, any spare time they have is occupied in thinking about their boy-friend and what he has done to them, will be doing or what they would like him to do. Take them to the brink of the act, let their minds enjoy the pleasure of what is to come and that will help their glands, because sex for women is something more than it is for men, they commit themselves.

As a man, you may take this committal very lightly, but it is everything to a woman, so do not underestimate it. Sex for them is much less of a physical need than it is for a man, but they live with it afterwards and relish the pleasure they have given and received. To treat sex cheaply is to destroy what a women most prizes, the fact that she is entitled to say no. Therefore put a value on the act of sex because your girl-friend does. She is letting you enjoy her most prized possession, so make her feel as though you hold her in esteem, even though you may not.

It was Shakespeare who said, 'If music be the food of love, play on, give me excess of it that surfeiting the appetite may sicken and so die.' Play to the mind for the best response from women, they will treasure what you put there in the hours and days to come. The idea of sex is vital to the act for both sexes so do not destroy the illusion, at least as far as women are concerned, that is too unkind.

THE ACT OF SEX

It almost seems unnecessary to write this chapter when nowadays you can see people performing sex on the stage, in films and magazines, and when almost every book you pick up is devoted to its ramifications, both natural and unnatural. But frequently the content of what such books have to say is so nauseating that it is necessary to dispel this taste and return the act of sex to an atmosphere of love. Otherwise we are not much better than the beasts of the jungle, coarse, crude and uncivilized.

Far be it from me to suggest that wenching is not great sport or that women fall into one's arms for the purpose of making love. That is very far from the case. I fully appreciate that one has to take one's pleasure with apparent thieving of the treasured prize, and that the act of stealing is supposedly done against the ladies' will; but there are ways of going about it which can satisfy a woman's honour and make her want to be robbed again. Sex is both Yin and Yang, it is male and female and cannot take place without the other's concurrence. This is surely the first lesson one has to learn about a satisfactory sex life, that it is no good being selfish about it.

The second lesson is that women nearly always have misgivings about making love. They want to please and give their best but they are never sure they have, so need assurance of this fact. If you tell them it was wonderful and that they are too, you will be doing yourself a service as well as pleasing and helping them. Do not forget that the risks involved are not yours, that you have not committed yourself to anything, in fact you may never be seen again. Even in marriage it is the same, women want to be loved and sex is one of their most important pieces in the jig-saw of love.

From what I have said so far it is obvious how different are the two approaches to sex, the male and the female. At a very early age boys seem to rather like their little female friends, but then comes a stage when they would not be seen dead with any of them, and regard women as much weaker and more feminine than they are. However that does not last long, next they are writing letters and wasting much of their time in pursuit of them. Their appetite increases till they make their first conquest and then they are hooked for life on this exhilarating sport. The chase becomes a fight and in the end they capture the wife they want and settle down to a steady married life with children, houses, gardens and pets. But on their way to accomplishing this they take advantage of whatever women will let them have their way.

Women think and dream of nothing other than marriage, children, homes, security and clothes, in that order. So any act of sex that they perform must fit into this scheme of things. I am not suggesting that once they have accomplished them all, as well as whetted their appetite with the enjoyment of the marriage bed, they will not then give their favours elsewhere. But that depends on them and on the rules and customs of society where they live.

However with women, sex always tends to go with the idea of marriage, they want to keep the person with whom they have shared their body and that makes sense, they do not give it for nothing! After all sex is not so important to them, they do not have to have it, whereas men do, at least up to a certain age if they have acquired the habit. Perhaps that is where sex should really begin, with the urge, for without it there would be no sex. It might be worth pursuing that great feeling further to discover how it comes about.

We have already had a glance at the mental side and discovered that the brain can nearly do the job alone, but equally that is true of the body. I suppose it depends upon the degree of sensitivity of the person concerned and their sensuality, but physical contact is the more swift and certain approach, as many women know all too well.

But there are two separate stages in sex, there is the mind's acquiescence and the body's fulfilment of that desire. Without the mind's willingness, the body cannot perform its task, therefore the urge may be there but its satisfaction blocked by the mind. In old age this happens the other way round, as also in disease or malfunctioning of the glands: the body cannot perform what the mind wants it to.

The physical side of the urge is a man's erection which a woman also has, but internally and on a diminutive scale. This gives the signal that all is set to go. From there it is a short distance to the final crescendo but without it no orgasm can take place. This is the outward and visible sign of the urge and where it all happens, but its activation is partly accomplished elsewhere.

Basically it is the senses which perform the act of sex, aided and abetted by the mind. Man's mind is full of pictures of the girls he has ravished, the happy memories associated with those moments and other pictures of the ones he would like to have seduced. It is these which help the act of sex, and make him do and want to do it at the time and in the future. But the senses are what produce the climax of the act and they all play their part to give man the greatest thrill he knows.

First he sees the beautiful girl, which is a general impression taking in her finer points of figure, grace of limb, her skin and hair, complexion, smile and sex-appeal. Next perhaps he smells her seductive scent, then hears her words of love. Finally he touches her soft and tender skin, then feels her seductive breasts and curves, and the thrill of contact excites him to ultimate consummation. Then the sensuous act is over in which all the senses played their part, except that of taste.

Of all the senses I suppose touch is the one most intimately connected with sex, for it is through this sense that the great crescendo takes place and without it nothing much would happen. Few are strong enough to resist the cumulative effects of the sense of touch, for once man and woman have laid hands on each other sex begins to play its tune till that contact is broken. This is almost more true for women than it is for men, in fact it is often said they cannot resist making love once you touch their breasts and vital parts.

Latin women are more quickly and easily excited and Northern ones more cold, whereas Negroes appear to be ready at a moment's call. Climate clearly has an effect on this, as it also does on the whole of the urge. 'The Long Hot Summer' was not written as a play on words, it is what happens in real life. Not only does the butter start to run in hot countries, but the blood also courses through the body with greater ease and the glands pour forth their secretions with a stronger will.

In the West Indies young boys make love shortly after puberty. On the continent of Europe they wait somewhat longer for older women to show them the ways of sex. In other countries I am ashamed to say the public schools become experimental grounds for boys with urges which they cannot satisfy: that can lead to all sorts of vice, perversion and a decadent display of sex. What a pity sex cannot be completely eliminated by the mind as is the case with many countries in the East, or alternatively treated in a normal healthy fashion like our need for food. To ignore it or to damn it as wicked and disgusting simply drives schoolboys to masturbation or to doing it with other boys, and doubtless the same is true for young girls.

If only sex could be withdrawn as a weapon for the politicians, then there might be a chance of it being accepted as normal or, even better, being eliminated from the habits of the young. Simply to make it a wrong-doing is to burden innocent children with a sense of guilt from which they cannot escape, and which does more harm than the act of masturbation.

Regrettably sex has been written into the system of domination in the West, so it is convenient that people should transgress this code. Apart from its use as a method of manipulating people, it also has a function in the permanent subjugation of society. Even by bringing it out into the open in such a depraved manner as we have today, we have done little to return it to its normal place but have made it abnormal and perverted.

If only young people could be taught about sex instead of frightened by it, if they could learn that it can be eliminated by the mind until nature has cause to make use of it, they might come to terms with it. But to let themselves damage their own minds and bodies by their experiments, only makes it likely that they will turn sex into a vice which will ruin their lives. Alternatively sex must be on sale like any other commodity which man has need of and in surroundings and at prices which are acceptable to all.

The urge to have sexual intercourse is one of man's strongest driving forces and one of his normal male characteristics. Without it he would not be a proper man, yet he is expected to pretend that the urge does not exist. Man's libido drives him to commit the act of sex, that is his need, his manhood, let it not be satiated in humiliating masturbation or some other more perverted way. We are not living in the dark ages of hypocrisy or false values, and although there may be many things wrong with the modern world, at least sex is no longer treated as a non-existent subject. Let us study that subject and find a logical answer to it.

So far I have talked only about men and their urge, because I am a man, but women also have this feeling, although perhaps not in quite the same way or for the same reason. Women want to be loved, that is one of their most urgent needs. The outward manifestation of that love is sex, and without it they feel unloved. I have already said that women rely much more upon their emotions than men, and they also tend to feel their way through life rather than reason things out. What they can feel, they understand, that is true to them, so they wonder how a man can love them unless they feel it and therefore unless he makes love to them. And women and their feelings are often right. When they have enough children to occupy their emotions, sex can take a second place and when they are older, they more than anyone else are aware of their own physical shortcomings.

So let us always remember that women also have an urge, sometimes stronger and more urgent than men but in a different way, and that if it is not satisfied, it will cause them much distress and physical concern. The fact that they are usually unable to reason their way out of situations makes them more vulnerable to lack of love and causes appalling neuroses. If they understood themselves, none of this would come about, but as they do not they collapse out of sheer frustration if their men are unable to supply the answer.

Also women usually find self-discipline hard to enforce, so their efforts to save themselves in the face of emotional crises are somewhat feeble. With the assistance of their man they can be much stronger. Without that support and with a state of chaos in their minds they are done for.

So urges must be answered, either satisfied or eliminated,

but never left to harm the body and destroy one's peace of mind. Self-discipline is probably the right answer and most of the great religions encourage people to subject their sexual urges to their mind's control, but for some this is easier than others, because we are not all the same. Therefore it is not possible to lay down a set of rules, but there is no doubt that moderation should be your guide. Excess of anything is bad, and excessive sex is a cause of illness according to traditional Chinese healing. Occasionally, sex is stimulating, but the strain of excessive sex on all the internal organs is harmful.

From this one naturally comes to that eternal question of how often should one indulge in sex. I have heard it so frequently asked, and indeed I also wondered the same when I was in my early twenties. One's appetite seems insatiable at that age and one's body capable of endless sex, but do not take more from the body than you put into it, namely nourishment. So now we have reached the food for sex, the actual edible stuff and not the mental kind which I have been describing up to now.

Once we have learnt to cajole our partner to the threshold of the bedroom door, having first created an appetite for love, then is the moment to learn what to have for dinner beforehand. The beasts of the field and the jungle do not need the same finesse, but it is rather a gratifying thought that we do. Why ever hurry what one likes to do? Much better savour all the mental aspects of it first before letting the body have its way.

You must let your body be your guide as to how often you indulge in sex. But it also depends on what you are doing and where you are. Holidays for the young marrieds are rather different from a climbing expedition for the middle-aged. Endurance and performance can both be built up with correct nutrition and additional vitamins and minerals.

Always remember that from a man's point of view, women can be the greatest pleasure on this earth, if they want to please, but equally they can also be the greatest headache if they do not. So give yourself sufficient time to relish all the joy they want to give. It is their hour, they are the star of the show, so enjoy the performance and reward them with a round of applause. Finally give them a standing ovation and send them flowers, because if they have given you pleasure they deserve it.

I suppose I cannot end this chapter without a word about the act of sex of the lesbians and the homosexuals because otherwise it would be incomplete. As far as the former are concerned they do exist and in my own experience are domineering, over-sexed women who cannot secure a man and therefore use their strong characters to dominate some gentle and usually beautiful girl.

It is hard to believe that any man could prefer boys to girls and I still do not believe it to be the case. The cult of homosexuals is something which has been artificially created (except perhaps at boys' boarding schools) and appears to be kept alive for the sole purpose of political and other forms of blackmail. In the East one seldom hears about it, although it was introduced into Japan at one stage. Their act of sex, if it really does take place at all, is no more than masturbation.

I am sorry to end this chapter on these particular problems because these unhappy people are so much to be pitied, but they are a part of the whole subject of sex and cannot therefore be left out. In properly regulated societies they do not exist. But other societies are controlled differently and there you find homosexuality on the increase and even encouraged.

Sex is easily turned into vice, in the same way as drink and drugs, smoking or any other stimulant. What the brain registers as pleasure, the body wants to do again. So many emotionally-deprived people slip into the habit of taking what is readily available to them. From there it is a short way for the weak to indulge in vice. Happy families are protected from all this, that is why they are the right solution for any society.

FOOD FOR SEX

GENERAL NUTRITION

Let me begin by saying that although there are foods which do help one's potency, and some which are essential to it, proper nutrition is the basis of it all. Unless you follow an all-round programme of healthy eating, a handful of this or a teaspoon of that is not really going to help you. So your first task is to discover the basic rudiments of nutrition, because unless you are healthy you will become impotent all too quickly.

Now impotence is usually glandular malfunction unless it is an inhibition of the mind, which is quite frequently the case. The glands can therefore be said to be the most important single factor in sex because even a slight imbalance in their output of hormones can completely change the sex life of a man or woman. The book *Glands of the Great* (which is now out of print) expertly explains all this, although it must be obvious from your own knowledge of the workings of the body, how and why this is. For example those with an overactive thyroid gland tend to be the world's great lovers, and those with an enlarged prostate are often unable to control their sexual urge. People do not usually start life in such a state of imbalance, but develop it gradually as a result of wrong living and eating habits.

Now glandular function largely depends on the minerals you obtain from the food you eat, as well as the essential unsaturated fatty acids (vegetable oils) which should also be a part of your diet. How therefore can you be certain of obtaining these in your daily round of eating? The answer to that is to be sure you eat only whole food, by which I mean food which has not been tampered with before it reaches your kitchen. No food which comes out of a tin, bottle or packet can be said to be completely whole because to some degree it has been interfered with to make it keep, and usually it is the enzymes which have been destroyed.

Since enzymes are the ferments which the body uses to digest food and thus turn it into flesh, hair, nails, sinew and all the other parts we need, we must then rely upon those which are produced inside the body, and they are an ever-decreasing supply. In this way our digestion degenerates and also the absorption of the vital elements of nutrition which we need to keep alive and healthy.

Enzymes are affected by heat and are often deliberately destroyed in this manner before deep-freezing food so it will not go bad. The same is done to all processed food which is intended to have a long shelf life. So my first piece of advice is to eat as much raw food as you can, in fact to have at least two-thirds of your diet uncooked, then you can also be sure it contains all the minerals and vitamins. (They too can be boiled away in cooking water and destroyed by heat.) Meat, fish and eggs are best cooked, but milk should never be touched before being consumed, nor should fruit and most vegetables, including nuts and seeds. If fresh vegetables are difficult to come by, sprout some mung beans or other legumes, or even sesame or other seeds. There is really no more you need to know about nutrition, for that is the basis of correct eating.

Of course there is a negative side too, such as not eating half-foods like sugar (particularly the white refined) or white flour (which has had its most nourishing and balancing portion milled away) or anything made from these two. Any food which has been processed like this will do you harm, because your body has to supply those missing elements from its own store and it cannot do this for long unless they are replenished.

Solid fats are dangerous because usually they consist of saturated fat (these include most animal fats) whereas vegetable fats (oils) are in general unsaturated and essential to the body. Fried food is bad for you for much the same reason that fat is, and added to this is the fact that heat changes the chemical composition of the fat and if used over and over again it becomes rancid. Most of the popular stimulants should be avoided. They are not foods but poisons. Coffee, alcohol (the word intoxicate means filling you with toxins,) and strong tea (very weak, unbrewed tea is better) all come into this category.

Finally, health not only depends on a sufficient amount of the correct food, but also on exercise and fresh air, sunshine and a good water supply. One's emotional life needs attention, as does the movement of one's bowels. Causes of unhappiness should be eliminated instead of left to fester, and one's way of life must include sufficient relaxation. Worry must be dispensed with (because it achieves nothing), and a positive, forward-looking philosophy developed.

There is not much more to health than that, except perhaps one's own determination and one's will to live and enjoy life. That cannot be bought or eaten, it must come from within. Without it no amount of food or any other elixir will help. You are the architect of your own health, and now you have the raw materials with which to build it. No one else can do it for you, they can only advise you. The rest is entirely up to you.

A BALANCED DIET

Having told you what to eat, I must now tell you how to organize your diet. The first thing you will presumably want to know is what you are balancing with what. The answer to this is the acid-forming foods against the alkaline ones. Generally speaking concentrated protein food like meat, fish, cheese and eggs are acid-forming, and fruit and vegetables are alkaline, thus meat and two vegetables and some fruit is a balanced meal. If you eat an excess of acids over alkalines, that excess must be eliminated from the body otherwise it will ultimately make you ill, so you need a working knowledge of how to achieve this. There is no need for complicated calculations or even very much thought once you have developed a pattern for eating, but the ratio of acid-forming food to alkaline should always be about 1 to 4; in other words you should have four times as much alkaline food as acid-forming. This is what we normally do in the West, because main courses often consist of a small piece of meat and lots of vegetables, followed by some fruit.

The principal ALKALINE foods are:

Basically all fruit and vegetables with a few notable exceptions such as beans, lentils, dried peas, fruit preserved with sugar in tins and bottles.
Pure honey, black molasses.
Most nuts and seeds.
Vegetable oils (but not animal fats).
Dates, raisins, dried apricots and figs.
Milk, cream, butter, soft white cheese (but no other), buttermilk.

The principle ACID-FORMING foods are:

Excess protein and all protein metabolism.
All bread, flour and cereals (in varying degrees).
Eggs, oysters and cheese (all particularly high).
Meat, bacon, liver, salmon, sardines (all high).

Shellfish, fish, poultry (not so high).
Beans, lentils, dried peas.
Jam, fruit preserved in white sugar, white sugar and sweets.
Lard, animal fats and food fried in it.

One's diet each day follows a fairly similar pattern, so it should not be difficult to limit oneself on the acid-forming side and be generous on the other. If you eat lots of fresh fruit and vegetables, even some cooked ones and potatoes, this helps to balance the equation, as does milk. White sugar is on the black list together with sweets and too much of any flour product, otherwise you are not likely to run into trouble unless you live on meat, eggs, cheese, fish, bread, sugar and flour products only.

Acids have to be eliminated from the body, because if they are not they cause diseases like arthritis, rheumatism, and kidney troubles. When there is excess acidity in your body you feel one degree under and lack energy, your glands and nervous system are upset and the process of metabolism and synthesis is interfered with. One of the best ways of correcting this imbalance is to fast for a day on water or fruit juice (one kind only) and water taken every two hours (one glass). Otherwise eat as much as you want but no more.

Should you find your hunger difficult to satisfy, you may be suffering from a calcium deficiency which can be put right with a biochemic preparation. If you ignore an acid state of your body, you are certainly heading for trouble because the effect is accumulative and ultimately reaches a point of no return. Be wise now. If necessary go to a health clinic and clean out the accumulation, but only do so if you are prepared to revise your eating habits afterwards, otherwise you are wasting your time and money.

VEGETARIAN OR MEAT-EATER

Before going any further I must clear up this issue of vegetarians versus meat-eaters, because there is so much misunderstanding and wrong thinking about it.

Many people are convinced that a thick juicy steak is a wonderful sex food as well as being nutritionally sound. They are quite wrong. The bull is a vegetarian, so are three-quarters of the world (either for religious reasons or because they cannot afford meat). Now the bull has enough sexual urge and male instincts, and the three-quarters of the world which is vegetarian breeds at nearly the same rate as rabbits, so there is obviously nothing wrong with their reproductive system. Added to this is the fact that Indians, Japanese and other Orientals are extremely brave warriors, and the bull does not seem to lack either courage or strength with which to fight.

In addition, meat is acid-forming, contains a lot of animal fat and its protein is not of such a high biological value as that from vegetables sources. All of these factors work against sex rather than for it, as indeed they also detract from health rather than help to built it up. The acids tend to make you feel lethargic which is the opposite of what is required for sex, because to some degree an excess of energy is part of sexual libido.

However it is true that the uric acid from meat may irritate the whole region of your sex organs, thus giving the impression of being an aphrodisiac. The animal fat tends to make you feel sleepy which is not a good portent for sex, and although you need fat for reproductive purposes, it is the unsaturated fat from vegetable sources, not the saturated fat from animals. Protein is another necessity for sex, but it is the biological value which matters, not the quantity, and vegetable sources can supply that (milk protein is one of the best).

Added to all this you have the vital fact that fresh, raw fruit and vegetables, nuts, seeds and milk contain all the vitamins, minerals, trace elements, intrinsic factors and other essentials for good nutrition, plus the essential enzymes with which to digest them. These foods are where you find the largest quantity of all these factors in their most easily accessible and digestible form. All of them are necessary for prodigious sexual strength as well as for optimum health, so the case for the vegetarian is not an entirely hollow one, particularly when you add to it the following information.

Nearly all the great cures in nutritional history have been accomplished by means of cleansing the body and then following that with a frugal fresh, raw vegetarian diet. Most of the household names in nutrition have themselves started in this manner, and it has been out of gratitude for what that diet has done for them that they have devoted their lives to passing on this information. I myself had the same experience, but I was not fortunate enough to be able to go to one of these famous establishments, I had to learn for myself the hard way which, on looking back, I am grateful for because it prevented me from being tied to any one particular school. Consequently I have taken what is good from them all without being educated into any prejudices, therefore I can still see the subject in perspective.

Were you to see the capillaries of a meat-eater and compare them with those of a vegetarian, there is no doubt that you would be immediately convinced of the advantages of foregoing meat. The former are like cork-screws, the latter completely straight as they should be. Now this may not sound vitally important to you, but it is, for this reason: the starting-point of the body is its cells, they are the basic ingredients.

The blood which courses round through our veins and arteries has the sole function of supplying those cells with nourishment and removing the waste products. It does this by means of the capillaries which are the final vessels to the cells. In good health their orifice is small and firm, enabling the cells to be properly serviced. In other states of health they become flabby and enlarged, making it difficult for the cells to survive, and easy for virus and germs to enter.

The best way of achieving healthy cells and strong capillaries is by a raw vegetarian diet. That ensures the cells are properly fed and their wastes removed, as well as maintaining the correct balance and degree of activity between sodium and potassium inside and outside the cell. This way you should be able to achieve immunity to disease. It is not a quick process because first the accumulated acids must be eliminated, but this is the only way that real and lasting health can be built.

The other three factors which finally seem to tip the scales are those I previously mentioned, the high biological value of vegetable protein, its alkalinity and freedom from saturated fat and cholesterol. Protein is made up of amino acids and it is the proportions and quality of these which determine whether a protein food is valuable or not. A certain number of amino acids can be synthesized in the body but ten cannot, so these are referred to as the essential amino acids, and food which comprises them is referred to as complete or first-class protein.

However providing all the essential amino acids are taken at the same meal (although in different foods) and in the right proportions, that protein has a high biological value and is therefore of the greatest value nutritionally. Meat and other animal food is first-class protein, but the combination of amino acids from vegetables and fruit produces a higher biological value, and is therefore not needed in such large quantities.

Meat may contain as much as 25% fat or more, as well as considerable quantities of cholesterol. That fat is saturated fat which is hard to digest and difficult for the body to process. The cholesterol, if taken in excess, may block up the blood vessels, so may the fat. On the other hand vegetables, fruit, nuts and seeds contain mostly unsaturated fat and, even more important, supply the essential fatty acids which the body cannot manufacture itself. Fat is needed for the complete combustion of sugar for energy, and it does not matter whether it is saturated or unsaturated fat for this task. Fat is also needed for the working of the sex glands, as well as all the other glands, in particular the essential unsaturated fats which come from vegetable sources. Since you can therefore supply your bodily requirements of fat from vegetable sources without running the risk of harming yourself, it would seem a logical choice to make.

Finally comes the question of the metabolic wastes from meat and other animal food. Meat starts to putrefy the moment it is killed and that process goes on till it is inedible. You eat it in whatever state of decomposition it happens to be. That is the first point. Next comes the fact that when the animal was killed it was pouring adrenalin into its bloodstream out of fear at what was about to take place. Adrenalin is poisonous and the body has to eliminate it, but in this case there was not time. You also consume with meat the various antibiotics and drugs which have been given to the animal and not eliminated. Finally, meat and most animal foods are acid-forming and it is those acids which, if allowed to accumulate, cause trouble in the end. Vegetables on the other hand are mostly alkaline in their reaction.

This therefore is the case for the vegetarian, but it is not a dogmatic one nor am I presenting it as such. After all the Esquimos would not find it very easy to follow nor would many other people. The only important point is to eat whole food as nature supplies it to you from the animal and from the ground, that is the real way to health.

It is incredible what one's body can make do with, and how it can transform the food you give it into what it wants. Only by interfering with the raw product and thus unbalancing nature do you endanger your health and spoil the quality of the food. This may sound like contradicting all I have just written about the vegetarian, but rather it is to explain that there is not only one answer to health. We are all different as are our circumstances, so we must do whatever nature meant us to within those limits.

SPECIFIC SEX FOODS

People have lived on water alone or just fruit juice and water for more than six months at a stretch, but during that time they would not have made very good lovers. The sick and the weary, the hungry and the undernourished have no great sexual desires. To feel sexy you need to have an excess of energy, not a lack of it, which is why general nutrition and a balanced diet are the first essentials. If you are saturated in harmful acids and lacking the necessary ingredients for glowing health you will not feel fit for anything, let alone sex. However, outside general nutrition there are certain foods and elements of food which are helpful to the proper workings of the whole reproductive system, these I have called specific sex foods and sex food supplements. The best known and the most commonly used are the following:

WHEAT GERM OIL AND WHEAT GERM

This comes very much top of the list and by far exceeds any other food used in the Western world as a stimulator of sexual activity. It actually stimulates the production of sperm in men and can not only help to stave off impotence but can sometimes reverse the process, as well as preventing miscarriages and premature births. It is given by farmers for infertility in cows and bulls as well as other animals, and sometimes as a prophylactic for sterility. It is a useful food for the change of life (menopause) because of its high Vitamin E content, and helps to prevent a great many of the unpleasant symptoms of this unhappy period. It is a tonic for the heart and helps the circulation as well as assisting the liver and kidneys. It has been used to cure diabetes and some writers claim that there is no condition of health or disease which it will not improve. I agree with them.

What was once called the Staff of Life could now be called the Staff of Death because present-day flour cannot support life. However the germ of the wheat contains all the goodness that the flour lacks, and in a concentrated form since it lacks most of the starch. For example half a cup of wheat germ has as much protein as half a pound of steak, and it contains a higher concentration of Vitamin E than any other food. It has an abundant supply of B vitamins, a lot of iron and many other minerals including copper, magnesium and manganese. Another of its vital qualities is lecithin which helps to metabolize fat and keep it in suspension, thus preventing arteriosclerosis and sometimes even curing that condition.

These are the known factors but it is strongly suspected that there are others, probably more important, that have not yet been isolated. The germ of any seed is what contains the life element as well as all the necessary food to support life until it can extract it from the earth and sky. Thereby may easily hang the secret of wheat germ, as also of all the other seeds.

Wheat germ is available from every miller who makes flour. It can also be bought from health food shops. Be sure it is fresh because it will do more harm than good if it is rancid, so keep it in the fridge (it should taste sweet not bitter). Wheat germ oil is not so easy to buy. It is manufactured in Germany and the United States, but I have never found any other source which tastes genuine. You will know immediately you have found the real product because it tastes like what it is. It is not necessary to take the oil in large quantities, one teaspoon a day is enough, or perhaps two.

This is your first sex food, because it contains all the necessary factors for the reproductive system in sufficiently large quantities for it to have a stimulating effect and to maintain it. No other single food will do quite the same. Wheat germ oil is the most potent, but the germ itself is as good if taken over a period of time. The latter as a breakfast cereal mixed with fresh apple and some dried fruit makes a good start to the day and ensures your supply of Vitamin E. Oxygen is vital to all the functions of the body, whether it be the brain, muscles, glands or the sexual organs and this is the principal role of Vitamin E, to conserve the use of oxygen.

NUTS AND SEEDS

Next on the list come nuts and seeds, principally because of their oil content, but also because they have an abundant supply of vitamins, minerals, trace elements and the 'life' factor of seeds (nuts are also seeds). Oil is fat and fat in one's diet is something to be particularly cautious about, because some are dangerous and others essential. The saturated fatty acids which come mostly from animal origin are the dangerous ones, the unsaturated fatty acids are the healthy ones and found in the largest quantities in vegetable foods. To an extent all fat contains some of each but for optimum health it is best to eat as little saturated fat as possible in relation to unsaturated, which is one reason why vegetarians follow the diet they do.

Here are a few examples to give you an idea of the big differences:

Seeds	Sat	Unsat	Veg Oil	Sat	Other	Sat	Unsat
Pumpkin	8%	37%	Corn	10%	Avocado	3%	9%
Sesame	7%	42%	Cottonseed	25%	Beef	12%	12%
Sunflower	6%	39%	Olive	11%	Steak	17%	17%
Almonds	4%	47%	Peanut	18%	Chicken	6%	11%
Peanuts	10%	34%	Safflower	8%	Cream	15%	10%
Pecans	5%	59%	Sesame	14%	Eggs	4%	6%
Walnuts	4%	50%	Soya bean	15%	Lamb	9%	5%
Hazelnuts	3%	44%			Milk	2%	1%
					Pork	9%	12%

If unsaturated fatty acids are not obtained in large enough

quantities all sorts of diseases can follow, including sexual disorders. The prostate gland is particularly affected by a deficiency because it cannot manufacture its fluid without essential fatty acids and therefore enlarges to compensate. The same applies to some extent to all the endocrinal glands (and therefore the sex glands also) which need these fats to remain healthy.

Apart from their oil, nuts and seeds are also storehouses of many other powerful food factors for sex and health generally. Like most vegetable oils they contain Vitamin E in large quantities and this is the sex vitamin. They also supply many minerals which are as important as vitamins, in particular zinc which is found in large quantities in sperm and in the prostate gland, as well as being known to retard sexual development in the young if deficient.

Pumpkin seeds are the best suppliers of zinc, but grain and other seeds are also adequate, particularly sunflower seeds and wheat germ. Outside these, zinc is available in yeast, oysters, herrings, eggs and onions amongst other foods. If you want to guard against the old man's complaint of prostate enlargement and the operation which usually goes with it, eat a handful of pumpkin seeds regularly and ensure an adequate supply of nuts and seeds.

Protein is also needed for sex, and nuts and seeds provide an ample supply as well as being high in the B vitamins. Vitamin B_1 in particular is needed to metabolize sugar and therefore produce energy, without which man would make a poor lover. The life factor is also a vital part of seeds and this is what creates new life, so it must also play a part in any form of procreation.

SESAME SEEDS

One of the oldest known virility foods are sesame seeds. They appear in many ancient writings and are still used to this day in Israel, the Arab countries, China, India and South America. These tiny seeds contain high proportions of all the food elements which you need for potent sex: Vitamin E, protein, unsaturated fatty acids, lecithin, minerals, the 'life' factor and other intrinsic factors. In particular they have more calcium than milk and cheese, a high concentration of the amino acid methionine. These qualities make them tiny atom bombs in the sex world although wheat germ oil is more concentrated.

There are many ways of eating them: I have them raw and chew them very thoroughly. Otherwise you can sprinkle them over salads or cereals, on to rolls or baked dishes. Even better have them as they do in the Middle East mixed with honey – a dish which they call halvah. To make this, grind up some sesame seeds and knead them into a paste with honey, and then roll them in the seeds to prevent them from sticking. This is a high energy food as well as one for sex. Halvah is much better for children than poisonous sweets made from valueless white sugar and synthetic substances. The calcium in halvah would help them grow, the complete sugar from honey give them energy, the minerals and vitamins make them healthy and the oil feed their glands.

Sesame seeds are a specific sex food and are special amongst the nuts and seeds for that purpose. They are easily obtained through health food stores or any grocery shop owned by Indians, Chinese or Middle East proprietors. They are cheap and nutritious and vital for those who do not drink milk because of their calcium content. Two or three teaspoons is quite enough each day because they are high in oil of which we do not need too much.

KELP

Kelp is seaweed and the principal reason for its inclusion as a specific sex food is because of its iodine content. Iodine has one vital function to perform in the body, and that is to supply the thyroid gland with the raw materials with which to make its hormones. Without a properly functioning thyroid gland there would be very little sex interest. The thyroid regulates the pace of one's physical and mental activity, one's rate of metabolism and growth. If it is overactive it produces the sex maniac or genius and if underactive, people who are sluggish, disinterested in sex and overweight. Without iodine in the diet people develop a goitre because the gland enlarges to compensate for what it is lacking.

So that is the first important contribution of kelp to the diet. It is also rich in minerals: calcium, potassium, iron, phosphorus, copper, magnesium, manganese, sulphur, trace elements and of course sodium from the sea. Whereas the soil is sometimes lacking in certain minerals, that is never true of the sea, so kelp is always full of them. It is eaten quite extensively in Scotland and Ireland where they make seaweed blancmange, and the Scandinavian countries have other recipes. In China they eat birds' nest soup which is principally made from seaweed and fish spawn and considered a great aphrodisiac. If you find some seaweed while swimming, chew a piece and also take a mouthful of sea water. Kelp also contains vitamins, including B_{12} which is seldom found in the vegetable kingdom.

HONEY AND DRIED FRUIT

Honey and dried fruit are coupled together because they supply principally the same basic ingredient, natural sugar, which is another essential for sex. Honey has other properties which makes it superior to dried fruit, and it has been prized as an aphrodisiac for many thousands of years.

Our principal energy food is carbohydrate and honey sugar is in the form of fructose. This is a simple sugar and does not need breaking down by the body before it can be utilized as energy, which makes it a quick stimulant of the right sort. It is also a specific for the heart, the brain, and muscles where energy is needed in large quantities at a moment's notice. However honey sugar is still sugar and an excess of it is just as bad as any other carbohydrate, whether it be for heart disease or anything else. Admittedly one reads of people gradually building up to taking a pound or more of honey each day, but they are usually athletes, runners or swimmers who are able to utilize what they eat, or have it as a first-line reserve.

Honey has other properties, such as its rejuvenating effect. This comes from its pollen and is apparently responsible for the longevity of many of the Russian centenarians. Pollen contains a hormone akin to the pituitary hormone which stimulates the sex glands, as well as plenty of vitamins and minerals. Unheated honey also has essential oils, so it is best eaten from the comb rather than creamed and blended. Honey is credited with increasing the haemoglobin count and thus assisting in anaemia, which may be partly due to its iron and copper content. The two organs which particularly need a ready supply of sugar, the heart and liver, are both strengthened by honey, the kidneys and the lungs are also assisted, as is the general feeling of well-being.

Honey helps to destroy bacteria and acts as a healing agent so is useful for ulcers and sores, it also attracts water which may be one of its healing properties, and the aspartic acid of honey has been used against lethargy and fatigue. Nearly 4% of honey has defied analysis, so it may well be this which makes it such a magic food as well as nature's oldest aphrodisiac. It does not take much imagination to see how honey can be mixed with sesame seeds to produce a most potent sex food.

First amongst the dried fruits come dates, because apart from anything else they do not have such a laxative effect as the others. At one stage in my life, when I was suffering from a calcium deficiency, I had a craving for sweet food which I satisfied with dates. The effect of an excess of dates was always aphrodisiacal, so I can personally recommend it as a sex food. Dates are good food in any case, because they contain natural sugar with all the necessary vitamins, minerals and intrinsic factors to digest it. They are extremely alkaline, have a high iron content, lots of calcium and an adequate supply of Vitamin B_1 (needed for sugar metabolism). They are a useful snack for children who seek the extra sugar and iron for energy and the calcium for growth. They are also inexpensive if bought in packets instead of pretentious boxes.

Other dried fruit is good too, particularly apricots which have more copper than most foods (without copper iron cannot be utilized by the body). They contain more iron than dates, a fantastic amount of Vitamin B_1 and Vitamin A, as well as natural sugar with its complements for digestion. Unfortunately they can be expensive, but a few go a long way and they do rate high by any standard as food, for health or for sex. Dried figs are noted for their laxative qualities due to their high indigestible residue, which also produces considerable flatulence. This is an unfortunate quality because they are a valuable food with a particularly high calcium content. They are extremely alkaline, have natural sugar, phosphorus, iron and other minerals and vitamins.

Raisins and sultanas have the special attribute of being able to increase haemoglobin (for those who are anaemic) and they contain iron, calcium, phosphorus, Vitamin B_1 and others. They are higher than dates in sugar content, with a considerable indigestible portion which can cause flatulence. There are other dried fruits too, such as pears, peaches, nectarines, bananas, apples and of course plums which are sold as prunes and which deserve special mention. Prunes have been noted through the centuries as a mild laxative and it is for this that they are famous. Although alkaline, they contain an acid substance which could be dangerous unless eliminated, so do not eat too many.

Fruit which has been sun-dried is best, although there are other methods which do not harm the food. Sulphur drying on the other hand is not so good. Dried fruit is always best washed before being eaten and if possible it is wise to soak them overnight to let them resume more natural proportions. Obviously they cannot be compared with fresh raw fruit but they are useful as an emergency or during the winter when fresh fruit is hard to come by. As a source of additional stimulating sugar for sex they are excellent, and do not forget that the right sort of sugar is needed for the manufacture of the male seminal fluid.

MILK AND BREWERS' YEAST

Milk and brewers' yeast come under the same heading because they are used as specific sex foods for the same reason, their protein content. Of course each of them is valuable in their own right as well, with many other attributes, but no other food has such a high biological value for its protein as milk, and yeast comes a close second. The amino acids in milk are of three kinds: casein, the most commonly known, is of extremely high value because it is so easily assimilated and can be used to make other protein foods, such as cereals, complete.

Two other amino acids have special functions such as preventing putrefaction in the intestinal tract and assisting in blood formation. Now protein is essential to sexual performance because all hormones are principally made up of protein structures, so without them they could not be formed. The easier the protein is to assimilate and the greater its integrity the better will the body be able to carry on its functions, including that of sex.

Outside its valuable protein, milk has much else to offer and not only because it is one of the few complete foods, although that is one great attraction. After all if it can keep the young of its species alive for the first few months of its life as its only source of nourishment, it cannot be lacking much.

However what milk contains must first be in the cow, and to get there it must be in its food which means healthy soil. To remain in the milk it must come to you raw and untampered with in any way, either by pasteurization, homogenization or any other process. Such treatment causes the calcium salts to change their composition and become less available to the body as do other elements, quite apart from the ones which are completely destroyed by heat. In its raw state milk has its own antibactericidal factors which make it an even more nourishing food when sour, but the same cannot be said of pasteurized milk as that only goes bad and will not sour.

Sour milk or yogurt are eaten because they assist the intestines to remain healthy as well as to manufacture B vitamins. In the process of souring or becoming yogurt, the protein is partly predigested and the calcium made even more available to the body. So those are two good reasons for taking your milk in that way. Of course milk itself has a good supply of B vitamins if taken raw, and it contains lecithin for the metabolism of its own fat, but this is lost when treated. Milk also has Vitamin B_{12} which is vital for vegetarians, who do not usually find it anywhere else in their diet.

Milk is a maid of all work in that it has a particular quality for assisting other foods and supplying what they lack. Goats' milk is most easily digested because the fat is distributed throughout the milk in tiny globules, whereas in cows' milk the fat must be broken down before it can be digested and utilized. Milk and dairy products are our best source of calcium, they also contain lots of potassium, some iron, as well as magnesium, phosphorus and some sodium. People who drink milk usually have good skins because of the Vitamins A and D which it contains. Riboflavin, one of the B vitamins, is also in abundant supply. This is good for the eyes, digestion, nerves and the skin, it increases resistance to disease and prolongs life as well as the prime of life.

So nutritionally speaking milk in some form is important to health as well as sex. Goats' milk comes top of the list and products made from it. Next comes sour milk from cows or yogurt, then raw milk. If none of these are available buy some powdered skim or whole milk, otherwise milk which has been evaporated in a vacuum. Finally, if you cannot buy any of these, pasteurized milk will have to do, but it comes well bottom of the list (calves fed on it as their only nourishment die within 3 to 6 months). Drink a pint a day if you are otherwise being well fed, because more than that will put on weight and anyway it may be too much protein, fat and carbohydrate. If you want a pick-me-up for your amorous desires add some honey to it and maybe take some wheat germ too, but since the latter takes time to digest do not be in too much of a hurry!

Yeast contains 40% protein whereas milk contains about 17 grams per pint (you need 1 gram per kilo of body weight). Two dessertspoons of yeast weigh about 20 grams which gives you about 9 grams of protein. Apart from its protein content, yeast is one of the best sources of the B vitamins and contains 14 minerals. Its calorie value is extremely low and it contains no fat. Torula yeast tastes the best but brewers' yeast can be mixed with milk to improve the taste (but nothing else).

RAW FRUIT AND VEGETABLES

Throughout this book I have given fresh raw fruit and vegetables pride of place as the givers of life and health, so it is not surprising that they should be included as special sex foods. For that reason alone they must have a place in the reproductive part of life, and also because it is necessary to include a reliable source of Vitamins A and D and all the minerals. Of course there are higher concentrations of A and D in the animal kingdom but they are all extremely acid-forming, contain a lot of cholesterol, saturated fat and other impurities and poisons. Were it not for that I might also have mentioned liver and kidneys, fish liver oil and eggs, although they cannot offer quite what fresh fruit and vegetables can, except at second hand.

Outside their vitamins and minerals, fresh fruit and vegetables contain that most valuable of all substances, 'liquid sunshine'. By this I mean that without sunshine fruit and vegetables would not grow. But the sun does not shine all the time, so they obviously have to make arrangements for the night. The green leafy vegetables contain chlorophyll, where radiant energy is packaged up to be used when necessary. Other vegetables and fruit have their own arrangements, but all have some method of storing away liquid sunshine which is in fact their energy supply, because the two fundamental reactions of life are storing it away and then using it up.

Now you may say that animals eat vegetables and we eat the animals, therefore we obtain our liquid sunshine that way. True enough, but that is not quite the same thing and anyway it is mingled with poisons and impurities as well as being acid-forming. Much better to have it fresh from the ground, then you also have the vitamins and minerals, trace elements and intrinsic factors as well as its natural water, the best which exists anywhere. There can never be any substitute for fresh, ripe, living fruit and vetetables.

SUPPLEMENTS FOR SEX

The following are called supplements because they supplement food in its action on the body. They obviously include those vitamins and minerals which have been isolated as well as trace elements, but they also include extracts from food which are particularly potent in one special factor. To make up a vitamin or mineral deficiency it is probably quicker to take some of these than go through the lengthy process of relying upon food, and anyway you would need to know a lot about nutrition to select the right ones. Out of this need has grown the health food trade which supplies these special foods, extracts and specific vitamin and mineral capsules.

Although certain vitamins play a greater part in sex than others, the fact is that all vitamins are interdependent so you need them all, not just one. Nonetheless you may have become deficient or your circumstances call for more of one than another, therefore taking one can help, although it would be better if you could also take all the others as well. The same is not so true of minerals because an imbalance of one is quite common, and if taken in the right form can be rectified immediately. Let me therefore give you a list of the supplements, in order of priority, which are important to your sex life.

VITAMIN E

This has been mentioned several times earlier in the book but since it is by far the most important factor to do with sex, it must appear again here. The fact is that it can often cure infertility and constant miscarriages and lighten the burden of menopause (change-of-life). It acts on the glands which are so necessary to sex functions and can sometimes rejuvenate them if they have started to atrophy. It has been found to reduce the pain of childbirth and prevent the stretch marks afterwards. It can even defrost frigid women by helping their internal organs to function in a normal feminine fashion. It can give back the libido to exhausted old men so that they are able to be proper males again.

For normal healthy people in the prime of life there is enough Vitamin E in the seeds they eat such as grain, oleaginous seeds and nuts. Unfortunately most of the goodness is processed out of grain, and nuts and seeds are infrequently eaten and then usually salted. The result is degeneration and then a need for vast doses of vitamins to replenish the deficiencies.

VEGETABLE OIL (Vitamin F)

Next in importance come vegetable oils because of their unsaturated fatty acids. These are vital to the whole process of sex as they are needed by the prostate gland to manufacture its liquid. All the other glands also need Vitamin F and they too play their part in sex. Do not forget that fat is also needed for the complete combustion of sugar into energy and sex is impossible without energy. Men need more of the unsaturated fatty acids than women, perhaps because of their particular sexual functions. For more information see earlier in this book.

ZINC

This often neglected mineral is one of the most important for the male reproductive system, because if it is deficient the prostate gland enlarges. This in most cases leads to its removal at an advanced age, when the body is least able to withstand such severe stress. The prostate is said to contain a higher content of zinc than any other part of the body, and it is further claimed that the function of the whole sexual system is dependent upon an adequate supply of this mineral.

Apart from the prostate, zinc is also present in the thyroid gland and forms a part of insulin which comes from the pancreas to cope with excess sugar. Deficiency of zinc is a factor in many cases of infertility and the retarded development of male gonads in children. Zinc is contained in male sperm, in the seminal fluid, although by far the highest concentration is in the prostate. It is present in large quantities in the livers of children but decreases as they get older, although it is a part of Vitamin B_{12}. Children do not grow at a normal rate if zinc is deficient, perhaps because it plays a part in the absorption of food from the intestines.

The reason zinc is so often deficient in the diet is the old story of food processing. All grains and seeds contain a good supply of it, but that disappears when the germ is removed and the seeds processed. Otherwise whole grains are a good supply but the best of all is pumpkin seeds, in fact a handful of these occasionally will ensure an adequate amount for all normal needs. Sunflower seeds, oysters, brewers' yeast, herrings, eggs and onions also contain some.

VITAMIN B COMPLEX

This vitamin appears here mostly because of its incredible powers as an energy-giver and excess energy, quite apart from enough of it, is a prerequisite for sex. The consumption of alcohol causes a deficiency of Vitamin B Complex, so does an excess of sex, so be sure your supply is adequate. It is best taken in food form or supplied from one's own intestines which manufacture Vitamin B, so read what has been said earlier about it.

VITAMIN C

Large quantities of this vitamin can definitely create a desire for sex. It is debatable if this is because of the additional energy it gives, the fact that it detoxifies the body and therefore makes you feel better or because it acts with calcium and other enzymes, but the fact is that it does. Vitamin C also acts on the adrenal and thyroid glands, both of which play a vital part in sex. It also maintains the health of the intercellular cement (collagen) which in turn makes for solid bones, muscles, blood vessels, teeth, skin and body organs. This keeps you in good condition, with everything functioning correctly, including the sex glands. During each orgasm a large amount of Vitamin C is excreted which must obviously be replaced if you are to remain healthy.

Vitamin C is a healer and mender, therefore it is not difficult to see how it plays its part in the reproductive cycle of life which is recreating cells. The easiest method of taking it is as ascorbic acid from the chemist, but since it is a complex like Vitamin B, it is best to have a food source also. Therefore rose hips or acerola berries or a specially prepared combination with buckwheat are helpful. All brightly-coloured fruits and vegetables contain good quantities: blackberries, strawberries, raspberries, oranges, lemons, red peppers and most green leaves.

VITAMINS A AND D

Vitamin A is sometimes called the youth vitamin because of its effect on the linings of the body which it keeps healthy, including the skin, and because it prevents premature ageing and even increases life expectancy. It is also a vital part of the nourishment of the cells of the body, without which they break down. It is not therefore difficult to see how it can be useful to the sexual system, in fact without it impotence sets in.

Vitamin D is essential for the absorption of calcium and phosphorus which are needed for bones and teeth, healthy nerves, muscles and skin, for glandular secretions and proper nutrition. Therfore it is also needed for sex.

LECITHIN

Lecithin is found in spermatoza and is a constituent of the brain and nerves. Its principal function is to emulsify fats and make it possible for the body to utilize them. By reducing the size of the fat globules, it makes them easily assimilable and prevents them being deposited where they are not needed and dangerous, such as in the blood vessels.

Lecithin can be bought at the health food shop or it can be taken as part of food such as wheat germ oil, nuts and seeds, cold-pressed vegetable oils or in soya beans. The body also manufactures it providing enough of the two B vitamins, Inositol and Choline, are eaten.

MINERALS

Since no process of the body would take place without minerals, they cannot be left out where sex is concerned. Zinc has already been mentioned, and the four great minerals: oxygen, carbon, hydrogen and nitrogen are all equally important, but there is less need to mention them since they form the bulk of food. However calcium, potassium, sodium, magnesium and iron, plus the trace element iodine, are also needed. Plants obtain them from the air, water and soil, animals from plants, air and water, and humans from animals, plants, air and water. But if the minerals are not in the soil in the first place they can never reach us.

The cause of most mineral deficiency is the method of preparing and storing food. By cutting and cooking, by freezing and washing, by picking and leaving, minerals as well as vitamins disappear. The best method of replenishing our supply is with food, providing the diet is adequate and sufficiently varied. For daily deficiencies, the Scheussler biochemic mineral cell salts are best because they act instantly. Never forget minerals in your diet or as far as sex is concerned.

GINSEN

This supplement comes from a root which is grown principally in the East. It is sold in the West as a rejuvenator and as a sexual stimulator. The East use it as a cure-all. There is no doubt about its sexual stimulating qualities and in this way perhaps it helps to rejuvenate. The Orientals take it during the winter to keep them warm, which is another of its attributes. (See under health foods.)

MORE ABOUT SEX

STIMULANTS

Since the beginning of time man has been searching for methods of stimulating his sexual urge, although why I sometimes wonder, as I have always had a need for the opposite. If a pretty girl does not excite you, then you would be better to look inside yourself and find the cause. However we are not all made alike and as I pointed out earlier, glandular function greatly regulates the urge, with the mind as its boss. If therefore the trouble is congenital the problem is more difficult, although the specific sex foods and supplements can play a great part in correcting it. The normalizing of glands is no great problem these days, providing it is done by natural methods and not with the knife or drugs, then the effete can become complete and the degenerate regenerated.

So let me begin by saying that there should be no need for aphrodisiacs and that any departure from normal is usually harmful. This is certainly the case with Spanish Fly, which has been known to be a killer, and other notorious concoctions which have anyway rather gone out of fashion. Of course abalone is sold at greatly inflated prices in the East and oysters are consumed in vast quantities in the West, both in the cause of sex, and there is certain nutritional sense in each case because they contain iodine, zinc and other essential minerals for the sex glands. However they are only stimulants if your body is deficient in them or if you believe ardently that they will stimulate.

However there are other things which do stimulate sexual desire, which I will enumerate now:

Excess Energy

Take the labourer away from his labour, the accountant away from his figures, the businessman away from his worries, anyone away from their outlet of energy and you will find a veritable sex maniac with the right partner at hand. Without enough energy to spare sex does not take place, as doubtless the wives of hard-working husbands have found out. There is no cure for it, nothing is wrong, so you just have to wait for different circumstances.

Adrenalin

However, should your hard-working husband by chance lose his temper and pour an excess of adrenalin into his bloodstream you may then find he badly needs you. One of the reasons for this is that fear, anger or any other strong emotion causes the adrenal glands to prepare us for fight or flight, and one of the processes is to make available a super-amount of energy for that fight or flight. So we are really back to excess energy again.

Hot Weather

Your other choice as a frustrated wife is to wait for the hot weather which very definitely loosens things up. Then with the right food and appropriate circumstances you can achieve your end.

Alcohol

There is no doubt that too many drinks is conducive to sex. This has been proved scientifically and by many others practically. However alcohol can also lead to impotence in excess, and not just temporary but permanent impotence.

Vitamin E

This is the natural stimulator for sex and it works whether you take it in the form of food or as a supplement. In conjunction with its natural complements it is best utilized, but as a straightforward vitamin it is very potent.

Vitamin C

Taken in large quantities for a period of time this vitamin definitely acts as a stimulant. There is no danger in taking a lot as any excess is lost in the urine. Do not mix it with alcohol to try and increase the effect, although you might take it after the alcohol to detoxify its poison.

Fasting

By dint of the fact that fasting increases your rate of metabolism and therefore stimulates your thyroid gland, it can be called a stimulant. I always fast one day each week and by the middle of the day I know how true this is.

Carbohydrates

Those who have ever had a craving for sweets will probably know that an excess of these can also stimulate sex. They can also be used as a replacement for sex: for women sweet food, for men alcohol. Dried fruit, honey, any concentrated carbohydrate will have the same effect.

INHIBITIONS

Everyone suffers from inhibitions of one sort of another, we cannot help it, because there are certain things we will not do and we have our reasons. Unfortunately, so far as sex is concerned, those reasons are usually not known, and therefore lie deep down inside the subconscious which makes them difficult to eradicate. It may be fear of inadequacy which was born from several unsuccessful attempts at intercourse or it may be just ignorance at what to expect or how to go about it, even lack of knowledge about youthful masturbation and its deleterious effects. Even feelings of inferiority about the size or performance of one's own equipment can sometimes inhibit satisfactory sex, although no male member in action varies much in size but it does at ease.

Then there are unfounded fears of the inability to perform intercourse with the frequency one reads about in sex novels, which of course is rubbish. The inhibition may be a domineering wife or a partner who nags, criticizes and abuses her man or she might simply fail to make herself attractive, either physically or mentally. Boredom also plays its part in inhibiting sex. There is no doubt that variety is the spice of sex. I am not suggesting that you change your bed-mate when you change the sheets, but a little imagination does help.

Then there are the old-fashioned taboos about the appalling iniquity of sex which are in themselves iniquitous, not the act they inhibit. With an open mind sex can be the greatest pleasure in the world with the person you love, but not if it is stifled by inhibitions and the suffocating effect they have. Introverts have the same trouble because they are always looking into themselves and trying to make things happen, which of course results in making them not happen. Sometimes what appears to be a lack of appetite for sex may simply be not enough energy which could come from overwork or poor nutrition. Whatever the cause, do not ignore unsatisfactory sex, it can ruin a marriage and cause much misery. Talk about it, consult a marriage guidance authority, even discuss it with friends or relations, but do not let it fester as a sore to destroy your marriage. If you are impotent, find out why. It might be the effect of mumps which can now be rectified. If it is glandular try some of the methods I have suggested.

There are other sorts of inhibitions as well, such as bad breath, unclean flesh, body odour, even bad manners, insensitivity and tactlessness. It is very often the smallest details which upset people, not only in sex but in other ways as well. After all sex is a relationship, it is a communication between two people and anything which upsets that will also spoil the act of sex. People sometimes forget that sex is a two-sided affair and maybe men are mostly to blame. By the very fact that they dominate their women and are catered for by them in their domestic needs, they are inclined to be thoughtless when it comes to sex, when they should be all the more considerate.

Sex is also a habit, so if you never fall into the habit you will not really miss it or even necessarily want it. However there are reservations about this because it depends on one's libido and that depends on age and the type of food you eat. On the other hand in marriage the habit can be acquired or discontinued, perhaps both during the course of its life.

However there is such a thing as the dialectic of sex, by which I mean the natural perversity of human nature, in that people want what they do not have but seldom what they have. This works in two ways: first by them preferring to conquer new sexual fields rather than graze happily in the one they have, and second by insatiable women wanting to be loved and the weary husbands making excuses, although it could be the other way round. Whichever way, the one is wanting and the other avoiding, which can become an irritation, even an inhibition. This, unless come to terms with, can cause trouble. But equally the same is true of all inhibitions, for once you know why they inhibit you it is only a question of understanding to overcome them.

PERVERSIONS

To pervert something is to turn it away from its proper use. Presumably the proper use of sexual intercourse is to produce children, at least that is what those who perform it unmarried spend their time trying to prevent. Any other method of having an orgasm must therefore in technical terms be called perversion. Masturbation is to create an orgasm for yourself and seems to cover someone else doing it for you also. These are therefore all termed perversions. It may be two women trying to have an orgasm, in which case they are called lesbians, or two men who are called homosexuals. All are trying to do the same thing, namely have an orgasm. Why?

Possibly it is physical, that their glands are forcing them to relieve themselves, and they cannot resist. Perhaps they are weak and have acquired the habit of sex or it has even become a vice. Perhaps excessive alcohol or excessive sex have demoralized them to the extent that they cannot resist. However perversion is not usually satisfying for the doer and very often they are bitterly ashamed of what they cannot help doing. How does this come about?

I believe most of it starts at school in certain countries

where those things are not frowned upon. On the other hand, if men had women to make love to there would be no homosexuals, because in the majority of cases no man could possibly prefer another man. The same must surely also be true for women. I say this so firmly because of the physical arrangements of man and woman. Since the object of making love is to have an orgasm there is only one satisfactory way of doing this for a man and for a woman. No other method could satisfy physically or mentally, it simply is not possible.

However there are women whose looks and behaviour are so aggressively male that no self-respecting man would go near them, and these are the ones who are attracted towards more feeble females with whom they practice lesbianism. The same is true of men, the more masculine they are the more they need their sex and the more determined they are to have it. If women are not available, whatever is at hand has to make do, as I said at the beginning of this section. The only true homosexual therefore is the effeminate young man who offers himself as a woman to a man.

However man's consuming and basic desire for sex has been used in recent times as a political weapon to gain dominion over him, to discredit him and in some cases to destroy him. The more refined are the politics, the more sophisticated are the methods used. In countries which do not play this sort of game the oversexed males are supplied with women, although in fact the need never arises because their social customs are different.

Unfortunately there is money in sex and power in being able to supply man with his pleasures, quite apart from the possibility of blackmail, so sex has become an inevitable weapon in the hands of the manipulators. In certain countries the front pages of most newspapers usually have a story of rape, homosexual opportuning or some other unusual sexual acts, whereas in other countries such things do not take place.

The fate of the pervert is an unhappy one. They admit it themselves. Unfortunately they are usually caught in their own net and cannot escape. The more they indulge their habits the stronger does the hold become. They can damage their health, distort their minds and pass on their habits to perfectly normal people. In some cases they become a complete menace to themselves and society because they only spread misery and dejection, not happiness. Admittedly only the minutest percentage of the world have a satisfactory sexual life, so people must either learn to dispense with it, which is probably the best answer or make a determined effort to put it right. Perversion is not an alternative in any shape, form or description.

CHANGE-OF-LIFE

The period of the change of life (menopause) can be a trying one for women with all its psychological and physical problems. The physical ones do no more than acknowledge the fact that the woman is no longer in a fit state to have children and therefore atrophy her reproductive organs. The psychological ones are much more alarming because although many of them may be attributed to glandular adjustments, the underlying cause is that the woman has come to the end of her useful and functional life and that she herself feels she may as well be thrown on the rubbish heap.

She can no longer offer man what he wants of a wife, the continuation of his own line by giving him children, and she has reached a stage when she is possibly no longer desirable. However well she may paint her face and disguise her body, sex is for the younger women, men do not want them after a certain age and no one knows this better than woman herself. So it is indeed a crushing blow to have reached only middle age and find your life has come to an end, at least that part of it which is important to a woman. It takes a lot of adjustment and since most women are not particularly good at logical thought, they have to feel their way rather carefully and the process hurts.

As always the physical and mental are closely tied together, so that if the physical side can be alleviated and even arrested for a short time, the mental process need not be so hurried and therefore so painful. That is precisely what nutrition can help to do, spread the change of life over a long period so that the psychological effects are gradually absorbed in the gentle, healing, all-absorbing arms of father time. Women can cope with most things if given time, it is shocks and pressures they find hard to absorb and which upset their balance and their frame of mind. The same is partly true of us all, but man is made to stand and fight and for that he must be able to deal with sudden emergencies. That is the difference in the sexes, we are not born equal, we react in completely different ways and although complementary to each other, we are not by any means the same.

Man is also said to have a change of life, a mental one if not a physical one, but I have my doubts about the truth of this claim. Of course it is possible for a man to lose his potency in middle life and doubtless the effect of that is hurtful to his pride which could have a psychological result; but I am inclined to think it is more the degeneracy of the man which causes this and nothing else. If man is healthy he can continue to sire children till at least the age of 100; this has been done on frequent occasions in many parts of the world.

Man does not lose his sex drive or his fertility simply by the passage of time, only by the degeneracy of his own body and that he can prevent by eating the right food and remaining healthy. Excessive alcohol and smoking will both play their part in ending his manhood, as will strong tea and coffee, not enough exercise and being overweight. All these as well as nutrition and other bad habits which contribute to an unhealthy life, gradually destroy a man and his virility.

But how to retain your sexual libido and your manhood, that is the question. First comes the need to keep your health or regain it, which I have already discussed earlier. Eat correctly, take exercise and be philosophical about life. This advice applies equally to man or woman, it is the basis of health as well as happiness. The other suggestions I have to make come after this has been followed. They cannot be used instead of it, although of course they will help and by degree prolong a virile life:

Vitamin E
This vitamin easily comes top of the list because it can prevent the hot flushes and other unpleasant symptoms which are mostly due to circulation troubles. It is also at the very basis of the workings of the sex glands so can therefore help prolong their life. For further information about this vitamin

see earlier in this section, or in other parts of this book.

Vitamins A and D

These are the youth vitamins and therefore help retain the youthfulness of the body, internally and externally. Obviously these vitamins are needed in anything affecting the ageing of the body. See earlier for more information.

Calcium, Potassium and Silica

These are the three vital minerals for everyone in advancing years. They are the three which become in increasingly short supply as the years pass by: calcium because it becomes more difficult to absorb later in life and because it is concerned with proper nutrition; potassium because the need for it is greater then, and silica because it will help to reverse the ravages of time. All of them are best taken biochemically for easy assimilation (particularly calcium) but the potassium and the silica can sometimes be had otherwise.

Vitamins B and C

These vitamins are always indispensable for health and they are the stress vitamins which help to counteract the enormous stress of change of life. Nerves, emotions, energy and the glands are all helped by these vitamins.

Magnesium

This mineral is nature's tranquillizer and can either be taken biochemically or with calcium in some form of bonemeal preparation.

Rest and Relaxation

Both of these are a tonic in trying times so you must learn how to accomplish them. Mind control through Yoga or Buddhism is one way, but doubtless there are others although they have to be learnt and practised.

THE PROSTATE

Instead of the problems of change of life, men can suffer an equally unpleasant and sometimes fatal complaint: derangement of the prostate gland. This frequently takes place later in life rather than earlier, and is brought on over a period of time partly by wrong nutrition. Since this gland is situated at the neck of the uretha it mostly affects the evacuation of urine: the inability to eliminate it all, a constant dribbling, a feeble flow, frequent night urination, sometimes a form of cystitis, pains in the legs and fatigue. Most of these are caused by the gland enlarging, thereby affecting the flow of urine, but the production of its fluid which is normally mixed with the semen is also interfered with. These are serious problems because the retention of wastes causes infection and its malfunction aids this condition.

For those who know nothing about nutrition or the other methods of nature cure there is usually only one answer: they have it removed by a surgeon, so freeing the flow of urine and eliminating the cause of infection. It is a major operation at an age when the body is least able to cope with such serious stress, and it needs tremendous resilience to return to normal afterwards, in fact most men never are quite the same again (in more ways than one).

But what else can you do? Your best course of action is to supply this gland with the raw materials it needs to function properly, the first of which is the unsaturated fatty acids (Vitamin F or vegetable oils). Next comes zinc, which is best supplied by pumpkin seeds, because there appears to be something else in these seeds which acts like magic on the prostate. Vitamin E must also be included because that is the sex vitamin and affects all the glands and functions of the reproductive system. Vitamins A and D are also useful because of their ability to help retain the internal youthfulness of the body. There are two other preparations which can also help if you can find them, one is any pollen product and the other is ginsen (the Oriental root). Both of these have met with success and apart from their action on the prostate, they have myriad properties for the prolongation of youth.

Although these vitamins and food supplements are the missing factors for a troubled prostate, it is always necessary to improve one's diet for the best results. The principal reason for that is to ensure an adequate supply of minerals and protein. However minerals are not always found in the food we eat, because we throw them down the drain in the cooking water and in other methods of preparation. I would recommend anyone with prostate trouble to take biochemic mineral cell salts, some of which are specific for hardened and enlarged glands and other conditions associated with them. Finally it is possible to massage the prostate, and this in conjunction with nutritional aids has sometimes helped, but it is necessary to find an expert to undertake the task and it should never be undertaken if the gland is cancerous.

DRINKING AND SMOKING

I have been asked by so many people to include some nutritional facts about these two habits that it seems worth doing, anyway drinking and smoking and sex are all rather tied up together. I used to indulge in both up to the age of thirty-five, when I was faced with the choice of either continuing to write or continuing to smoke and drink, and it did not take me long to decide. Fortunately I was in the East at the time, where it is easier to see the subject in perspective, or rather I was able to see the two sides of the picture more clearly by contrasting Western and Eastern cultures.

So far as smoking was concerned, the difficult thing I found was to actually make the decision: it was so easy to say tomorrow, why should I say today, so I did it gradually till there were only two or three cigarettes a day to finally give up. Drinking just meant not having one when I was offered it, so that was quite easy to do, except when my friends were bores about it, which they frequently were so I had to dispense with some of them.

As far as the effects of giving up these habits are concerned, I can only say I did not notice drinking because living alone in a foreign country and writing books one did not drink anyway, so there was no immediate change. Smoking on the other hand gave me all the withdrawal symptoms of a drug, and for a short time the desire was always there. Finally I had one relapse, mostly the cause of a beautiful Canadian nurse, but it did not last long and I have never looked back from that day.

The tremendous feeling of lightness and energy are the two things I remember best about giving up smoking, because I really did feel so much better, particularly on waking in the morning. Had I known as much as I do now about nutrition I would have probably been able to help myself through the trying period and not had the relapse to contend with, so perhaps what I have to say now will be of some help to those who want to give it up, as well as those who intend to continue with both.

Smoking

If you give up smoking you must be able to replace the lift it used to give you, or rather you must be able to do without that lift. This is a question of being able to keep a constantly high level of blood sugar, which, unlike what it may sound, does not depend on eating sugar, rather the opposite. You must give up sugar, take only small amounts of carbohydrate with protein and fat frequently, and replace your urinary loss of potassium with a biochemic or other preparation. Consult a nutritionist or health food shop and see earlier in this book.

One of the most pernicious effects of smoking is that it positively eats up the supply of Vitamin C in your body at the rate of about 25 mgs per cigarette. Presumably this happens because the toxic substances from smoking have to be nullified, so if you are going to smoke you must pour Vitamin C into your body. Refer to Vitamin C saturation earlier in this book.

Smoking also causes scar tissue to be formed in the lungs and this is blamed for lung cancer. If you must go on smoking at least take Vitamin E which has the ability to soften scar tissue which already exists, and to prevent the formation of new. This vitamin will also ward off the onset of arteriosclerosis which is encouraged by smoking.

Cancer is the disease most associated with smoking nowadays and I wonder very much whether the taking of potassium as I have suggested earlier, may not be helpful here, because a great many cancer patients are deficient in potassium and saturated with sodium chloride (common salt). These two minerals go together, inside and outside the cells (see earlier).

Some people think that smoking calms the nerves but that is not true, in fact it does actually destroy the nerve centres. This effect is constant, accumulative and permanent until it reaches the point of no return.

Drinking (Alcohol)

This is no place to advocate the pleasures of drinking against the advantages of not doing so. I have done both under totally different circumstances, and I can only say that I am glad I did not miss my ten years of tasting the sensuous pleasure of drinking, smoking and for that matter sex. I do not suppose I would have been a complete person without this period because one cannot go through life without knowing what it is all about.

The young must learn to live and this they can only do by making mistakes, and if they come out whole the other end they are twice the people they would have been otherwise. But I think they must do it, they must have a past as well as a present and a future otherwise they are only part of what they should be. There is a risk that they will not come through, but that is a risk one takes in any battle, and life is no less than that. In war one may be wounded or even lose one's life, but wounds help to create the character of a person if taken in the right way, otherwise they destroy them. So do not be afraid of living but learn by your mistakes, and when you have had a good time settle down, get married and have some children.

The physical effects of alcohol are accumulative, although when you are young you do not notice the ill effects so much, but gradually they make themselves felt. Alcohol attacks the liver, because that is the organ which has to detoxify the poisons from it; when you are intoxicated you have simply filled yourself with poison and if it was not eliminated you would die. A healthy liver can continue to do this for a certain period of time, depending on the amount of liquor consumed, but if it does not receive the right raw materials with which to operate, its life is limited.

Alcohol is 100% carbohydrate without the necessary minerals or vitamins to digest it, that is why in certain countries people never drink without eating something and why they usually remain healthy in spite of it. However if you want to do even better, you should see that you have an extra large supply of B vitamins when you drink, because it is these which are necessary for the utilization of carbohydrate.

After that you should avail yourself of an enormous quantity of Vitamin C (in any form) which has the power of combining with toxins and so nullifying them. This will greatly assist your liver. Finally you should secure some reliable supplement of magnesium (combined with calcium) because it is a deficiency of this which cause the trembling hands, jitters, nervousness and tension of drinkers.

The liver has tremendous powers of regeneration: more than three-quarters of the liver can be destroyed yet it will regain its full capacity given the right materials and the right circumstances. The first material needed for this is protein, so enough must be supplied by the diet (1 gram per kilo body weight). To prevent the damage from scarring which is likely to take place if you maltreat your liver, take Vitamin E. This will also help to detoxify poisons, prevent arteriosclerosis which usually follows excessive drinking and maintain the fluidity of the blood.

An overworked liver also becomes sodium-depleted but this cannot be rectified by taking common salt, in fact that would probably have the opposite effect. However biochemic minerals in the form of sodium sulphate will help, so will other preparations of mineral cell salts.

Apart from these basic raw materials which are absolutely vital, the best treatment for an impaired liver is complete rest. This is accomplished by giving it no work to do: by not expending too much energy or giving it any food or metabolic wastes to cope with. Fasting on water or juice or even one sort of fruit for a day is useful.

Remember that alcohol, like any other stimulant or drug, is addictive and that the effects are accumulative.

9. More Food for Thought

MORE FOOD FOR THOUGHT

In conclusion let me say that to destroy a nation it is necessary first to destroy its people and this is not done by the sword but by their own living habits. That is the importance of a way of living, as a means of survival. The same is true for the individual, because no one can survive without his health and that depends on what he eats, what he thinks and what he does. The Jews learnt this from their years of slavery in Egypt, so they drew up a code of living to which they still adhere. That is why they do not eat pork, eels, shellfish or the hindquarters of meat, and why they have remained a nation in spite of having no country up till quite recently and in the face of adversity.

That is also why the Eskimoes were a healthy and hardy race, until we took them our semi-foods and decadent ways of living. No one can survive the way the Western world lives today, unless their diet is extremely varied and their code of living extraordinarily resistant to the vices of our times. Of course they will live but not with any degree of health, and they are more than likely to die a harrowing death from cancer, heart disease or one of the other degenerative complaints.

The challenge of life, for nations as well as individuals, is to remain healthy and to be happy, because most of the rest of what we think we want or need is an illusion, and it is our lust for that illusion which destroys us. But we are not wise enough to see our folly and the need for progress outweighs our wisdom. However we could be wise and still progress if we paid a little more attention to our way of living, and used the law to defend the health of our people instead of legalizing the most appalling abuse of food. This is something which needs studying in depth, because to continue along this haphazard road will certainly end in ruin.

In the East it is their pride that people are taught to be

content with very little, and that is their strength. In the West it is the other way round, by advertising and insinuation people are encouraged never to be satisfied with what they have but to want more. Even worse than that, films, television and literature even suggest you steal it if you cannot obtain it any other way. It is not surprising therefore that few people are happy. This is not living, but a form of slavery to money which brings neither health nor happiness. The communists have a different form of slavery which is equally materialistic, and seems to be based on the destruction of the individual which is the acme of oppression. This is proved by the twenty million Russians who were killed by Stalin from 1934 to 1953, and the 46,000 scholars slaughtered in China in an even shorter period.

None of this is necessary if people would learn to control their minds which would then make them independent and unconquerable, secure and at peace, unaffected by the daily inequalities and hurts of life. That way everyone could also find happiness. Our health is as readily obtainable, because we could all be healthy with only a few cups of wheat or rice each day, providing it was whole and not separated from its vital germ which contains all the goodness. Of course we should add to that whatever vegetables, fruit and other food we can afford. But none of this is the case, so no one is completely happy nor remotely healthy.

You cannot escape the fact that everything becomes what you make it. A piece of paper becomes a poem or a picture, the earth a garden or an orchard, a house a hovel or a home, a person someone or nothing. It is not by chance but by design that this happens and we have control over its destiny. From the idea comes the implementation, but without the idea nothing is achieved. Life is creation, from a mother's womb to the building of a man, both require a struggle and some pain but it is the effort of accomplishing this which keeps us alive. However everything in life has to be learnt, whether it be walking or reading and writing, so we must learn how to build healthy bodies and minds because they will not take shape by chance. That is our challenge and in part the responsibility of those who govern us.

So learn to become the hero of your own life and not its

victim, it is so easily possible. Learn to create something on the blank canvas of life which lies before you, instead of letting circumstances guide your timid hand. Be the master of your own destiny and instead of being oppressed or even destroyed by misfortune, turn it to your own advantage. There are always two sides to everything because right can come from wrong and good from bad, as indeed one learns from one's mistakes. It is only those who are afraid to live who achieve nothing, because the spark of life is needed to ignite the fire we live by, without it there is no life.

The problems we meet each day are our challenges and how we answer them is the test of what we are. It is this which gives us independence, which is the only sort of freedom we can ever have, and from it we obtain our happiness. A healthy body and a controlled mind can tackle anything and always win, even if the person dies in the process, that is the extent of physical and mental health. Anything short of that is sickness in one degree or another. So learn the art of positive thinking and correct eating which alone can create a healthy body and mind, instead of destroying both as you go along.

Index

Abscesses, 83
Absorption, poor, 217
Abortion, 38
Acerola berries, 231
Acid-alkaline, balance, 41, 43, 49
Acod-forming foods, 328-9
Acidity, 329
Acne, 83
Adrenal glands, 232, 234
Affections, 139-40
Ageing,
   Vitamin E, 38
   Iodine, 48
   Ginsen, 80
   Wheat Germ Oil, 243
   Pollens, 247
Aimlessness, 87
Air, fresh, 65
Alcoholism, 34, 43, 84
Alkaline foods, 328
Alkalinity, 213, 236
Allergies, 35, 84
Anaemia, 60, 85-6
   B complex, 34
   Vitamin C, 36, 232
   Calcium, 42-3, 238
   Yeast, 219
   Liver, 247
   Vitamin E, 38
   Salt, 44
   Iron, 45
   Molasses, 217
   Dried Fruit, 220
   Pernicious, 51, 73
   Bleeding from, 246
Angina, 43
Antibiotics, 33, 69
   Natures, 79, 242
Anti-stress factors, 51, 78, 247
   Milk, 213
   Sources of, 51
   Facts about, 164
Anti-stress foods, 77-81
Apathy, 87

Appreciation, 127-9
Appetite, 247
Arteries,
   Hardening of, 37
Arterosclerosis, 234, 245
Arthritis, 86-7, 329
   Molasses, 217
   Cider vinegar, 224
   Vitamin C, 35
   Vitamin D, 37
   Vitamin E, 38
   Water, 67
   Lecithin, 80
   Bioflavonoids, 245
Ascorbic acid
   see Vitamin C
Assimilation, 43, 242
Asthma, 84
   Honey, 216-17
   Cider vinegar, 224
   Garlic, 242
   Pollens, 247-8

Baby foods, 226
Balanced diet, 462-4
Barker, J. Ellis, 81, 89
Beauty, 87
Bieler, Dr Henry, 81
Biochemic Tissue Salts, 239-41
   Function of, 239-40
Biochemistry, Dr Scheusslers, 39-40, 71-2
Bioflavonoids:
   Facts about, 245-6
   Functions of, 245-6
   Sources of, 245
   Medicine for, 246
   Dosage of, 246
Bircher-Benner, Dr, 86, 89
Births, premature, 38
Blackheads, 260
Bleeding gums, 35
Blisters, water, 44-5
Bloating, 44

Blood:
　Impure, 34, 83, 219, 224, 230, 232
　Clotting, 35, 37, 42, 233
　Minerals, 41
　Supply of, 68
　Formation of, 231
Blood pressure, high, 46, 79, 242
Blood sugar, 87, 93
Blood vessels, 34, 47, 80
Boils, 80, 83, 231, 242
Bones, 88
　Broken, 37
　Diseases, 37
　Structure, 41, 238
　Brittle, 46, 239
Bone meal, 238
Books, health, 210–11
Brain function, 37, 234
　Lecithin, 244
Breast feeding, 279
Breathing, 65–6
Brewer's yeast, 78, 159
Bronchitis, 47, 88, 242
Bruises, 35, 36, 89, 231, 246
Buddhism, 81
Burns, 37, 50, 68, 88, 234

Calcium:
　Utilization of, 37, 42, 51, 72, 231, 232
　Deposits, 42
　Sources of, 42, 43, 72
　in milk, 213
　Absorption of, 238
　Deficiency symptoms, 239
Cancer:
　Vitamin E, 38
　Salt, 45
　Raw food, 68
　Garlic, 79, 242
　Bioflavonoids, 246
Capilliaries:
　Strength of, 35
Carbohydrate, 27–30
　Overweight, 29
　Metabolism, 43
　Facts about, 162
　Description of, 28
Carbuncles, 83
Catarrh, 79
Cells, body, 82

Cereals, 158
　Facts about, 165–6
　Food value, 166
　Preparation of, 179–80
　in diet, 187
　Sources of, 214
　Medicinal qualities, 215
Change-of-life, 90, 354–6
　Vitamin E, 38, 233, 344, 355
　Vitamins A and D, 356
　Vitamins B and C, 356
　Magnesium, 356
　Rest and relaxation, 356
Charcoal, 80, 208
　Facts about, 243
　Functions of, 243–4
　Doseage, 244
Chapman, Dr J. B., 81
Chilblains, 90
Child birth, 344
　Stretch marks, 344
Children:
　Breast feeding, 279
Chin, receding, 37
Chlorine, 44–6, 73
Cholesterol, 35, 260
　Reduction of, 43
Circulation, 42, 66, 67–8, 234, 239
Civilization:
　meaning of, 16
Cobalt, 46–7, 73
Coffee, 221
Community responsibility, 282
Conjunctivitis, 47
Convalescence, 36, 42, 91, 231, 239
　Honey for, 217
Copper:
　in liver, 78
Cold:
　Reactions to, 48
　Feeling of, 80
Colds, 45, 67, 68, 90
　Honey for, 217
　Garlic for, 242
　Bioflavonoids, 245
Cold sores, 45, 91
Constipation, 91
　Molasses, 217–18
　Yeast, 219
　Salt, 44, 220
　Royal jelly, 247
　Vitamin B, 34, 230

Potassium, 46
Coronary problems, 43
Cortisone therapy, 108
Cosmetics, natural, 209
Cramp, 45, 92
Cuts, 68
Cures, famous, 330–31
Cystitis, 38

Dairy produce:
  As Health Food, 212–13
  Facts about, 167–8
  Food value, 169
  Preparation of, 180–81
  In diet, 188
Dandruff, 92
Davis, Adelle, 81
Dental caries, 37
Depression, 34, 92
Diabetes, 92
  Vitamin C, 35
  Vitamin E, 37, 38, 70, 234
  Ginsen, 80
  Bioflavonoids, 245
  Food for, 223
  Wheat Germ Oil, 243
Diarrhoea, 80, 93, 242, 243–4
Diet, 18
  My own, 185
  Suggestions for, 186–7
  Summarized, 191–2
  National responsibility, 292
  Balanced, 328–9
Digestion, 46, 48, 67, 80, 84, 242
  Poor, 34, 67, 79, 217
  Dairy products, 33
  Cider vinegar, 224
  Yeast, 219
  Aids for, 208, 248
Discipline, 280
  Self-discipline, 280
Diseases, 18, 59–63, 82–3
  Suppression of, 15
  Vitamin A, 33
  Causes of, 39, 59, 60, 62, 63
  Animals, 59
  Resistance to, 229, 231, 246
  Curing of, 60, 62, 64
  Treatment of, 59–63
  Drugs, 61–2
  Prevention of, 62, 63, 286
  Freedom from, 288

Degenerative, 216, 234
Diuretics, 35
Doctors:
  Training of, 60
Doubts, 130
Don'ts, 164, 192
Dried fruit, 220–21
  For sex, 338–40
Drinking, 358–61
Drowsiness, 44
Dryness, excessive, 44
Diptheria, 242

Eczema, 45, 84, 245
Education, nutritional:
  need for, 290–91
Eggs:
  Facts about, 166–7
  Food value, 167
  Preparation of, 180
  In diet, 188
  Acid forming, 214
Ego, 138–9
Elimination, of wastes, 67, 68
Emotions, 77, 93, 279
  Negative, 131
Encephalitis, 35
Energy, 88, 93, 329
  From food, 29, 50, 78–9, 212, 260
  Lack of, 34
  Production of, 30, 42, 43
  Supply of, 47, 106, 219
  From honey, 216–17, 230
  Wheat Germ Oil, 243
Endurance, 36, 38, 231, 243
Environment, 133–4
  Our creator, 13, 280
Enzymes, 50–51, 72, 212, 248
  Destruction of, 51
  Preservation of, 51
  Sources of, 51
  Facts about, 164
Epilepsy, 43
Example:
  Parental, 281
Excesses, 104
Exercise, 66–7, 177, 244
  Constipation, 91
Exhaustion, 104
Extreme heat or cold, 104
Eyes, 94
  Watering of, 44

Eyes (contd.)
    Bags under, 45
    Ulcers on, 45
    Protruding, 48
    Vitamin A, 229
    Royal jelly, 247
    Diet, 260

Fasting, 74–5
Fat:
    Description of, 29
    Metabolism, 43, 80
    Facts about, 161–2
    Unsaturated, 30
    Uses of, 29–30
Fatigue, 34, 46, 80, 217, 243
Fear, 104, 131
    Of living, 194–5
Feet, cold, 48
Female frigidity, 38
Fertilizers, artificial, 403
Fevers, 35, 47, 50, 68, 94, 246
Fish, 160
    Facts about, 175–6
    Food value, 176–7
    Preparation of, 184
    In diet, 190
Flour, white
    Vitamin B deficiencies, 33
Flu, 94, 242, 246
Food, wholeness, 68
    Available groups, 158–60
    Selection of, 160–65
    Not to eat, 160, 164
    Values, 165–77
    Preparation of, 177–84
    Raw, 178–9
    Cooked, 179
    Supplements, 207–8, 227–8
    Marketing of, 286–7, 291
    Alkaline, 328
    Acid forming, 328–9
Fresh air, 177
Frigidity, female, 344
Fruit, 159
    Oxidization of, 51
    Dried, 159
    Facts about, 170–71
    Food value, 171–4
    Preparation of, 177–8
    Raw, 342–3
    As Health Food, 211–13

Gall stones, 32, 38, 43
Garlic, 79, 208
    Facts about, 242
    Functions of, 242
Gastric complaints:
    Charcoal, 243
Ginsen, 81, 348
Gout, 95
Goitre, 48, 106
Glandular Health, 38, 43, 67, 80, 218, 245
Glass, Justine, 81, 89
Glands, 94
Grievances, 284–5
Growth, 42–3, 71
Gums, 95, 231, 246

Habits, 16, 17, 19
Haemorrhages, 36, 39, 246
Haemorrhoids, 101, 107–8
    Vitamin C, 36, 231
    Vitamin E, 37, 234
    Iron, 47
    Bioflavonoids, 71, 245
Hair, dry, 45, 48
Hang-nails, 45, 95
Hands:
    Clammy, 48
    Cold, 48
Han Suyin, 132
Happiness, 13, 15, 17, 109, 116
    Ingredients for, 116–25
Hauser, Gaylord, 81
Hay fever, 84, 248
Headache, 84, 95
Healing wounds:
    Vitamin C, 35
    Salt, 45
    Water, 50, 67
    Vitamin E, 70–71
    Garlic, 79
    Bioflavonoids, 246
Health, 13, 14, 59, 66–7, 126–7
    Responsibility for, 15
    Stepping stones to, 18
Health Foods, 18, 203–49
    Generally, 203–4
    Specifically, 205–7
    Individually, 211–27
Heart, 43, 66, 67, 96, 230
    Fat against, 29
    Disease, 34, 37, 70, 80, 234

Beat, 42, 43, 46
Palpitation, 47
Eggs, 214
Coffee, 221
Vitamin E, 233
Wheat Germ Oil, 243
Lecithin, 244-5
Bioflavonoids, 246
Heat:
    Reactions to, 48
    Intolerance to, 48
Herbal remedies, 209
    Facts about, 248
Hepatitis, 97, 257-9
Highly strung, 48
Hives, 84
Homeopathy, 76, 209
Honey, 159
    Facts about, 176
    Food value, 176
    Preparation of, 184
    In diet, 190
    For heart, 216-17
    For liver, 217
    For sex, 338-40
Hope, 131
Hopelessness:
    Feeling of, 45
Hormone production, 38
Hunger, violent, 45, 270

Impotence, 234
Indigestion, 45, 96, 244
Infection:
    Immunity to, 34, 35, 36
    Constant, 229
Infertility, 37, 38, 234, 243, 344
Inflammations, 47, 50, 68
Inhibitions, 351-2
Insanity, 43
Insect bites, 45, 50, 68, 87, 220
Insomnia, 97
Intestinal flora, 213, 248
Intoxication, 232
Iodine, 48-9, 74
    Sources of, 48
Iron:
    Assimilation of, 35
    General, 46-7, 73
    Sources of, 47, 73
    Absorption of, 47, 231
    Inorganic, 47
    In liver, 78
    In green veg, 78
Irritability, 34, 43, 48, 230
Itching, 45

Jam, health food, 223
Jaundice, 97, 257-9
Jaw formation, 37
Joints, 98, 231
Juices:
    Fruit and Veg, 79

Kelp:
    Facts about, 237
    Functions of, 237-8
    Deficiency, 238
    Dosage, 238
    For sex, 337
Kidneys, 37, 66, 80, 98
    Damaged, 45, 329
    Enlarged, 46
    Stones, 32, 38, 43
    Facts about, 175
    Eggs, 214
    Food value, 175
    Cider vinegar, 224
    Vitamin E, 233
    Bioflavonoids, 246
Knock knees, 37

Lassitude, 87
Laxatives, 221
Lecithin, 80
    Wheat Germ Oil, 77, 243
    For sex, 347
    In nuts and seeds, 216
    Facts about, 244
    Sources of, 244
    Functions of, 244
    Dosage, 245
Legs, bowed, 37
Life, value of, 16-17
Lips, 99
    Cracked, 34, 44
    Abnormalities, 230
Liver, 78
    and fat, 30, 35, 37, 38
    Function, 34, 66
    Anti-anaemia, 78
    Lecithin for, 80
    Facts about, 175, 271

Liver, (*contd.*)
　Food value, 175
　In diet, 190
　Yeast for, 219
　and coffee, 221
　Cider vinegar, 224
　Vitamin B, 230
　Vitamin E, 234
　Desiccated, 247
Living, art of, 154–6
Living alone, 151–3, 156–60
Loneliness, 13–14
Lung problems, 242
　More facts, 73, 79
Leukemia, 38, 246

Magnesium, 42–4, 72
　Sources of, 72
　Functions of, 43
　Deficiency symptoms, 43
Malnourished states:
　Milk for, 213
Manganese, 48–9, 74
　Sources of, 48–9
Marketing of food, 287, 291
Maternal instinct, 48
Meat, 160
　Facts about, 175–6
　Food value, 176
　Preparation of, 177–8
　In diet, 190
　Case against, 329–33
Medicines, natural, 63–4
Mechanical aids, 211
Memories, festering, 130
Memory, 34, 42, 48, 99, 239
Meningitis, 35
Menopause, 38, 90, 233, 344, 355
　(also Change-of-life)
Menstrual problems, 38, 233, 234
Mental strain, 85
　Health, 99
Menus:
　Preparation of, 184–90
　Non-vegetarian, 191–2
　Vegetarian, 191
Metabolism, 41, 99, 106
　Poor, 48
Mind, 76–7
　For survival, 16
　Control of, 77

Minerals:
　General, 39–42, 74
　Body proportions, 40
　Trace, 40
　Action of, 41
　and water, 67
　Groups of, 41
　Functions of, 41
　Therapy, 71–2
　Facts about, 163, 236–7
　Generally, 207–8, 212
　In nuts and seeds, 216
　For sex, 347–8
　Sources of, 237
　Supplements of, 241
　Biochemic, 239–41
Milk, 159
　Pasturization of, 51
　Facts about, 167–8
　Food value, 168
　Preparation of, 181
　For protein, 213
　For calcium, 213
　Anti-stress factors, 213
Miscarriages, 38, 233, 234, 243, 246
Molasses:
　Minerals in, 217
　Vitamins in, 217
Mouth abnormalities, 230
　Blisters round, 44–5
　Dry, 45
　Sore, 34
Mumps, 35, 100
Mung beans, 168–9
Multiple sclerosis, 38, 234
Muscle, 41, 42, 66, 100
　Tone, 37, 234, 243
　Weakness, 46
Muscular dystrophy, 38

Nails, 48, 100
　Hang-nails, 95
National Health Service, 14
Nature, laws of, 296–7
Nature cure, 62
Nerves, 100
　Vitamin B, 34, 230
　Vitamin D, 37
　Vitamin E, 37
　Calcium, 43
　Magnesium, 43

Iodine, 48
Yeast, 219
Lecithin, 244
Nervousness, 87-8
Nettlerash, 45
Neuritis, 101
Neurosis, 80
Nolfi, Dr Kirstine, 89
Nose:
  Bleeds, 36, 47, 231, 246
  Drips, 44
  Running, 84
Nutrition, 17, 25-6, 42, 325-8
  and salt, 45
Nuts, 80, 159
  Facts about, 169-70
  Food value, 170
  Preparation of, 182
  In diet, 189
  As Health Food, 216
  As sex food, 336-7

Obesity, 270
Oil, vegetable, 159
Organ meats, 159
  Facts about, 175
  Food value, 175-6
  Preparation of, 183-4
  In diet, 190
Over-weight, 48
Overwork, 85, 104, 106
Oxygen, 65, 233

Pantothenic Acid, 33, 69
Pain, 43, 101
  Sensitivity to, 239
Peace of mind, 129-32
Perversions, 352-4
Phlebitis, 37
Phosphorus, 42-4, 72
  Sources of, 43
  Utilization, 51, 72
Pigeon chest, 37
Piles (see Haemorrhoids), 101, 107-8
Pimples, 83
  On arms and thighs, 229
Pneumonia, 35, 79, 242
Poisons, 102, 242
  Neutralizing, 231
Poisonous bites, 35
Poliomyelitis, 35, 43, 246

Pollen, 208
  Facts about, 247-8
Potassium:
  Versus sodium, 44
  Sources of, 46
  Deficiency of, 46
Potassium chloride, 46
Premature births, 38
Problems, 104-5, 193-4
Prostate, 48, 102, 218, 248, 336, 356-8
  Infection of, 35
  Enlargement, 357-8
  Supplements for, 357-8
Protein, 26-7
  Incomplete, 27
  Deficiency symptoms, 27
  Intake, 160-61
  Selection of, 161
  Facts about, 161
  Concentrated, 248
  Supplements, 208
  in milk, 213
  For aged, 213
  In nuts and seeds, 216
Pulses, 159, 215-16
  Facts about, 168-9
  Food value, 169-70
  Preparation of, 181-2
  In diet, 188

Reproductive organs:
  Damage to, 37
Respiratory infections, 47, 80, 102, 246
Rest, 65
Relaxation, 65
Rheumatic fever, 246
Rheumatic pains, 47
Rheumatism, 102, 224, 329
  and eggs, 214
Rice:
  Preparation of, 180
Rickets, 37, 232
Rose hips, 231
Royal jelly, 208, 247

Saliva, excessive, 44
Salt (see Sodium Chloride), 159
  As health food, 220

Scars, 37, 103, 233, 260
Scheussler, Dr:
  Biochemistry, 39, 81
Schizophrenia, 231
Scurvy, 34, 232
Sea sickness, 242
Security, 129, 132-3
Seeds, 80, 233
  Facts about, 169-70
  Food value, 169-70
  Sex food, 335-7
  Sprouted, 179, 187
  Preparation of, 182
  In diet, 189
  As health food, 216
Self-respect, 131
Sensitivity, 142-3
Sex, 13, 14, 18, 37, 38, 95, 103, 233, 245
  Male characteristics, 38
  Glands, 48
  Reduced urge, 48
  Rejuvenation, 80
  Degeneration, 234
  and Wheat germ oil, 243, 333
  Morality of, 305, 309-10
  The idea of, 310-19
  Dreams, 317
  The act of, 319-25
  Food for, 325-8
  Specific food for, 340-43
  Nuts and seeds, 335-6
  Sesame seeds, 336-7
  Kelp, 337-8
  Honey, 338-40
  Dried fruit, 338-40
  Milk for, 340-42
  Supplements for, 343-8
  Libido, 234, 344
  Vegetable oils, 344-5
  Zinc, 345
  Vitamin B, 345-6
  Vitamin C, 346
  Vitamin A and D, 346-7
  Lecithin, 347
  Minerals, 347-8
  Ginsen, 348
  Perversions, 352-4
Self-discipline, 193-4
Shelton, Herbert, 81, 86
Shock, 38
Sight, poor, 37

Sinus, 84, 104
Shyness, 103
Skin:
  Eruptions, 34, 80
  Wrinkles, 38, 232, 233
  Cancer of, 38
  Greasy forehead, 45
  Health of, 48, 66, 229, 245
  Problems, 80, 104, 218
  Rash, 84
  Dry, 220, 229
  Beauty, 233, 260
Sleep:
  Problems, 34, 43, 80, 97, 247
  Unrefreshing, 44, 48
  Normal, 46
  Constant desire to, 48
Sleeping pills, 33
Smell, loss of, 44
Smoking, 34
Snake bites, 35, 76
Sodium, 44-6
Sodium chloride, 44-6, 72, 73
  Toxicity, 44
  Versus potassium, 44
  and Anaemia, 44
  Deficiencies, 44, 45
  Excess, 44
  Quantities needed, 45
Soya beans, 79, 168-9, 215-16
Soy sauce, 226
Spirits, low, 47
Sprains, 50, 68
Stammering, 107
State of mind, 134-7
Stimulants, 348-50
Stress, 104, 284
  Vitamin C, 35, 231
  Vitamin E, 38, 233
  Magnesium, 43
  Salt, 45
  and Food, 51, 77
Stones:
  Kidney and gall, 32, 38, 43
Sugar, white:
  Malnutrition, 29, 33
Sulphur drugs, 33, 69
Sulphur, sources of, 48, 74
Sun burn, 68
Sunshine, 66
Sunstroke, 45, 105
Suppuration, 83

Surgery, 34, 37, 104
  Honey for, 217
Survival, 14, 15
Sweets, craving for, 43
Sluggishness, 48

Taste, loss of, 45
T.B., 79, 242, 246
Tea, 222
  Herb, 222
Teeth, 105, 238
  Loose, 35, 231
  Holes in, 37
Tension, 87, 247
Tetanus, 35
Tetany, 43
Thirst:
  Violent, 45, 50, 67
Thyroid gland, 72, 106
  Vitamin C, 35
  Vitamin E, 38, 233
  Iodine, 48, 237–8
  Vitamin D, 232
Tongue, 106
  Abnormalities, 34, 230
  Dry, 45
Toxins, 34
Trace elements, 74
Trembling, 87, 107
Typhus, 242
Twitching, 107

Ulcers, 37, 107, 217, 233
Unhappiness, 17, 114, 140–42
Unsaturated fatty acids, 72
  Facts about, 235
  Nuts and seeds, 216
  Wheat germ oil, 78, 243

Varicose veins, 107–8
  Vitamin C, 36
  Vitamin E, 37, 233
  Bioflavonoids, 71, 246
  See Piles
Vegetables, 159
  Cooking of, 51
  Value of, 66
  Leafy green, 78
  Facts about, 170–71
  Food value, 171–4
  Preparation of, 183
  In diet, 189
  Concentrated, 208, 248
  As health food, 212–13
  Raw, 342–3
Vegetable oils, 218, 344–5
Vegetarians, 85
  and salt, 46
  and iron, 47
  Foods, 223
  The case for, 329–33
Vinegar, cider, 224
Vitamins:
  General, 30–32, 39–40, 203, 207, 212
  Enemies of, 30
  Quantities of, 30
  Balanced diet, 31
  Therapy, 68
  Facts about, 162–3
Vitamin A, 32–3, 69, 179
  Sources of, 32, 69, 229
  Deficiency symptoms, 32, 229
  and disease, 32
  In liver, 78
  In wheat germ oil, 78
  For sex, 346–7
  Functions of, 229
Vitamin B complex, 33–4, 70
  Self-production, 33
  Deficiency causes, 33, 70
  Sources of, 33, 70
  Deficiency symptoms, 34
  Quantities, 34
  In wheat germ oil, 78, 243
  In liver, 78
  In brewers' yeast, 78, 219
  In yogurt, 213
  Functions of, 229
Vitamin B12, 33, 51, 69, 73, 247
  Sources of, 74, 175
Vitamin C, 34–7, 70
  Complex, 35
  Sources of, 35, 36, 232
  Amount needed, 35
  and Vitamin P, 35
  Deficiency symptoms, 35
  and kidney damage, 36
  As antibiotic, 36
  Functions of, 231–2
  Dosage, 232
  and sex, 346

Vitamin D, 36–7, 69, 72
  Sources of, 36, 66, 232
  Functions of, 320
Vitamin E, 37–8, 70–71
  World authority, 37
  Sale of, 38
  Destruction of, 38
  Sources of, 38, 234
  Dosage, 70, 234–5
  Antagonists, 70–71
  In wheat germ oil, 79, 243
  In nuts and seeds, 216
  For sex, 344
Vitamin F, 71
  Sources of, 71
  Facts about, 235
Vitamin K, 39
  Sources of, 39
  Facts about, 235

Warts, 108
Water, 49–50, 67–8
  Amount needed, 49
  Softened, 50
  Excessive drinking of, 50
  Sources of, 67
  Facts about, 177
  In diet, 191
  Balance, 40, 50, 68
Waterbrash, 44
Waterlogging, 48, 50, 108
Watery exudations, 44

Weakness, 87
Wheat germ, 215
Wheat germ oil, 77, 208, 333–4
  Facts about, 243
  Functions of, 243
  Dosage, 243
White sugar, 33, 43, 68, 360
White flour, 33, 43, 68, 263
Whole food:
  Need for, 68
Worry, 97, 104, 130–31
Wounds:
  Healing of, 231, 260
  Sceptic, 242

X-ray damage, 35

Yeast, brewers:
  Facts about, 174
  Preparation of, 183
  In diet, 189–90
  As Health Food, 219
Yoga, 81
Yogurt, 33, 213, 248
  Vitamin B, 213
  Calcium, 213
  Protein, 213
  Digestion, 248

Zinc, 48, 74
  Sources of, 48
  For sex, 345

Also in Unwin Paperbacks

LET'S HAVE HEALTHY CHILDREN
Adelle Davis

Let's Have Healthy Children is an invaluable guide for mothers and expectant mothers. Adelle Davis's classic child guide gives useful advice on every stage of pregnancy, including the prevention and overcoming of nausea, leg cramps and fatigue and the problem of weight gain. This new edition has been fully revised and updated by Marshall Mandell MD with the help of advice from a team of experts including UK practitioners.

'Sound advice on the management of feeding problems in young children.' *Health Education Journal*

'A complete guide to nutrition for a mother . . . valuable information.' *Housecraft*

LET'S COOK IT RIGHT
Adelle Davis

Let's Cook it Right is one of the most popular, helpful and widely praised cook-books ever published. It is dedicated to the principle that foods can be prepared to retain both flavour and nutrients. Hundreds of basic recipes for preparing every type of food are included together with many more easy-to-fix variations on them. A major emphasis is the reduction of solid fats to a minimum and an increase in the use of vegetable oils. Adelle Davis has also eliminated any ingredients likely to contain cancer-producing additives, such as those found in some colourings, preservatives, bleaches, artificial sweeteners, flavourings and dyes.

'This is not merely a book to show how delicious foods may be prepared but a book which is a necessity for the young and inexperienced no less than for older cooks who may have forgotten the principles of nutrition.' *Woman's Choice*

LET'S EAT RIGHT TO KEEP FIT
Adelle Davis

Let's Eat Right to Keep Fit is a practical guide to nutrition designed to bring about good health through a proper diet. Adelle Davis discusses, in detail, the 40 or more nutrients needed by the body to build health, and explains the foods that supply them in the most concentrated form. There are chapters on essential vitamins, on the importance of reducing blood cholesterol and on nature's own tranquilllizer 'magnesium'. Adelle Davis included her own specific recommendations for a balanced diet.

'An expert but very readable guide to nutrition.' *TV Times*
'Adelle Davis knew how to inspire enthusiasm for wholefood living.'
She

LET'S GET WELL
Adelle Davis

Let's Get Well explains how a well chosen diet, which provides the most needed nutrients, can repair and rebuild a sick body. A proper diet can restore health and Adelle Davis shows in simple, non-technical terms, that recuperation can be hastened by the proper selection of natural foods supplemented by vitamins. There are full medical references. Many illnesses are covered including heart attacks, ulcers, diabetes, arthritis, gout and anaemia. Adelle Davis explains the function of nutrition in disease related to the blood system, the digestion, the liver, the kidneys and the nervous system.

'A good overall picture of the relationship of nutrition to health . . . highly recommended.' *Good Health*

GROWING UP WITH GOOD FOOD
Edited by Catherine Lewis
The National Childbirth Trust

Growing Up with Good Food is a guide to good eating for young families. It provides ideas and recipes for meals for the entire family together with material on a good diet for pregnant and breastfeeding mothers, as well as on the preparation of baby foods. The book aims to make the reader more conscious of nutritional matters.

'Clear and forthright nutritional guidance and recipes to match.'
Penelope Leach

MINERALS AND YOUR HEALTH
Len Mervyn

Minerals and Your Health is written for everyone concerned about the effects of modern food processing. It will interest particularly mothers of young children and anyone concerned with nutrition. It explains how minerals can be absorbed most effectively, why we should care about the level of trace minerals in our bodies and how a diet poor in minerals can lead to chronic illness. It is the first book to describe how hair analysis can reveal mineral deficiencies.

THE NATURAL FOODS PRIMER
Beatrice Trum Hunter

Here is a clear and concise introduction to natural foods – foods free from artificial colouring, preservatives and other additives. Beatrice Trum Hunter shows how you can buy and cook natural foods and explains why it is important to make them the basis of the family's diet. With the help of this book, you can begin to enjoy a nourishing, satisfying and healthy diet.

'There is no more practised hand to guide the beginner through the natural foods jungle.' *The Vegetarian*

'For those seriously intending to adopt healthfood principles. Makes it sound not just easy but positively inviting.'
The Times

WHY ENDURE RHEUMATISM AND ARTHRITIS?
Clifford Quick

More people suffer from arthritis and rheumatism than from any ailment other than colds and 'flu. Clifford Quick, who has spent a lifetime treating and studying rheumatic complaints, describes how you can treat yourself effectively without recourse to drugs or medicines. He explains why drugs and pain killers are harmful and why the diet and exercises he recommends lead to generally improved health.

Also in Unwin Paperbacks

Acupressure Slimming Book *Frank Bahr*	£1.75 ☐
Challenge of Homoeopathy *Margery G. Blackie*	£2.50 ☐
Do-It-Yourself Shiatsu *Wataru Ohashi*	£3.95 ☐
Family Medical Handbook *David Kellett Carding*	£1.95 ☐
Growing Up with Good Food *Catherine Lewis*	£1.95 ☐
Let's Cook it Right *Adelle Davis*	£1.50 ☐
Let's Eat Right to Keep Fit *Adelle Davis*	£1.50 ☐
Let's Get Well *Adelle Davis*	£1.50 ☐
Let's Have Healthy Children *Adelle Davis*	£1.95 ☐
Menopause: A positive approach *Rosetta Reitz*	£2.95 ☐
Minerals and Your Health *Len Mervyn*	£1.75 ☐
Natural Foods Primer *Beatrice Trum Hunter*	£1.25 ☐
Phobias *Joy Melville*	£1.50 ☐
Take Care of Yourself *D. M. Vickery, J. F. Fries, J. A. Muir Gray and S. A. Smail*	£3.95 ☐
Why Endure Rheumatism and Arthritis? *Clifford Quick*	£2.50 ☐
You Are Beautiful *Shirley Lord*	£3.50 ☐
You Must Relax *Edmund Jacobson*	£2.25 ☐

All these books are available at your local bookshop or newsagent, or can be ordered direct by post. Just tick the titles you want and fill in the form below.

Name ....
Address ....
....
....

Write to Unwin Cash Sales, PO Box 11, Falmouth, Cornwall TR10 9EN.

Please enclose remittance to the value of the cover price plus:

UK: 45p for the first book plus 20p for the second book, thereafter 14p for each additional book ordered, to a maximum charge of £1.63.

BFPO and EIRE: 45p for the first book plus 20p for the second book and 14p for the next 7 books and thereafter 8p per book.

OVERSEAS: 75p for the first book plus 21p per copy for each additional book.

Unwin Paperbacks reserve the right to show new retail prices on covers, which may differ from those previously advertised in the text or elsewhere. Postage rates are also subject to revision.